I got a copy of Mike Gunderloy's book *Coder to Developer* yesterday and started looking at it and then started reading it and then continued reading it in bed before I went to sleep. I have been programming for 20 years, but it is still interesting for me to be reading this book because it refreshes ideas about certain things and gives me new ideas.... Also, it is great to see how other programmers (who have been at it for a long time and who I have a lot of respect for) go about their development process. The book is geared at taking people who know a lot about coding, but do not really know about the scope of developing a project. These are skills that it takes years to evolve through experience, and it's a perfect book for someone like Mike to write.

—Julia Lerman
Julia Lerman Blog

As freshly minted computer science majors pick up their diplomas, they should buy, beg, or borrow this book. *Coder to Developer* will take them from the mindset of interesting but academic code problems into the trenches of achieving professional success in this globalized world. *Coder to Developer* pulls together all the aspects of being a successful programmer who delivers solid code on time. Other reviewers have said this is only a .NET programmer book. Not true. While .NET programmers will benefit the most from buying *Coder to Developer*, Java, VB6, and even open-source diehards will find more than enough to be worth their while.

—Bob from Sonoma, California
(Courtesy of Amazon.com)

After three days of reading and digesting the information in the book, I must say that it is one of the best computer books I have ever read (and one of the very few that I have read cover-to-cover, and not only cover-to-cover, but cover-to-cover to the exclusion of all else). After reading the first couple of chapters, I decided to put aside the software application that I was working on, and read the entire book. I will now go back to the start of my application and apply the lessons from the book to the project. I don't feel that I have "lost" the time working on the software project, because I think that what I learned in the book will more than pay for itself in saved time during development.

—Eric Brunsen from Colorado Springs, Colorado
(Courtesy of Amazon.com)

Coder to Developer was a great read and a definite addition to my must-read list for others.

—Scott Watermasysk

Developer to Designer:
GUI Design for the
Busy Developer

Developer to Designer: GUI Design for the Busy Developer

Mike Gunderloy

SYBEX

San Francisco · London

Publisher: Joel Fugazzotto
Acquisitions Editor: Tom Cirtin
Developmental Editor: Tom Cirtin
Production Editor: Rachel Gunn
Technical Editor: John Mueller
Copyeditor: Nancy Sixsmith
Compositor: Laurie Stewart, Happenstance Type-O-Rama
Proofreaders: Jim Brook, Nancy Riddiough
Indexer: Nancy Guenther
Cover Designer: Ingalls + Associates
Cover Illustrator/Photographer: Rob Arkins, The Image Bank

Library of Congress Card Number: 2004109306

ISBN: 0-7821-4361-X

Manufactured in the United States of America

10 9 8 7 6 5 4 3 2 1

For Fru, who keeps calling me.

Acknowledgments

S ome people finish a book and say "Never again." After I finished this one, I said, "Let's do another one." That's because of the truly superb editorial team that helped me complete the project. So I'd like to start by acknowledging Tom Cirtin, who signed me up for this project, as well as Susan Berge, Rachel Gunn, Nancy Sixsmith, and John Mueller. After they were done making me justify my stands and clarify places where I was unclear, this book was much better than when I thought I was finished with it. And even after that, of course, the production team at Happenstance took over and turned the manuscript into the final printed product that you're holding today.

My notions about user interface design have come mainly from designing user interfaces and finding out what works and what doesn't. Time and again, I've discovered that the interfaces I thought were completely obvious were in fact opaque (by using the simple stratagem of sending them out for testing). So thanks to all my customers for helping me improve my design skills by refusing to pay for inferior work.

Thanks, too, to the Microsoft Office team, who hired me several times to work on obscure corners of the product. Struggling to keep up with the Office quality bar is a great way to understand just how difficult it is to write good applications in general, as well as a great way to learn about interface design.

On the home front, my family has (as always) been very understanding of the long hours and occasional fits of grumpy cursing that go into writing a book. Even as I finish this list of acknowledgments, there are two kids sleeping on the couch behind me, having given up hope that dad was going to find more play time tonight. But I do take time whenever I can; Adam, Kayla, and Thomas are all much more fun to play with than any amount of software. And finally, Dana Jones gives me the love and support that I need to keep going at all.

Contents at a Glance

Contents

Introduction

When I'm not writing books, I'm a software developer myself. In fact, I spend more time writing code than I do writing books, though sometimes it's a close thing. My hope with this book is to fill a hole by writing about user interface issues that software developers care about, based on real-world software (specifically, applications for Windows and the World Wide Web). I'm not a graphics designer, usability specialist, or market researcher; I get right down into the code and grub around. So although you won't find many specific code snippets in this book, you'll find ideas that you should be able to implement without too much work.

To be clear, there are a few things that you *won't* find in this book, even if they're almost a tradition in user interface design books:

- I'm not going to redesign Microsoft's own applications to show how smart I am when not faced with budgets, delivery dates, tradeoffs, and other constraints.

- I'm not going to present "ivory tower" user interfaces built with nonexistent controls.

- I'm not going to redesign Windows itself. Instead, I'll show you how to work with what's already there.

My goal is to provide a mix of descriptive and prescriptive content that you can apply immediately to building user interfaces for your own applications. I'll describe how the standard Windows and web user interfaces work, and then I'll tell you which parts I think you need to pay attention to. My advice, combined with your own common sense about how Windows and web applications ought to behave, will help you create applications that end users can use without confusion or anxiety.

How This Book Is Organized

This book contains 15 chapters (organized into three parts) plus an appendix. There's no particular need to read every chapter in order; for the most part, they stand alone. Feel free to jump around or to dip in if you need a quick course on a particular topic.

The first part includes eight chapters that discuss the static design of user interfaces for Windows applications. Chapter 1, "The Big Picture," covers my basic philosophy of user interface development, with some advice on general principles. This chapter is a good starting point, no matter which other parts of the book you're interested in. Chapter 2, "Putting Words on the Screen," is about labels, ToolTips, and other text that you display to the user. Chapter 3, "Managing Windows," discusses the mechanics of application windows, including the management of multiple windows. Three chapters follow to discuss the individual controls that make up a Windows user interface: buttons (Chapter 4, "Command Buttons"), text boxes (Chapter 5, "Using Text Input Controls"), and other controls (Chapter 6, "The Other Controls"). Chapter 7, "Dialog Boxes," offers general advice for assembling these individual controls into task-focused sections of a user interface. Finally, Chapter 8, "Common Windows User Interface Elements," discusses some of the things that people expect in a Windows application, including menus, toolbars, Wizards, and status bars.

The second part of the book has three chapters that discuss the interaction between users and the user interface of a Windows application. Chapter 9, "User Input and Navigation," discusses keyboard, menu, and toolbar command techniques. Chapter 10, "Common Interaction Patterns," covers such topics as drag and drop and cut and paste. Chapter 11, "User Choice, Customization, and Confusion" reviews some of the ways in which many Windows applications allow the user to customize the user interface.

The last part of the book turns from Windows applications to web applications. Chapter 12, "The Web Is Not Windows," is an overview of the changes that you need to make to your mindset as you move from Windows design to web design. Chapter 13, "Building a Web Page," includes the basics of HTML design and similar techniques for the developer who's new to the Web. Chapter 14, "Common Web Design Patterns," discusses common web design patterns including common page types such as home pages and search pages, which let you make your web application seem more familiar to new users. Chapter 15, "Common Interaction Patterns" gives advice on handling forms and search in your web applications.

Finally, there's an appendix, "Looking Forward to the Next Generation: Designing User Interfaces for Avalon." This appendix goes over the information that we currently know about Windows "Longhorn" and discusses how user interfaces will change when Microsoft releases this version of the Windows operating system.

Staying in Touch

I welcome feedback from my readers. If you find any problems with this book, or have any questions or suggestions, I'm happy to hear from you via email. You can reach me at MikeG1@larkfarm.com. Of course, I can't guarantee an answer to every question, but I'll do my best.

CHAPTER I

The Big Picture

- User Interface Design for the Busy Developer

- Thinking About Software

- Finding a Few Guiding Lights

- Basics of a Good User Interface

My goal with this book is simple: to help you design and improve user interfaces for your Windows and web applications. By designing better user interfaces (UIs), you can improve user satisfaction and make users more productive. Ultimately, this will make you more appreciated and in demand as a developer. Along the way, I'll pass on lots of little tips and drill into many of the details that make for a good user interface. Most of the book will focus on little things, from toolbar buttons to laying out a web application. But before getting into the details, it will help to have an overall framework for thinking about user interface design. That's where this chapter comes in.

User Interface Design for the Busy Developer

Depending on the size of your development team and the workflow in your organization, several people may be responsible for designing an application's user interface:

- If you have project managers whose responsibilities include writing software specifications, they may include user interface mockups in the specification.

- If you're using extreme programming (XP) practices, you might have a customer representative dictating the design of the user interface.

- If the organization is sufficiently large, you may have user interface design specialists who do nothing but work on these issues.

- If the user interface isn't completely specified at the time that the code has to be written, it falls on the developer to make the initial design decisions. This is not usually the best possible situation. Without user feedback, it's hard to come up with a good design. But the task still needs to be done.

I'm primarily a developer myself, so if you're in that last category, I empathize. Designing the user interface is just one of the dozens of things that most developers have to do in the course of their jobs. Even if it's not your primary focus, you need to understand enough about user interface design to get the job done.

But remember: Designing a good user interface does not relieve you of the responsibility to develop a working application. You can't afford to invest all your development time in making the user interface pretty. That approach would sacrifice functionality. Instead, it's your job to strike a balance among all the competing demands on your time.

Take heart, however. Although you may never have thought about user interface design in detail, the basics are fairly straightforward. And like any other skill, they can be learned. I offer these words of comfort for the busy developer faced with user interface design:

TIP   If you can learn a computer language, you can learn to build a functional, usable, and reasonably attractive user interface.

Thinking About Software

What do you think about when you think about software? Ones and zeroes? Loops and conditional statements? Although these may be good ways to think about the internal construction of computer programs, they don't do much to illuminate the task of building a good user interface for an application. In this section, I'll guide you through some alternate ways of thinking about your software. These ways have proven helpful to me in the past when I've had user interface design work to do.

Software as a Conversation

One way to think of your software is as a conversation between the developer and the user. The user starts the conversation by running your application. You return with an opening gambit that lists the things you're ready to talk about. The user selects one, and you respond. The interchange of the user taking an action and then you responding (through your software) continues through the life of the application.

Thinking about software as a conversation makes it clear that you need to communicate with the users of your application. It's unrealistic to expect users to figure out what the application does and how to make it work by guesswork alone. Fortunately, there are several ways to communicate with the user: help files, printed documentation, and the user interface all contribute to your end of the conversation. Of these, the only one that you can depend on the user "hearing" is the user interface itself. Help files can be closed, manuals can be left unread, but it's the rare user who can fire up the application and then ignore the user interface completely.

But don't push this way of looking at things too far. Although you do communicate with users through the user interface of your application, it's a very limited kind of communication. You don't have any way to react to the user's facial expression or body language. You can't tell from timing whether they're understanding your intentions or missing them wildly. Despite these limitations in the software-as-a-conversation model, there's one big lesson to be learned here. In a real-life conversation, you wouldn't arbitrarily start speaking Esperanto or Hungarian without some indication that listeners are expecting the switch. Similarly, in software it is very dangerous to suddenly discard well-known user interface conventions without a good reason. A confused user is an unhappy user.

Similes, Metaphors, and Software

Another way to think about software is to compare it to some real-world object. This is a familiar tactic for making computer programs less scary—and their functions more obvious—to users. For example, Windows was originally designed as a sort of electronic rendition of an office worker's desktop, with file folders and documents and a calculator and a clock. You can move documents from one file folder to another, or discard them into a recycling bin. You can punch buttons on the calculator to do simple math, or set the time on the clock.

This may all seem quite obvious to you as a Windows user in the first decade of the 21st century. But when Windows first came out in the early 1990s, it was a revolutionary way to interact with computers. The similarities between the Windows desktop and a physical desktop helped many of us figure out how to use this new breed of software.

Sometimes software developers speak of this sort of thing as coming up with a *metaphor* for their software. But they're wrong: the relation between applications and the real world is one of *simile*, not metaphor. Think back to your middle-school English classes, and you may recall the difference between a metaphor and a simile:

- A metaphor is a figure of speech in which one thing is equated to another, as in "Windows is an office worker's desktop."

- A simile is a figure of speech in which one thing is said to be like another, as in "Windows is like an office worker's desktop."

The distinction is important, because these comparisons between applications and parts of the real world inevitably break down at some point. For example, you can't keep a pint of whiskey in the bottom drawer of the Windows desktop or spill ink on the letter you're writing. But the Windows desktop lets you change the label on a file folder without needing an eraser or a typewriter—something that would be quite a trick in the real world. The point is that the Windows application is not identical to the real world. At best, it is similar to the real world.

Another way to think about this is to consider applications as analogies to the real world. One dictionary definition of analogy is as a similarity in some respect between things that are otherwise dissimilar. We know that computer applications and the real world are two different things, and they are wildly dissimilar: The real world is made up of atoms, and applications are made up of bits. But there are areas where the two are similar. Thus, the Windows desktop does have an analogy to a real desktop, and by conjuring up the image of a real desktop in the user's mind, it suggests to the user how the Windows desktop can be manipulated.

Because applications are at best similar to the real world, users are forced to construct a map (a set of correspondences) between the application and more familiar objects. That is, some reasoning takes place of the sort "this application behaves like X, so I should be able to do Y," either consciously or unconsciously, as the user tries to figure out which parts of the real world experience are applicable to the software at hand. Not all such mappings are created equal. Figure 1.1 shows schematically how two different applications might compare to their real-world counterparts.

 The upper part of the diagram demonstrates an application that maps very closely to its real-world model. There are a few things about the application that aren't in the real world, and vice versa, but the overlap between the two is substantial. The application behaves mainly as if it were a part of the real world. In the lower part of the diagram, a second application is a much less precise match to its real-world partner. Many things about the application can't be understood by reference to the real world.

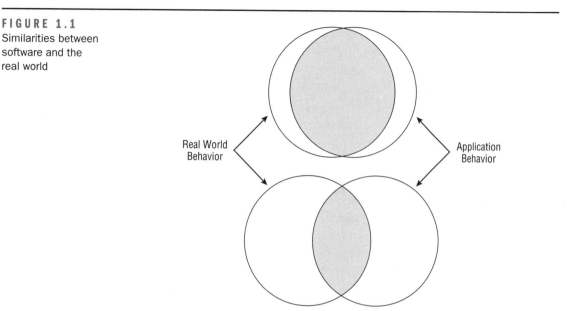

FIGURE 1.1
Similarities between software and the real world

Real World Behavior

Application Behavior

It's tempting to suppose that more an application will be better and easier to use if it is a more precise match to its real-world model. This in turn implies that the user interface should mimic some portion of the real world. But that is not necessarily true. Remember Microsoft Bob? That was Microsoft's most "realistic" user interface to date, and it was a resounding flop. Among other problems, imposing too much of the real world on the way the system worked led to very difficult navigation, with artificial constraints to traveling around from one part of the application to another. That's fine in a game, but not in an operating system.

Another reason to beware of software similes is that they can lead to tunnel vision. If you're trying to exactly mimic some piece of real-world hardware in a software application, you may well miss opportunities to add and extend functionality that would benefit users. So if you start with a simile in mind, make sure that you don't stop there.

Software as a Means

As a final way to think about software, remember that software is a means rather than an end. The chance that a user will be running your application just because they want to run your application is almost zero. Instead, they will have some goal in mind, and your application is a way to reach that goal. Even when a user launches your application to explore its capabilities, they usually have a goal in mind, such as evaluating whether the application will meet their needs.

Keeping this principle in mind is a good way to avoid making your software overly cute at the expense of usability. Spending effort to add a photorealistic three-dimensional user interface inspired by your favorite movie may make you feel extremely clever, but if users can't find the menus among the clutter, it's a step backward for your application. Users also don't care about how clever your code is, or how much work went into the program. They just want to reach their goals. If your program is the best means to that end, great. If not, there are plenty of other programs out there to try.

This is an area where a good user interface can give you a boost in the market. If your application is easy to use, then it will be a more natural means. This can translate directly into happier users and more sales.

Finding a Few Guiding Lights

The next step beyond thinking about applications is to thinking about user interfaces. Some applications, of course, have no user interface (or so little user interface as to be practically none at all): Windows services are a prime example of such applications. But most applications display information to the user and allow the user to interact with the application in turn.

Before getting into specific guidelines for what constitutes a good user interface, there are three overall principles that you ought to keep in mind:

- Task orientation
- Idiom reuse
- Intuition isn't

I'll discuss each of these principles in turn.

Concentrating on the Task

Just as user has a long-term goal in mind for their overall use of your application, they have a short-term goal to focus on at any given point. Writing a letter in a word processor, for example, might be broken down into three steps:

1. Choose an appropriate template to create the skeleton of the letter.
2. Type the text of the letter.
3. Print the letter.

Although the user wants to write a letter through this entire process, they need to perform a number of tasks along the way. The user interface is their only way to convince the application to perform these tasks in the right order. Making sure that the user can always perform their next desired task is part of the job of building a user interface.

At any given point, a good user interface will offer ways for the user to perform the next task that they have in mind. In most cases, though, you won't know precisely what the user wants to do next, so the user interface must offer choices. Even so, sometimes you can target your choices. Figure 1.2 shows the task pane that Microsoft Excel 2003 displays when you first launch the application. At this point, it's a good bet that the user wants to either create a new document or open an existing document, so the choices are focused in those directions.

FIGURE 1.2
Excel 2003 attempts
to make likely tasks
easy to perform

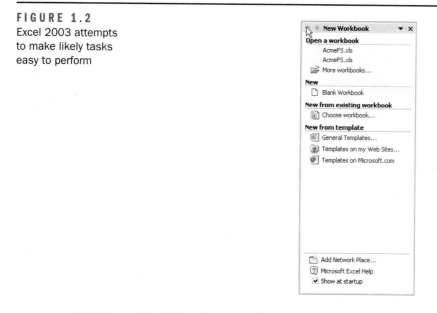

Task panes like this strike a nice balance between making common tasks easy and making uncommon tasks possible. Most users can probably get to their proper starting point by choosing an option in this task pane, but the task pane doesn't block access to the other menus and icons within Excel. If you have some other starting point in mind, and you know what you're doing, the task pane won't get in your way.

If you're having trouble figuring out the tasks that a user might want to perform with your software at any given time, try writing some scenarios. A *scenario* is just an informal story about what a user might want to do with your software. For example, if you're writing the perfect application for sending out spam, a couple of your scenarios might read this way:

"Judy is a new spammer who isn't quite sure how to get the maximum returns from her ads for dubious imported pharmaceuticals. She launches SpamOVator and tells it to create a new spam e-mail. She then types in the text of her ad and presses the Analyze button. SpamOVator automatically inserts misspellings and obfuscates the URLs, while keeping the sense of the message intact and suggesting some subject lines. Judy selects a subject line from the list, presses the Send button, and spews out 100,000 copies of her ad."

"Bob is an experienced spammer who has limited time to get things done. He starts SpamO-Vator and imports his ad text from a Microsoft Word file. He's already crafted his own keywords to get past Bayesian filters, so he simply types in his subject line, hits Send, and goes on to his next project."

In a real product specification, each of these scenarios would be much longer, and there would be others to supplement them. The key to writing a good scenario is to focus in on a particular real-world user and describe their interaction with the software. From the scenarios, you can then derive a list of tasks that might be performed at any given time. For example, it's already clear that SpamOVator must both allow creating new messages from scratch and importing messages created in other applications, and that both of these tasks should be possible to perform as soon as you launch the program.

Using Common Idioms

The dictionary offers several definitions of the word *idiom*; the one that concerns me here is "The specific grammatical, syntactic, and structural character of a given language." (Thanks to the fourth edition of the *American Heritage Dictionary of the English Language* for that wording.) When pressed into service for user interface design, idioms are those broad patterns of behavior that persist across many programs. Take a look at Figure 1.3. If you've had any substantial experience with Windows at all, you're likely to agree that one of these applications looks right and the other looks wrong.

The word processor at the top of the figure has its menu at the very top of the window, with toolbars directly beneath that. The one on the bottom has these parts of the interface scattered around willy-nilly. Although both applications have the same functionality, users are likely to be much happier with the one on the top because it uses the idioms with which they are already familiar.

NOTE   Ironically, both of these word processors are really Microsoft Word 2003. A few versions ago Microsoft went somewhat crazy with customization, and ever since then the Office applications have allowed you to move the menus to any place you might want them. I'll discuss this aspect of user interface design in Chapter 11, "User Choice, Customization, and Confusion."

Any given operating system is full of common idioms, from the arrangement of menu items (you're expecting New to be above Open on the File menu, right?) to toolbar button images, to the way drag-and-drop operations work. The more that your application can take advantage of these common idioms, the more comfortable your users will be. A large part of this book will go toward teasing out the ways that Microsoft Windows applications work in the Windows XP and Windows 2003 era.

Another way to think of a language idiom is as an expression in which the meaning isn't derived from the literal meaning of the words themselves, but from a cultural understanding of the aggregate expression; for example, "She heard it straight from the horse's mouth." This is useful in talking about software design because much of what "makes sense" to us are simply conventions that we've learned to understand and use. For example, it makes no literal sense to have a trashcan on a desk (unless you're a night janitor), but we've come to accept it and find it useful. The literal meaning of the trash can on screen is pretty silly, but so is the literal meaning of a language idiom. Similarly, why would a user have a menu, unless he works in a restaurant? It doesn't make a lot of sense, but because everyone has gotten used to the convention and finds it very useful, software designers keep it. A designer could change the convention to something that made more literal sense, but that would probably be a lot more trouble than it's worth—and it would confuse users to boot.

FIGURE 1.3

Common idioms used and abused

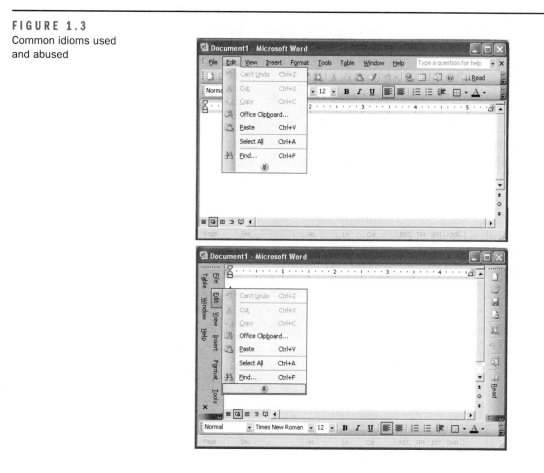

Debunking the Myth of Intuition

A lot has been made of the supposedly intuitive nature of various computer operating systems and applications. I won't say that this is all nonsense because I haven't tried out every application under the sun. So to be charitable, I'll simply quote Sturgeon's Law:

> *Sure, 90 percent of science fiction is crud. That's because 90 percent of everything is crud.*

I could tell you a lot of stories to illustrate my point, but I'll start with one from the earliest days of Windows. Back in the prehistoric era (around the release of Windows 2.0), I spent part of my time teaching 3-hour night school classes in Windows Basics. We got a wide variety of computer users, from hobbyists to business users. Many of them had never worked with a computer mouse. Perhaps you think the mouse is an intuitive device. It probably is, for you, right now. But then why did so many of my students attempt to move the cursor by waving the mouse in the air?

As another example, Figure 1.4 shows a new toolbar button that showed up in the Office 2003 user interface. Does your intuition help you guess what this button does?

FIGURE 1.4
A mystery toolbar button

The icon is a combination of the New Document icon and the international Stop symbol. Don't allow new documents? Stop others from making new documents? Insert a new stop sign icon in the document? Take a break from word processing? When faced with a new icon like this, intuition is pretty worthless, no matter how obvious things might have seemed to the developer.

That's why a good user interface offers hints. Things can be "intuitive" the second time you see them as long as they're explained the first time that you see them. Microsoft invented the ToolTip as a way to provide user interface hints. Hover your mouse pointer over the mystery icon, and you'll see the ToolTip shown in Figure 1.5.

In fact, this icon opens the Permission dialog box, which allows you to set rights management properties for the document. A few years from now, the icon will be intuitive—but only because you had a chance to learn what it does.

FIGURE 1.5
The mystery explained

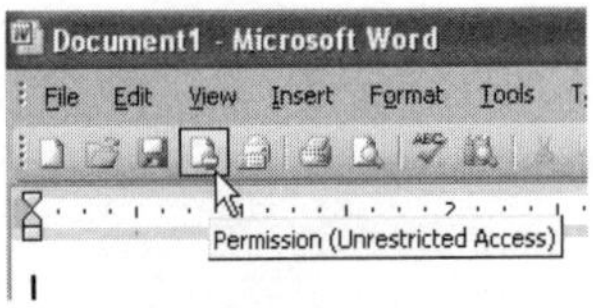

The bottom line is this: Nothing is intuitive unless you're a wild beast; for humans, everything is learned. Therefore, one of the differences between good and bad GUI design is simply how easy the software is to learn for the targeted user.

Basics of a Good User Interface

There are many ways to define "good" when it comes to user interfaces. Is it one that is esthetically pleasing? Is it one the works like a Microsoft application? As an overall rule, I'm happy with this definition:

RULE   A good user interface is one that lets the user accomplish the task that they want to accomplish, without putting obstacles in their way.

In this book, I'll teach you to construct user interfaces that meet that definition of "good." As a starting point, here are my guidelines for what goes into a good user interface:

- Respect the User
- Keep Things Simple
- Be Direct
- Be Forgiving
- Be Consistent

Respect the User

Without the user, your application is useless. That's why I put respecting the user at the top of my list. You need to obtain the user's cooperation to get them to continue using your application. The application's user interface can play an important part in obtaining this cooperation. If users have a positive experience with an application (it does what they want, it's easy to use, and so on), they're more likely to use it again in the future.

In some rare cases, you may have a captive audience and be able to ignore this precept. For example, if you're building internal applications in a Fortune 500 corporation, and your boss is experienced at corporate politics, it's quite likely that people will be told to use the applications whether they're any good or not. But even if you can get by with not respecting the user, you ignore this guideline at your own peril. It's entirely possible that you won't have that luxury at your next job, and it's hard enough to write software without having to unlearn bad habits.

One element of respecting the user is to leave the user in control as much as possible. Remember the task pane that you saw in Figure 1.2? The task pane makes it easy to perform common tasks, but it does not limit the user to performing only common tasks. The rest of the Excel user interface is still available in case the user should feel the urge to perform an uncommon task.

One way to keep the user in control is to make your application modeless (as opposed to modal). In a *modeless* application, the user has access to the full range of program functionality no matter what's going on. In a *modal* application, what the user can do is determined by the mode that the program is in.

Although you'll sometimes see modeless applications recommended as an absolute good thing, reality is a bit more complex. As a trivial example, some modes are mutually exclusive. For example, when you're working with many Windows applications, the Insert key toggles data entry between insert and overwrite modes. If you're inserting characters, you can't overwrite characters without switching to the other mode. Well, you could define some strange keystroke combination to insert characters while in overwrite mode or vice versa, but then you'd be ignoring a common Windows idiom.

On a less trivial level, modes can be useful in limiting the complexity of your application when the user is focused on performing a particular task. For example, most wizards (and similar interfaces, whatever their names) are modal. When the user is working through the steps in a wizard, it's a good bet that they're trying to perform a specific task through following the steps that you lay out in code. In that case, it's only a distraction to make the rest of the application's functionality available while the wizard is on the screen.

NOTE   I'll discuss wizards in Chapter 8, "Common Windows User Interface Elements."

Finally, modes can reflect underlying limitations in your code. For example, you might simply not be able to show changes to the underlying document while a print preview window is open on screen because your preview rendering code doesn't get called correctly. In such cases, modal behavior is far preferable to wrong or crashing behavior.

The other important element of putting the user in control is to assume that the user is intelligent (if perhaps not experienced). It's up to you not to waste the user's time with unnecessary steps and wasteful dialog boxes. The key is to come up with a user interface that works for both inexperienced and experienced users. In general, you can achieve this through careful hinting. (You already saw one example of this in Figure 1.5 earlier in the chapter.) ToolTips act as hints for less experienced users while remaining invisible (and therefore unobtrusive) for more experienced users.

Another area in which hinting works well is with explanatory dialog boxes. You can't depend on users to read the help file before using your application, but sometimes there is extremely important information that you want like to convey. For example, consider the status message shown in Figure 1.6.

The problem with status messages like this is that they age quickly. If the user hasn't looked at the manual, this is useful information the first time that the message pops up. If they have, it might be a slight annoyance. If it keeps popping up, the message rapidly escalates into a major annoyance, with users shouting at the screen, "I know that, you stupid program!"

You can remove most of the annoyance potential with one simple change, shown in Figure 1.7.

This change puts the user back in control. With a single mouse click, they can decide that they know enough about this aspect of the application and have it stop bothering them. Now the original message is a piece of information rather than an insult to their intelligence.

TIP   You could improve this piece of the user interface even more by rewriting the text to use normal English instead of computer jargon.

This example illustrates another aspect of user interface design as well: Design decisions have consequences. What if the user accidentally turns off the notification? You should provide some way to turn these messages back on (short of removing and reinstalling the entire application). One way to handle this is to add a check box labeled "Show all warning and informational messages" to your application's customize dialog box. Thus, you could turn off each message individually, but if you ever went too far in disabling all messages, you could get them all back together.

Keep Things Simple

Some applications are overwhelmingly complex. Figure 1.8, for example, shows a portion of the options settings dialog boxes for Microsoft Outlook 2003. By clicking a few buttons, I've gotten modal dialog boxes stacked five deep, and this is just a small part of the hundreds of options that Outlook offers its users.

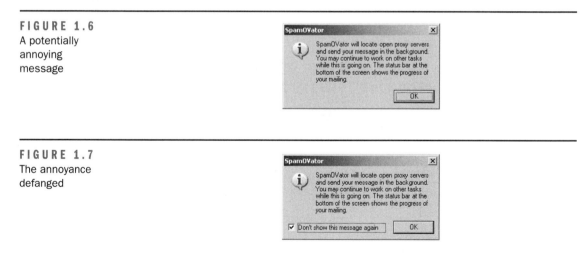

FIGURE 1.6
A potentially
annoying
message

FIGURE 1.7
The annoyance
defanged

FIGURE 1.8
Outlook offers too
much complexity for
most users

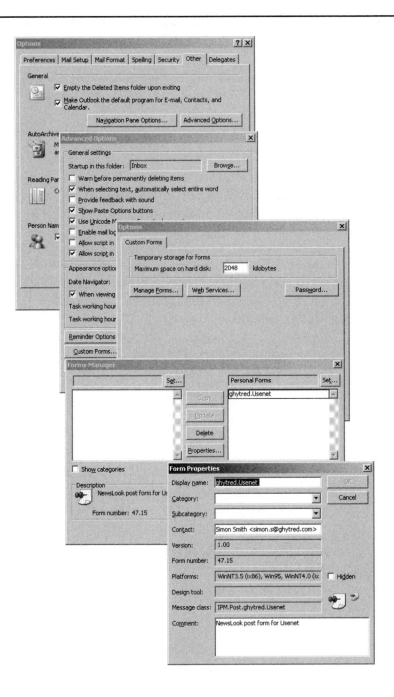

The designers and developers of Outlook would probably defend this interface by saying that every option in it is useful to some of their target audience, and that if they remove any control, users complain. And, of course, I did just recommend leaving the user in control. But the experience I have with Outlook users is rather telling. There are quite a few people who know that I've been using Outlook since the very first release, and I get instant messages and phone calls whose general subject is "how the heck do I do X with Outlook?"

Now, I'm not going to pretend that I have the solution to reorganizing Outlook's rat's nest of options into a more manageable format. But I do think that users are not given any meaningful measure of control by being presented with hundreds of options that they do not understand and cannot find. Part of what's going on here, I think, is a confusion of two different dimensions of user interface design. If you think of control as requiring complexity, your mental map of these factors looks like Figure 1.9.

FIGURE 1.9
Two dimensions
collapsed into one

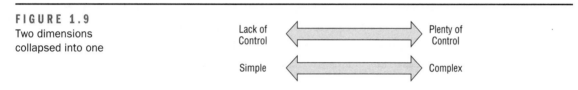

If you think that simplicity and lack of control are the same thing, it's going to be hard to keep the user in control and have a simple application. But thinking a bit deeper, you'll probably agree with me that the situation is better represented by Figure 1.10, in which simplicity and control are two distinct dimensions that can be independently varied.

As Figure 1.10 suggests, you can have a simple system in which the user has a high level of control (for example, the Segway human transporter) or a complex system that offers little control (for example, the stock market). For software, the sweet spot is to have a simple system that still offers the user enough control to perform all the tasks that they have in mind for your software. You're unlikely to design the perfectly simple application that keeps the user perfectly in control, but it's a goal worth striving for.

To make life even more confusing, simplicity itself is not a simple concept. When you try to make an application simpler, you might be doing any of these things:

- Removing extra controls from the user interface
- Minimizing the lines of code in the application
- Removing functionality from the application
- Adding hints or help to make the application easier to use
- Organizing controls into logical groups
- Hiding controls until they're needed

- Adding wizards to step the user through tasks
- Breaking up large dialog boxes into smaller ones

Any of these activities is a reasonable way to decrease the complexity of an application. But remember, the goal isn't just to make the program simpler: it's to make the user's interaction with the program simpler. One way to test whether you're moving in the right direction is to go back to the scenarios you've constructed for using the application. Imagine that you've built the application, and now you need to explain to one of your prototypical users how to use it to accomplish their tasks. Given two choices of user interface, the one that's easier to explain is almost certainly the simpler one.

There's one other test you should perform when using scenarios to test simplicity. Print out the user interface on paper, and work through your scenarios. As you use each piece of the interface in carrying out the users' tasks, cross that control out on the printout. When you're all done with scenarios, inspect the printout. If any controls are not crossed out, there are two possibilities. Either they're superfluous and your application's user interface can be simplified further, or you've missed an important scenario and should write it up for your master list.

FIGURE 1.10
A better way to think about simplicity and control

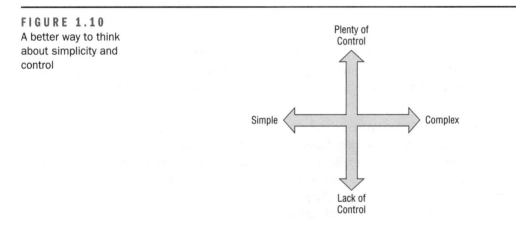

Be Direct

Consider the problem of applying formatting to text in a word processing application. What would you think if the user interface shown in Figure 1.11 were the only way to format text?

Certainly you *could* format a document this way—but it would be exceedingly tedious and painful. You'd need to count character positions, then open the modal dialog box and fill it in, and then hit OK. If you made any mistakes, it would be back to the dialog box. Each time you had to make a change it would require the same process, interrupting your train of thought.

Now compare this with the way that Microsoft Word actually handles this task, as shown in Figure 1.12.

Word's approach to the formatting problem is much more *direct* than the modal dialog box. You select the text that you want to format, and then click controls to dictate the formatting. Feedback is instantaneous, and you're not prevented from working on other tasks while you're deciding on formatting (this is an example of a modeless approach, as discussed earlier in the chapter).

In general, indirect user interfaces seem to appeal more to developers, whereas direct user interfaces are better for end users. As coders, we're used to writing instructions to tell the computer what to do. But for people who live a bit closer to the physical world than we do, it's more natural to pick an object and apply a tool to it. Most people would rather grab a hammer and take a whack at a nail than write detailed instructions telling someone else how to do it.

Directness in user interfaces comes into play any time there is some object that can be selected within the application. Note that I'm using "object" here in a rather naïve end-user sense, rather than in the technical sense of object-oriented programming. From the user's point of view, an object is anything (a database row, a cell in a spreadsheet, a paragraph of text, a rectangle on a drawing) that they can select. If it can also be dragged around the screen with the mouse, the illusion of objecthood is enhanced.

Given a set of end-user objects within an application, a direct user interface allows the user to select an object, and then choose a tool or operation to apply to that object. For example:

- Select a database row and click the Delete toolbar button to remove the row.
- Select a cell in a spreadsheet and use the Format menu to change the cell's background color.
- Select a paragraph of text and choose a font for the text from a drop-down menu.
- Select a rectangle and pour a new color into its interior with a paint bucket tool.

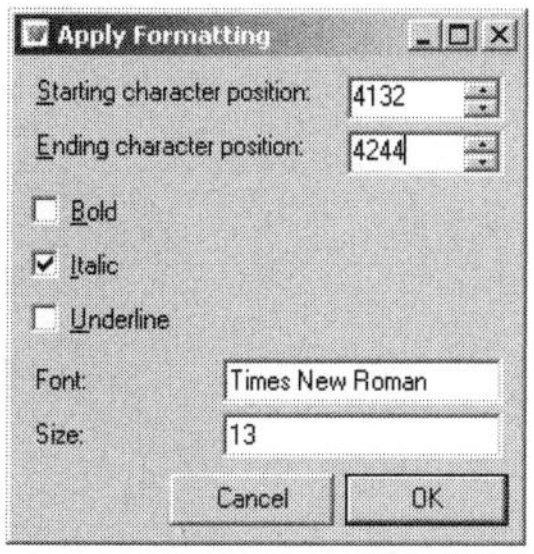

FIGURE 1.11
Indirect text formatting

FIGURE 1.12
Direct text formatting

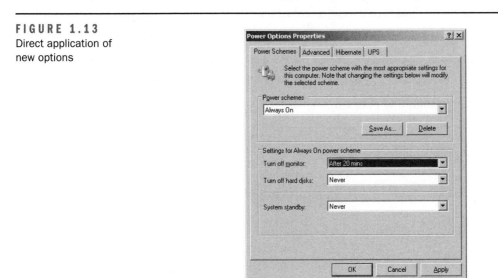

There's a common noun-verb pattern here. More informally, you might call this idiom "grab-this-do-that." My experience has been that this idiom is easy to explain, easy to remember, and a good fit for the way in which most users work with the computer.

WARNING   Remember, though: No matter how direct you make your interface, the computer is not the real world. Don't be afraid to abandon directness if an indirect interface makes more sense.

Another approach to directness is illustrated by many of the Windows Control Panel applets, such as the Power Options dialog box shown in Figure 1.13. When you make a change in options here, the Apply button is available to save the changes.

The three buttons at the bottom of this dialog box have three distinct functions:

- OK saves the changes and closes the dialog box.

- Apply saves the changes and leaves the dialog box open.

- Cancel discards the changes and closes the dialog box.

FIGURE 1.13
Direct application of
new options

Although this is by now a well-established Windows idiom, and it fits the "grab-this-do-that" pattern, it tends to be confusing to new users. If you choose to use this idiom in your own applications, you'll want to make sure you explain the difference between Apply and OK somewhere in the application's help file.

Be Forgiving

As Alexander Pope reminds us, to forgive is divine. Although your application probably doesn't aspire to divinity, forgiveness is still a virtue well worth keeping in mind. Users will rapidly develop a dislike for your application if it seems to be unforgiving of mistakes. This is an area that deserves particular attention because developers tend to develop blind spots to the unforgiving parts of their own applications. When you've written all of the code, it's quite easy to run through a usage scenario without making any missteps. But if you do this, you'll miss the places where one bad menu choice or errant toolbar button click can wipe out substantial work.

There are three main strategies that you can use to make applications more forgiving. The first is to make sure, as best you can, that users want to perform potentially destructive actions. Figure 1.14 shows the prompt that Windows XP displays when you tell it to delete a file.

Such prompts help make sure that a user actually intends to delete a file, but they can get annoying after a while. If you do opt to use confirmation prompts, you should provide a way to suppress or sidestep the prompts. This might involve a check box to suppress prompts in the future or a special key combination such as Alt+Delete to delete without prompting.

The second way to make your application more forgiving is to move rather than destroy information. Even if you tell Windows to go ahead and delete a file, it doesn't *really* delete the file. Instead, it moves the file to the Recycle Bin, from which you can recover it later if you change your mind. As with confirmation prompts, there are potential problems with this approach. In particular, you need to be sure that the user understands the consequences of their actions with respect to confidential information. You need to provide a way to do a real, permanent deletion of sensitive material. In fact, Microsoft does provide a way to really delete a file: Press Shift+Delete instead of Delete. But there isn't any easy way for most users to discover this shortcut.

FIGURE 1.14
Confirming a
destructive action

The final step toward application forgiveness is to implement some sort of undo facility. Most experienced Windows users have the Ctrl+Z keyboard combination wired into their fingertips because it's the most common shortcut for undo. Building undo into your applications allows users to recover quickly from mistakes by reversing the mistaken actions.

Some applications supply more sophisticated undo facilities than a simple reversal of the most recent action. For example, the Windows Recycle Bin preserves everything that you delete until you decide to empty it. As another example, Figure 1.15 shows the Undo drop-down list in Microsoft Word, which lets you reverse a whole set of actions at once.

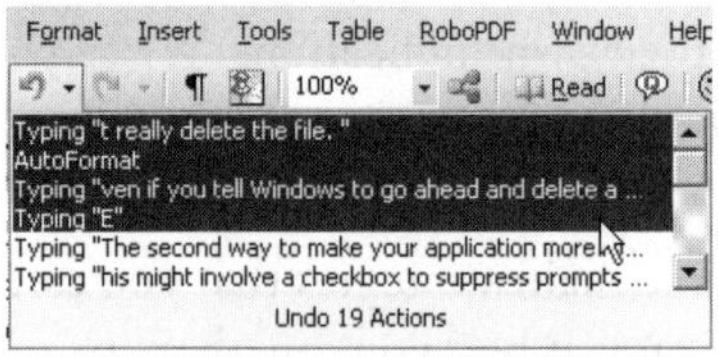

FIGURE 1.15
Multiple undo in
Microsoft Word

Be Consistent

If I had to choose just one guideline for good user interface design, it would be this one: Be consistent. I briefly mentioned this earlier in the chapter when discussing common idioms, but it's a topic worth a more extended discussion.

Consistency in software programs comes in at three different levels:

- Internal consistency
- Suite consistency
- Platform consistency

Internal consistency refers to an application's consistency with itself. If you implement ToolTips for toolbar buttons in the application, you should implement them for every toolbar button in the application. If you use pale yellow to indicate missing information on one dialog box, use that same color for the same purpose throughout the application. The goal of internal consistency is to establish a set of standards for the application that your users can depend on. This helps them build up their knowledge of how the application works more quickly and contributes to reaching a comfort level with your program.

Depending on the application, suite consistency may or may not come into play. If you're producing more than one program, and if they're meant to work together, you need to consider suite consistency. Microsoft Office is the prime example of how suite consistency works. If you know how an operation (such as multiple-level undo) works in one of the Office applications, you likely know how it works in all the rest. Office's suite consistency isn't perfect, but it is way ahead of that found in most groups of applications. By developing your own set of standards, you can make it easier for users of one of your applications to pick up on others. That tends to translate to increased sales, which is always a good thing.

Finally, platform consistency is concerned with making sure that your applications feel like they belong on the operating system (Microsoft Windows in the case of this book). To take a trivial example, Windows uses Ctrl+C for copy, Ctrl+X for cut, and Ctrl+V for paste. Your application should implement those same key combinations for those operations. To do otherwise is to leave users baffled and angry.

TIP   Microsoft has published an entire online book, *The Windows User Experience*, which discusses the standards for Windows applications. This book is available online (`http://msdn` `.microsoft.com/library/default.asp?url=/library/en-us/dnwue/html/welcome` `.asp`) and on the MSDN Library CD-ROMs, and should be required reading for anyone building Windows user interfaces.

Why is consistency so important? Because it cuts the learning curve for applications substantially. Whether they've been using Word and Excel or Notepad and Calculator, the chance is that users know something about the Windows standards. Any part of those standards that they can apply to your program is one less thing to learn. Similarly, suite consistency and internal consistency make it easier for people to figure out how your application works in the context of your other applications, or as a stand-alone program.

Summary

In this chapter, I tried to give you a broad overview of user interface design as it's practiced by developers. You learned some ways to think about software, some overall principles, and some basic guidelines. The rest of the book will show you how to apply these principles and guidelines to user interface construction in more detail. I'll start the process in the next chapter by looking at some of the issues surrounding the simple display of text on the user's computer monitor.

CHAPTER 2

Putting Words on the Screen

- Guidelines for Window Titles

- The Basics of User Interface Text

- Messages and More Messages

- Using ToolTips and Other Instant Help

- Dealing with Multiple Languages

- Text versus Images

'll start my tour of detailed design issues with a look at one of the simplest (yet most often overlooked) parts of user interface design: dealing with words on the screen. Between window titles, labels, ToolTips, and other controls, the average application has plenty to say to the user. This is a great place to start thinking about adhering to conventions and making the most of the available screen real estate.

Guidelines for Window Titles

For the most part, applications with a user interface display information in one or more windows (there are other possibilities, such as an application that runs only in the notification area of the Taskbar, but I'm not concerned with them right now; you'll learn more about using the notification area in Chapter 3, "Managing Windows"). Each of these windows is identified by some text in the title bar of the window, between the icon at the upper left and the system buttons at the upper right. Choosing the right text for this purpose is surprisingly tricky if you want to adhere to all the Windows guidelines. It turns out that the rules change depending on the type of window:

- Windows without documents
- Windows containing a single document
- Windows containing multiple documents

WARNING   Keep in mind that although there are rules for designing title text, it's depressingly easy to find applications—even Microsoft applications—that ignore these rules. For example, if you compare the title bars of Microsoft Word and Microsoft Excel, you'll see that they disagree on whether the application name (in Excel) or the open file name (in Word) should come first. According to the standards, Word does the right thing and Excel does the wrong thing.

Windows Without Documents

For applications that don't create or edit data files, the rule is simple: Display the name of the application in the title bar. For example, the Windows Character Map application, shown in Figure 2.1, places its own name and icon in the title bar.

But this rule, although simple, isn't universal because many applications use the title bar to indicate the current *context* of the application—an indication of what the user is doing or using right now. The Windows guidelines allow this when the title bar can convey useful information. An obvious example of this is Windows Explorer. Although Explorer doesn't create or edit files, it displays the name of the current folder in the title bar, as shown in Figure 2.2.

FIGURE 2.1
Title bar for an
application without
data files

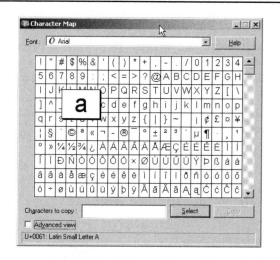

FIGURE 2.2
Title bar in Windows
Explorer

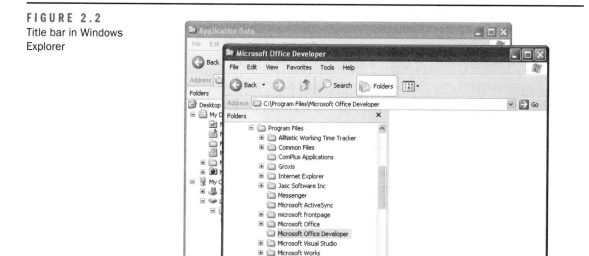

Because Windows also displays the title bar text on the Taskbar, using the folder name as the title bar text makes it easy for the user to select the Explorer window that they want from the Taskbar if they have more than one such window open.

NOTE   Explorer is a fertile source of incompatibilities between versions of Windows. If you open Explorer windows on Windows 2000 or Windows Server 2003, you'll discover that the title bar includes the full path to the selected folder. On Windows XP, the Explorer title bar includes only the name of the selected folder. The best advice I can give you is to think about the context (if any) that's important for your users and to standardize one title bar text across all operating systems.

WARNING   Think carefully before you adapt the practice of using the title bar to convey application context. Doing so means that minimized windows change title depending on what you were doing in the application, and you must recognize the application icon to select the correct window. This can be troubling for users with visual disabilities and confusing to everyone.

Single-Document Interface Windows

Applications designed to edit only one file at a time are referred to as single-document interface (SDI) applications. Notepad is a simple example of an SDI application. For an SDI application, the rule is to display the name of the data file, followed by a dash and the name of the application, as shown in Figure 2.3.

There are some additional rules that you should follow when constructing title bar text for SDI applications:

- If the user hasn't yet saved the document, use a default name in the title bar. For example, Microsoft Word uses `Document1`, whereas Notepad uses `(Untitled)` as its default.

- Display the filename exactly as it appears in the file system, including upper- and lowercase letters.

- Don't display the file extension unless the user has chosen to display file extensions in Windows Explorer.

It's easy to comply with the last two rules, because Windows supplies the GetFileTitle application programming interface (API) call. Calling this API with a filename shows you the title that Windows itself will use for the file, which is also the title that you should use in your own applications.

FIGURE 2.3
SDI application with
an open file

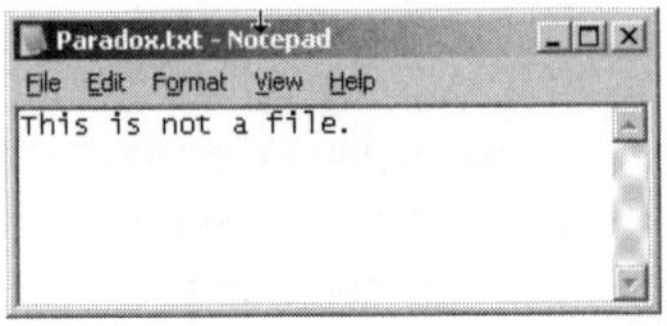

Multiple-Document Interface Windows

Some applications support viewing or editing more than one file at the same time by using multiple child windows within a single parent window. These applications are called multiple-document interface (MDI) applications. With MDI applications, there are two rules:

- If a single document is maximized in the workspace, the title bar text should consist of that document's name, followed by a dash and then the application name.

- If no document is maximized in the workspace, the title bar text should consist only of the application's name.

Microsoft Visio is a good example of an application that takes this approach. Figure 2.4 shows Visio with a document maximized in the work area. In this configuration, the document name is on the title bar. Figure 2.5 shows the same Visio session with the document restored to its smaller size within the Visio workspace.

Classic MDI applications have been declining in popularity over the last few years, led by Microsoft's movement of its Office suite away from MDI. Some Microsoft applications such as Excel still use a traditional MDI interface, but others, such as Word, have a separate window and taskbar for each open document. This has led to a variety of ways to handle multiple windows. Many applications use a tabbed user interface to display multiple windows within a single workspace. There don't seem to be any real standards for what to display on the title bar in this case. Microsoft Visual Studio .NET, for example, displays both the name of the loaded project and the name of the active window, as shown in Figure 2.6. In general, I'd suggest you treat separate windows as though they were MDI windows with maximized documents.

FIGURE 2.4
MDI application with a maximized file

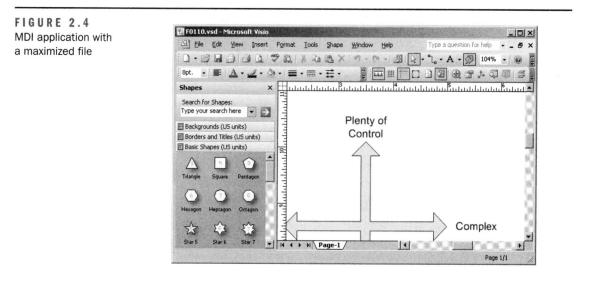

FIGURE 2.5
MDI application without a maximized file

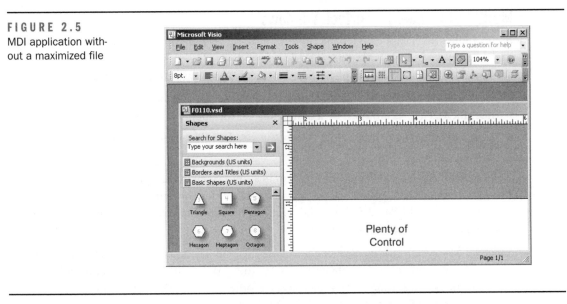

FIGURE 2.6
A non-standard MDI title bar

The main purpose of the title bar is to help users find your application if they have many windows open at the same time. This means that you should consider what's needed to identify the application (and to distinguish between multiple instances of the application) and then use that information on the title bar.

TIP Don't place extraneous information, such as status messages, in the title bar. There are other places (such as the status bar at the bottom of your application) for such information. You'll learn more about using the status bar in Chapter 8, "Common Windows User Interface Elements."

The Basics of User Interface Text

Moving down from the title bar, you come to the text in the application's windows and dialog boxes. Broadly speaking, there are two purposes for user interface text: identification and instruction. Some text serves to identify the purpose of other controls. Other text serves to help the user carry out a task. Of course, there are standards that apply to both of these areas.

Thinking About Text

There are many different genres of writing in the world, each with its own conventions. A classical Greek tragedy, the official rules for the game of basketball, and a romance novel each have certain standards that help identify their intended purpose and audience. So too with user interface writing. Placing text on the user interface tends to be guided by constraints on time and space. Computer users tend to be rushed for time; they don't want to read long chunks of text on screen. And in any case, most users don't have sufficient screen resolution for extensive paragraphs of text to be visible at the same time. These limitations of writing for user interfaces lead to some rules that you should keep in mind.

First, it's incredibly important to keep your text short, simple, and direct. Every word that you place on the user interface should have a reason for being there. You should also strive to make the text instantly understandable to any user of the application. Remember that you're distributing your application in a global market. Particularly if you don't make localized versions available, the application can be used by people whose English skills are not perfect. Avoid uncommon contractions and unusual terms unless they're absolutely necessary.

Because space is limited, you should avoid duplicating text. If the labels on buttons and other controls already explain what's going on, there's no need to add additional text confirming their use. An exception to this comes when you're designing a wizard or other task-based user interface that's designed to walk the beginning user slowly through a process.

Use standard verbs when writing about user actions:

- *Click* for the act of clicking the mouse, or to describe any other way of selecting a command button, hyperlink, menu, or similar control.
- *Select* for the act of selecting an item in a list box, combo box, or listview; or for checking a check box.
- *Clear* for the act of removing the check from a check box.
- *Press* for the act of pressing a key on the keyboard.
- *Choose* for the act of selecting one item on a menu.

Identification Text

Figure 2.7 shows some of the common standards for identification text.

If you inspect this figure carefully, you can see several different standards in use:

- Labels for text boxes (and other controls that are identified by text to their left) use sentence case with a colon at the end.

- Labels for combo boxes and option buttons (that is, controls that are identified by text to their right) use sentence case with no colon or other punctuation. This standard also applies to the text of list box and combo box items.

- Text on command buttons use title case. This standard also applies to ToolTips, column headings, toolbar buttons, and window titles.

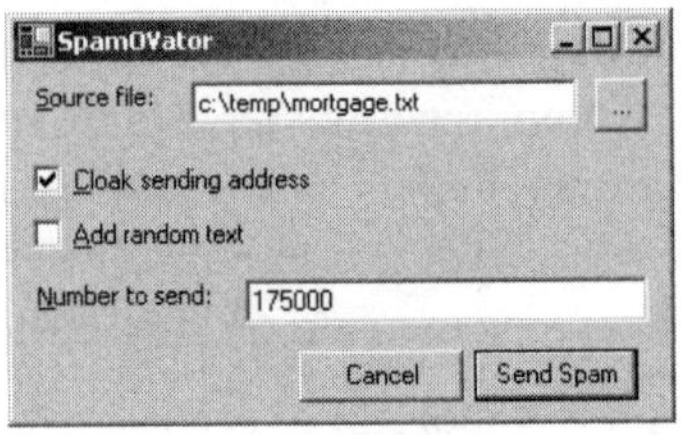

FIGURE 2.7
Identification text
on a form

TIP   When using sentence case, you capitalize the first letter of each sentence. When using title case, you capitalize the first letter of each word except for prepositions of four letters or fewer.

Will your application function any differently if you ignore these rules? No. But your users might end up thinking that it looks funny or be confused by your non-standard ways of doing things. Computer software is hard enough to use without putting this sort of artificial barrier in the way of your users.

Instructional Text

Figure 2.8 shows a bit of user interface with some instructional text. In this case, the text is displayed while the user is working with a wizard, and it describes the actions to be performed in this step of the wizard.

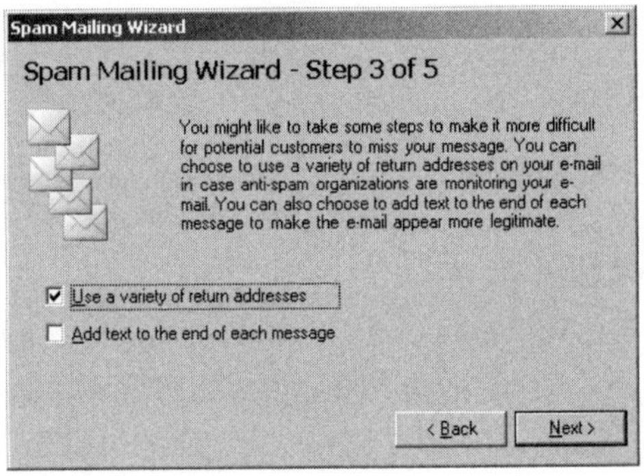

FIGURE 2.8
Instructional text
on a wizard

Generally, you'll see instructional text on parts of the user interface that are geared to less-experienced users: wizards, task panes, and the like. You should use full sentences and regular punctuation here. In addition, it's a good idea to keep your instructional text task-based. This is the place where you want to tell users how to perform the particular task that they're trying to carry out. Background information or notes on how your product stores data should be relegated to the help file and other reference documentation, not imposed on the user interface.

Messages and More Messages

Of course, words displayed as a regular part of your user interface are not the only text that you'll need to share with users. Most applications end up needing to display transient information, such as warnings or questions, during the course of their work. Figure 2.9 shows the four standard types of message box built into Windows to handle these needs.

Each of these types of message box is intended for a specific purpose:

- Information message boxes contain information that the user should acknowledge to confirm that they understand what's going on with the application.

- Warning message boxes contain information about unexpected results or problems that do not prevent the application from continuing.

- Question message boxes are used to elicit short input from the user.

- Error message boxes contain information on problems that (at least potentially) prevent the application from continuing.

WARNING Microsoft recommends that you avoid the question icon type entirely, and instead use one of the other types of message boxes (depending on severity) for questions. I don't happen to agree with this recommendation myself; I've seen too many users confused by a warning or error that asks them a question.

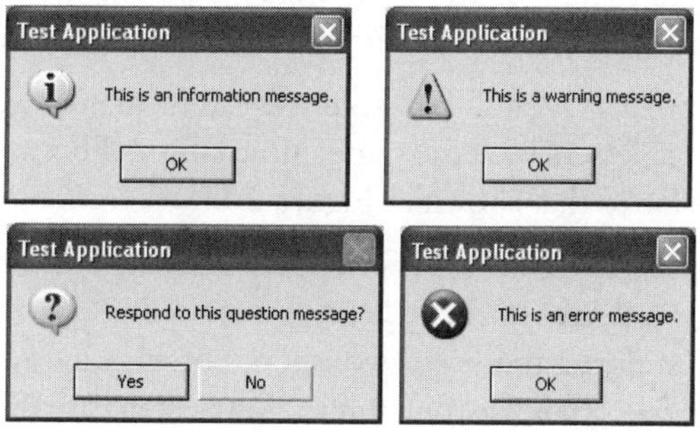

FIGURE 2.9
Information, warning,
question, and error
message boxes

NOTE   The icons shown in Figure 2.9 are the most recent versions supplied by Windows XP. Older versions of Windows use different icons for the same concepts, such as a stop sign for errors.

Message boxes are provided by Windows itself, and most programming languages supply a way to invoke them. For example, in the .NET languages you can use the Show method of the System.Windows.Forms.MessageBox class to display a message box. Windows also supplies a standard selection of sets of buttons that you can show in a message box:

- Abort, Retry, Ignore
- OK
- OK, Cancel
- Retry, Cancel
- Yes, No
- Yes, No, Cancel

It's important to keep message box use to a minimum. If a program is too "chatty," it will be perceived as interrupting the user's work. For example, successful operations generally do *not* require an information message box. Figure 2.10 shows an example of a message box that's not needed.

FIGURE 2.10
An annoying and superfluous message box

Users have a justified expectation that your program is functioning properly unless you go out of your way to tell them otherwise. Confirming that all systems are operating correctly quickly gets to be a nuisance. The problem is that message boxes interrupt the smooth flow of the application; no matter what users were doing before you decided to display a message box, they have to stop and deal with your information or question.

In some cases, you'll want to present information geared to new users while not bothering experienced users with the same information. This requirement can be handled with an interface similar to that shown in Figure 2.11.

Unfortunately, adding a check box to a message box isn't a part of the standard system message box, so you'll have to create your own form if you want to follow this path. Also, if you provide a way to suppress messages, you should provide a way to turn them back on (perhaps in the Options dialog box for your application) just in case the user has second thoughts about turning the messages off.

FIGURE 2.11
A message that can
be suppressed

FIGURE 2.11
A message that can
be suppressed

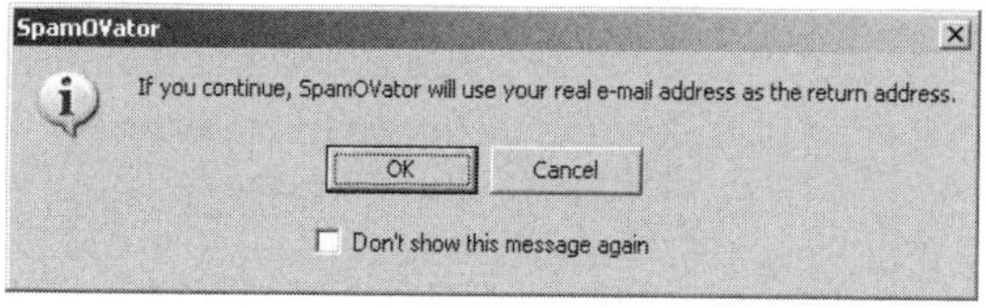

Another source of annoyance is the infamous "Are you sure?" message boxes that some applications like to present to the user. If there's no other way to handle potentially destructive actions, you might be forced to such confirming message boxes. The problem is that it's difficult to get users to actually read "Are you sure?" messages. After just a bit of exposure to your application, most users will just automatically click Yes when such a message box appears, robbing it of its hoped-for effect of inducing thought. A better path is to add an Undo capability to your program that lets the user back out of destructive changes if they decide they've made a mistake. That way, you don't annoy the experienced user and you still protect the novice.

Some other guidelines for message box use:

- Always include the application name in the message box title. If they have multiple applications running, users might not immediately realize which application displayed a message without this help.

- Use complete sentences in the message itself.

- If you're warning the user of a non-fatal problem, give them as much information as you can about correcting the error.

- As with other user interface text, keep message boxes concise and free of extraneous information.

- If you can automatically fix a problem, give the user the opportunity to do so. Figure 2.12 shows two versions of a message box; the second is preferable to the first because it offers to fix the problem.

FIGURE 2.12
The message box on
the bottom is better
than the one on top

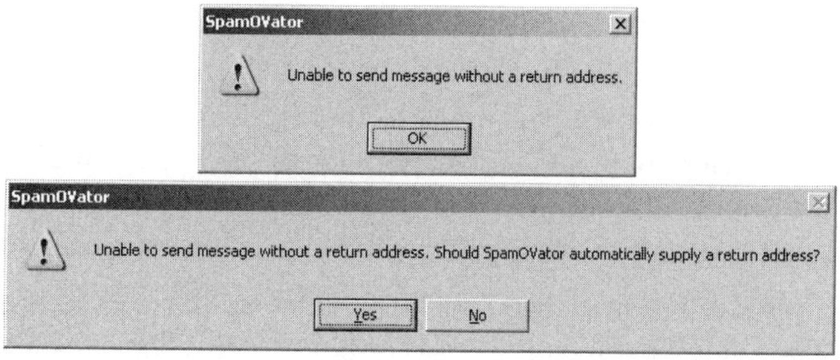

Using ToolTips and Other Instant Help

Some bits of text are short and transient—but that doesn't mean that you can ignore them. In this category, I put ToolTips, context-sensitive help, and text on the status bar.

Using ToolTips

ToolTips exist because of one simple problem: toolbar buttons are simply not large enough to tell every user what they do. Some buttons (for example, those for common functions such as cut, copy, or paste) are familiar to almost every user. But others, particularly those that lead to new features, might be completely opaque. Consider Figure 2.13, which shows a portion of the Microsoft InfoPath 2003 user interface. Without the ToolTip, would you know what the highlighted button does?

FIGURE 2.13
ToolTip as a source of identification text

By now, ToolTips are so common that users expect them to go with any toolbar button. You should consider them a required part of the user interface if your application includes toolbars. The text in a ToolTip should be in title case with no punctuation.

Some development environments let you add ToolTips to other controls, as shown in Figure 2.14. This is generally not a good idea. The ToolTip in this figure doesn't add any information. It's just a redundant nuisance that gets in the way of other controls.

FIGURE 2.14
A pointless ToolTip

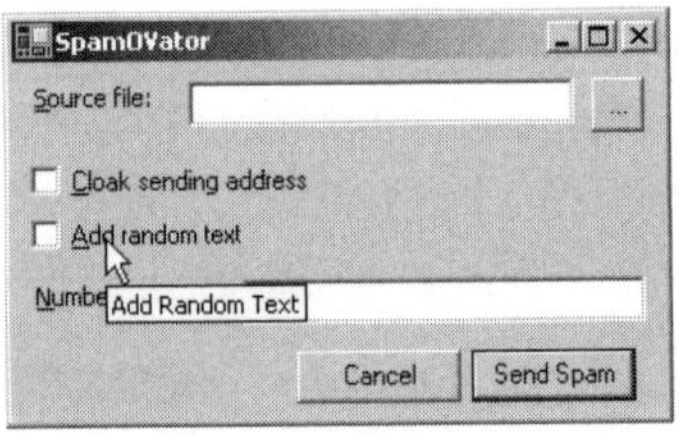

You might be tempted to use a ToolTip like the one shown in Figure 2.14 to provide additional instructions and explanations for the user. But remember, a ToolTip pops up whenever the user hovers the mouse for a while. You're better off using a less-intrusive mechanism, such as context-sensitive help (discussed next) for this purpose.

Also keep in mind that ToolTips are essential to most accessibility aids such as screen readers. Though I'm not focusing on accessibility in this book, it's worth keeping in mind that many users may not be seeing the interface the same way that you do. Screen readers, for example, will identify controls by reading their ToolTips. If you neglect to set a ToolTip for a particular control, the screen reader won't be able to "see" that control, and the user won't be able to interact with it. This is another good reason to keep ToolTip text succinct. If you were using a screen reader, you'd much rather wait for "Display options" than "Click here to display options for the current application."

Supplying Context-Sensitive Help

Context-sensitive help is sometimes called "What's This?" help. Windows applications can enable context-sensitive help in any or all of these ways:

- Through Help ➤ What's This?
- Through a What's This? toolbar button
- Through a What's This? button on the title bar of a dialog box
- Through a What's This? shortcut menu item
- Through the What's This? shortcut key, Shift+F1

In most cases, these actions will change the cursor to the help cursor, which is a combination of the regular pointer and a question mark (the exception is the shortcut menu item, which immediately displays the message for the control whose shortcut menu is being shown). Clicking the help cursor on a control displays the help for that control, as shown in Figure 2.15.

Keep these points in mind when using context-sensitive help:

- Use complete sentences with punctuation in the help messages.
- Keep help messages concise because they block the user's view of other parts of the interface.
- Supply messages for every control on the form. It's frustrating to click the help cursor on a control and have nothing happen.
- Try to answer the questions "What is this?" and "Why should I use this control?" for the user.
- Don't supply help for portions of the user interface that don't do anything (such as labels).

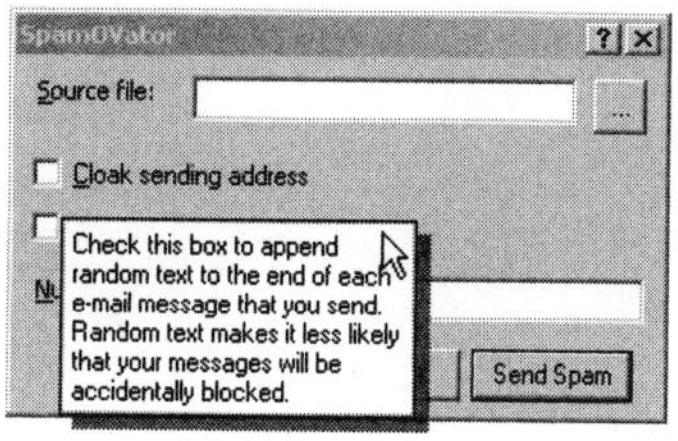

FIGURE 2.15
Using context-sensitive help to provide extra information

Working with the Status Bar

A third way to supply bits of information to the user is through the status bar at the bottom of the application's main window. Not every application has a status bar, but many do. Figure 2.16 shows a typical status bar in Internet Explorer 6.0.

The experienced user can tell several things from this status bar:

- IE is currently displaying a web page.
- The cursor is hovering over a hyperlink, and the destination address is shown.
- The current page is secured by SSL.
- The current site is in the Internet zone.

The status bar is a good place for non-critical information that the user might or might not want to know. It is not a good place for critical messages and notifications that the user must acknowledge. That's because text in this area can be very easy for users to overlook. The status bar is also a good place for text and indicators that should not interrupt the user's work. For example, Word uses the status bar to display the current page number and the total number of pages in the document. It can update this information without interrupting whatever the user happens to be typing.

FIGURE 2.16
An application with
a status bar
(Image copyright
1999–2004
QuiltIndex.com,
used by permission)

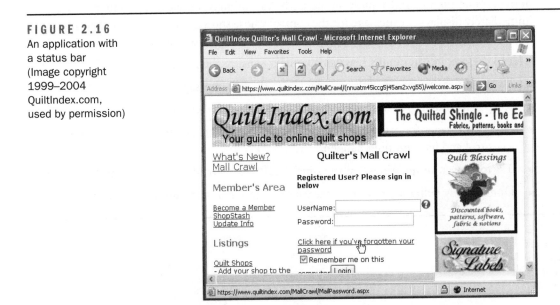

Dealing with Multiple Languages

When you're designing a user interface, you need to be aware of the possibility that it will someday be translated into another human language, even if you plan to produce only an English-language version to start. Although I won't cover localization in any depth in this book, there are some things that you can do to make it easier to localize an application.

The key to easy localization is to set things up so that translating the user interface text does not require any other changes to the application. That way, you can send out the translation job to some company that specializes in such things and not have to rearrange controls to hold the translated text when they're done. The first thing to realize in this regard is that translated text will often be as much as 30 percent larger than the English version, so you need to leave room for the expansion. When placing labels and other controls containing text on the user interface, make sure that you allow for this growth.

Keep in mind, too, that word order might be different in other languages. Figure 2.17 shows two possible ways to prompt for a number in an application. The second of these ways is preferred because it won't require moving the text box control around to accommodate different word orders and sentence lengths.

Planning for localization is another good reason to keep your user interface text simple and direct. To make life easier for the translator, you should avoid idioms that might not translate well. For example, "You have completed the process!" is more easily localized than "That's the cat's pajamas!" No matter how direct your language, though, you should make yourself available to help sort out difficult translation issues.

Text versus Images

Designers sometimes try to replace the text in a user interface with images. For example, the toolbar in Internet Explorer uses large flashy icons to indicate major functions within the application (Figure 2.18).

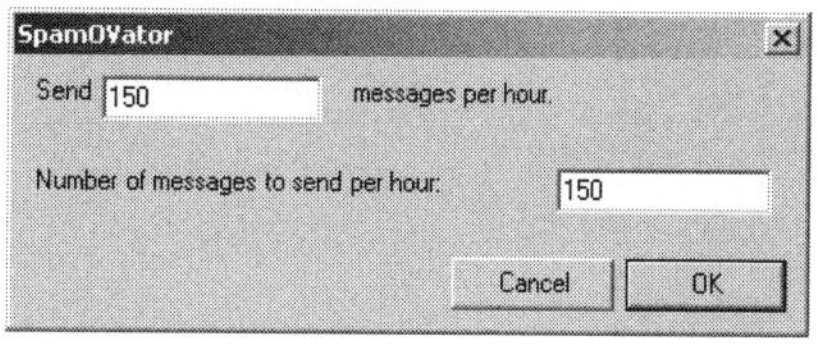

FIGURE 2.17
The lower set of controls is more easily localized than the upper set of controls

FIGURE 2.18
The Internet
Explorer toolbar

Notice that Internet Explorer doesn't depend solely on images, however; it defaults to showing text with some of the buttons. You can turn this off in the application's options, but Microsoft made a wise decision to make text the default; otherwise, no one would figure out what the star icon was for (and the clock icon is still opaque).

Even this limited use of images in place of text doesn't move well from the toolbar to the rest of the application window. This is a good example of the failings of the supposedly intuitive user interface that I discussed in Chapter 1, "The Big Picture." Images alone don't convey the same thing to every user, even in the developer's home country, let alone around the world. And if you will add text to explain the images, what's the point of the images?

My advice is to leave the images for decoration. Images serve a purpose on some parts of the user interface. For example, the wizard screen that you saw in Figure 2.8 is made easier on the eyes by the inclusion of a relatively large graphic. But in general, you should make sure that the text of the user interface tells users what to do and how to do it, rather than trying to depend on images.

Summary

In this chapter, you learned the basics of working with text on the user interface. Whether you're assigning a title to a window, presenting labels to identify part of the user interface, or popping up messages or ToolTips, there are standards that all Windows applications share. Remember that text exists to identify parts of the user interface or to instruct the user. You should ruthlessly prune all other text from your application's interface to make it as easy to use as possible.

I briefly touched on the issue of window management in this chapter (in the discussion of SDI and MDI applications). But there's a lot more to know on that topic, which is the subject of the next chapter.

CHAPTER 3

Managing Windows

- Why Windows?

- Types of Windows

- Arranging Windows

- Working with Windows

Windows provide the fundamental way in which a user views and interacts with data. Consistency in window design is particularly important because it enables users to easily transfer their learning skills and to focus on completing their tasks rather than on learning new conventions. To a large extent, Microsoft Windows itself will take care of managing your application's windows. For example, you don't need to write any code to handle the mechanics of turning a full-sized window into a minimized icon, or to display the window contents while it's being dragged around the screen. But you still need to decide which windows your application needs to work effectively for your users.

Why Windows?

Back in the dark ages (that is, a bit over a decade ago), those of us using Microsoft software used DOS as our operating system. Over the years, DOS evolved in sophistication, but for the most part it was a single-task operating system. We ran one application, worked with it for a while, and then shut it down to use another application. But we programmers (being the sneaky people that we are) gradually worked out ways to run more than one application at a time. One popular dodge was the terminate-and-stay-resident (TSR) program. TSR programs pretended to DOS that they were done, but they really lurked in memory, waiting for the press of a key to pop up on screen and do something useful.

The experience of working with TSR programs convinced many of us that using more than one application concurrently made good sense. But it was pretty obvious that you couldn't just jumble the information from all of those applications together on screen in one untidy heap. The answer was (and has remained) the window: a rectangular area on screen that is owned by a particular application. With an operating system (such as Windows) that supports windows, you can run as many applications as you like, each with its own window on the screen. Of course, Microsoft wasn't the only company to come up with this idea. You can trace the history of windowing systems back to places like Xerox's Palo Alto Research Center, and into consumer product like DesqView that provided windowing environments on the PC before Microsoft did.

Most Windows applications with a user interface will display at least one window on screen (the exception being applications that run entirely as an icon in the notification area of the Taskbar and full screen applications such as screen savers). This is the application's *primary window*, which delimits the application's area on screen. A primary window might contain controls that the user directly interacts with, or it might be home to *secondary windows* (such as document windows if your application allows users to open more than one document at a time).

NOTE	The notification area is a region at the end of the Taskbar opposite the Start button in which various icons for running applications are displayed. You'll often find the notification area referred to as the *tray* or the *system tray*, but those names are wrong according to the official Windows documentation. They're in widespread use, though, wrong or not. For a discussion of this terminology issue, see `http://blogs.msdn.com/oldnewthing/archive/2003/09/10/54831.aspx`.

Windows come in a variety of forms. In addition to displaying information and documents to the user, a window might be used to

- Accept input and parameters necessary to complete a particular action such as opening a file.
- Display the properties of an object.
- Supply a palette of options or tools.
- Warn the user of an error or other problem.

In many of these cases, you don't need to worry about the look of the window at all. Warnings, for example, are normally shown in a message box window, so although you need to choose an appropriate icon, message, and buttons, Windows takes care of formatting the window for you.

Types of Windows

Ordinarily, most of a user's interaction with an application is with the primary window of the applications. But any application might also include a variety of secondary windows. In this section, I'll present a selection of window types and discuss the ways that they ordinarily function.

Primary Windows

There are some features you (and your users) should expect to see as a part of any primary window. These include the following:

- Window frame
- Title bar
- Title bar icon
- Title bar text
- Title bar buttons
- Scroll bars

NOTE   Of course, a window with just these listed features is essentially useless. In any real application, you'll have some combination of text and images to communicate with the user, and controls to let the user interact with the application. Chapters 4 through 8 cover the things that you can put inside of windows.

You're undoubtedly familiar with these elements simply from working with Windows, but let's take a closer look. Knowing how the standard elements work keeps you from wasting time by duplicating features elsewhere in your application.

When there was only a single version of Windows in use (for example, when Windows 3.1 had the bulk of the market share), it was possible to give strict guidance about how these various elements should be drawn. If you wanted to create your own window, for whatever reason, you would draw a rectangle of a specific color and thickness. Now, things are not so simple because windows appearance changes with different versions of the operating system. Figure 3.1, for example, shows a portion of a Notepad window (greatly enlarged) on a Windows Server 2003 system.

Figure 3.2 shows the same portion of the same application on a Windows XP system. The shading is different, the title bar font is different, and the corner of the primary window is curved (to name the more obvious changes).

To make things even more complex, all current versions of Windows leave the details of window styling—such as fonts and colors—up to the user. One user with visual disabilities might prefer 36-point type in the title bar; another with a particular sense of style might like lime-green text on a fuchsia background. The practical outcome of this state of affairs is that you should just let the operating system format the windows, and you can concentrate on the content, such as the particular text and controls inside of each window. If your application's design calls for "fake" windows (for example, showing a bitmap picture of a window in place of the actual window), you should seriously rethink the design.

FIGURE 3.1
Notepad on Windows
Server 2003

FIGURE 3.2
Notepad on
Windows XP

The top portion of the application's primary window is reserved for the title bar. This bar serves to identify the window, as well as to support standard functionality that should be present for every primary window. Figure 3.3 shows a typical title bar.

FIGURE 3.3
Title bar for Notepad

Untitled - Notepad   _ □ ×

At the far left of the title bar is the window's icon. If the application is not structured around document management, this should be the icon of the application itself. If the application is structured around document management, the window's icon should be the application's icon if no document is loaded or a document icon if any documents are loaded.

Clicking the primary mouse button on the window's icon, clicking the secondary mouse button on the title bar, or pressing Alt+Space opens the system menu for the application. As the name implies, the system menu (which is the same for every primary window) contains these commands:

- Restore
- Move
- Size
- Minimize
- Maximize
- Close

To the right of the icon, you'll find the title bar text. I discussed choosing the proper title bar text in Chapter 2, "Putting Words on the Screen."

The title bar buttons are located at the far right of the title bar. There are always three of these buttons grouped together. The first and second buttons are right next to each other, and there's a small gap before the third button:

- If the window is maximized, the buttons are Minimize, Restore, and Close.
- If the window is minimized, the buttons are Restore, Maximize, and Close.
- If the window is neither maximized nor minimized, the buttons are Minimize, Maximize, and Close.

Under most circumstances, you can't see the buttons when the window is minimized because under current versions of Windows, all minimized windows are automatically relocated to the Taskbar as buttons. But theoretically they're still there, and in future versions of Windows, they could be visible again, as they were in versions of Windows before Windows 95.

The functions of these buttons are ordinarily quite standard. The maximize button expands the primary window to occupy the entire screen (and, in so doing, hides the window frame). The minimize button minimizes the window to its smallest possible size. The restore button reverses the effect of a maximize or minimize operation to return the window to an intermediate size. However, there is one special case that you'll encounter fairly frequently for the minimize button. Rather than minimizing to the Taskbar, some applications minimize to an icon in the notification area of the Taskbar.

This behavior is typical of utilities that run in the background but still need to present both status information and a full user interface. For example, consider Hardware Sensors Monitor (http://www.hmonitor.com/). This utility monitors CPU temperatures and other important hardware information. During ordinary operation, Hardware Sensors Monitor provides feedback via a notification area icon that changes color when a sensor is out of its optimal range, as shown in Figure 3.4.

FIGURE 3.4
Hardware Sensors
Monitor in the
notification area

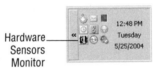

When the icon changes color, Hardware Sensors Monitor has more information to display. In this case, double-clicking the notification area icon will show the full user interface, which you can see in Figure 3.5.

When you're done inspecting the actual values, you can hit the minimize button, and Hardware Sensors monitor minimizes back to the notification area.

FIGURE 3.5
Hardware Sensors
Monitor expanded
to the screen

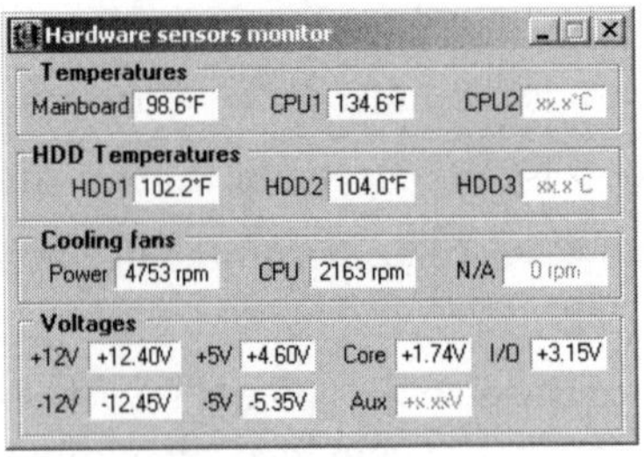

Although this behavior is useful in a utility whose user interface you want to see only occasionally, it's certainly non-standard. There are two guidelines you should follow if you decide that this (or any other non-standard use of the title bar buttons) is right for your application:

- Make sure that the user understands that your application behaves in this non-standard way by explicitly documenting the behavior somewhere obvious (such as in the readme file, the application's splash screen, the help file, the written documentation, or all of these).

- Make the behavior optional. For example, provide a check box on your Tools ➢ Options dialog box to enable or disable the "minimize to Taskbar tray" behavior.

The last piece of the standard primary window interface that deserves a mention is the scroll bar. A window might have no scroll bars (or one, or two, depending on whether it allows horizontal or vertical scrolling). Like the other standard widgets, Windows draws scroll bars differently depending on the version of the operating system. Figure 3.6 shows scroll bars under Windows XP, and Figure 3.7 shows the same scroll bars under Windows Server 2003.

FIGURE 3.6
Windows XP–style
scroll bars

FIGURE 3.7
Windows 2003–style
scroll bars

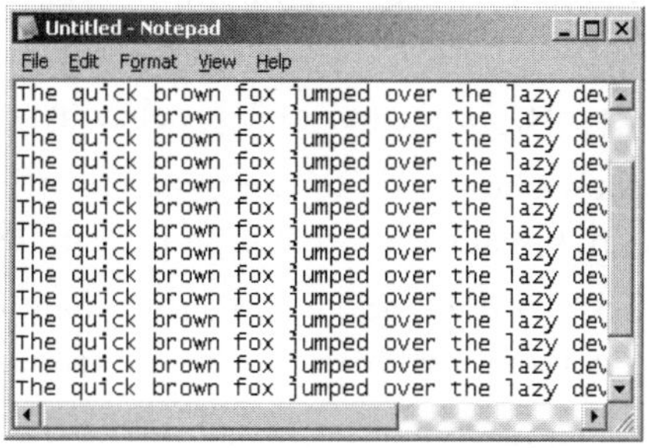

If a primary window will contain more information than can fit on the screen at one time, scroll bars provide the standard way to display the additional information. The same is true of secondary document windows. In addition to giving the user a way to get to the additional information, the scroll bars provide an important clue that the additional information exists.

Scroll bars are not the only way to display additional information. Dialog boxes in particular are not normally drawn with scroll bars. Instead, these windows can use an unfolding mechanism (as I'll discuss in the "Dialog Boxes" section later in this chapter).

Secondary Windows

Almost any application has one or more secondary windows to support the operations of the main window. Secondary windows come in many varieties. In this section, I'll discuss the ones that you should be familiar with when designing your own applications:

- Document windows
- Dialog boxes
- Task panes
- Property sheets and property inspectors
- Floating auxiliary windows

In addition to these windows, which are usually long-lived parts of the user interface, most applications make use of message boxes to communicate important information to users. (For more information on message box design, refer to Chapter 2.)

Document Windows

Document windows are used by applications that allow editing more than one document at the same time (see "Multiple Document Interface" later in this chapter). Figure 3.8 shows a user interface with one primary window and two secondary document windows (in this case, the application is Paint Shop Pro, http://www.jasc.com).

For the most part, document windows behave just like primary windows—with a few differences:

- Document windows use an icon indicating the document, rather than one indicating the application. Usually the two are similar but distinct, as shown in Figure 3.8.
- Right-clicking on the title bar of a document window usually reveals a more extensive shortcut menu than right-clicking on a primary window.
- Document windows get *clipped* (cut off) by the edge of the primary window. You can't drag a document window out of the primary window.
- Document windows minimize and maximize within the boundaries of their parent primary window.

FIGURE 3.8
Document windows in
a parent application

In document-oriented applications that allow editing multiple documents at the same time, users typically do all or most of their work in document windows. Menu items and toolbar buttons in the primary window apply to the contents of the active document window in this case.

Dialog Boxes

Another form of secondary window that you'll encounter frequently is the dialog box. Figure 3.9 shows a typical dialog box.

FIGURE 3.9
Using a dialog box to
collect user input

By convention, dialog boxes have a distinct look and feel:

- The border of a dialog box is not resizable.

- The title bar of a dialog box contains only the title text, the close button, and an optional "What's This?" help button. The title text is usually the name of the command that opened the dialog box.

- A dialog box should contain a single button to commit the changes shown and to close the dialog box. The caption of this button is OK and it is the default control (so that it responds to the Enter key).

- A dialog box might contain a button to discard the changes shown and to close the dialog box. If it contains this button, it should be labeled Cancel and respond to the Escape key.

Although dialog boxes do not have a resizable border, they can sometimes be resized. This is accomplished through a process known as *unfolding*. Consider the standard color picker dialog box shown in Figure 3.10. By default, it lets you pick from one of 48 basic colors.

But Windows is capable of displaying far more than 48 colors. When you click the Define Custom Colors button in the dialog box, it unfolds to display the additional controls shown in Figure 3.11.

Note the visual cue offered by the chevrons (>>) on the Define Custom Colors button. In many cases, you can use one button to both unfold and refold a dialog box by adjusting the caption. For example, when the dialog box is in its folded state, the button could read Show Advanced Properties >>; and when the dialog box is in its unfolded state, the same button would read Hide Advanced Properties <<.

FIGURE 3.10
The Edit Colors
dialog box

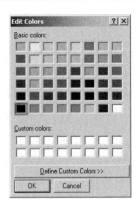

FIGURE 3.11
The Edit Colors dialog
box after unfolding

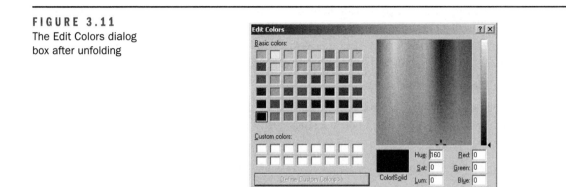

Dialog boxes are *modal* (while a dialog box is displayed on screen, the user cannot interact with other parts of the application). This capability makes dialog boxes most suitable for tasks that must be completed without interruption by other activities in the same application.

Task Panes

Microsoft introduced task panes as a new type of secondary window in Office 2000. Figure 3.12 shows a typical task pane (in this case, from Microsoft PowerPoint 2003).

FIGURE 3.12
A typical task pane

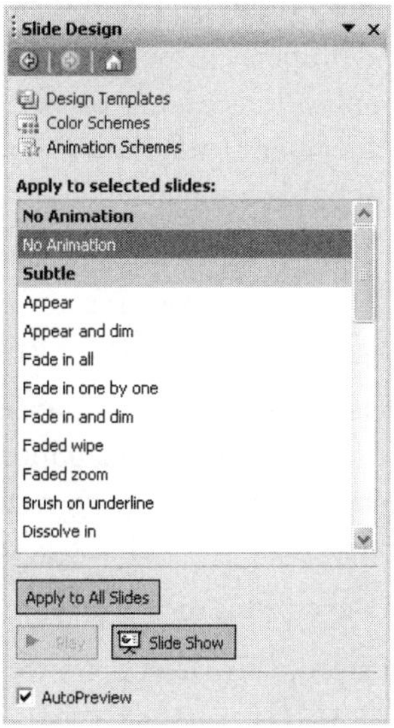

Task panes are designed to provide help and controls necessary to accomplish a particular task. For example, the task pane in Figure 3.12 helps a user apply animation schemes to one or more PowerPoint slides. Unlike dialog boxes, task panes are non-modal, so you can continue to work with the rest of the application's user interface while a task pane is open.

Conventions for task panes include the following:

- A task pane appears as a separate window within the application's main window. This secondary window is normally docked to one side of the application's workspace, but (like toolbars and other docking windows) it can be undocked and moved around.

- The Ctrl+F1 key combination opens the task pane window.

- All task panes use the same secondary window. A drop-down list at the top of the task pane lets you choose which task pane to display.

- Task panes include hyperlinks to other task panes (for example, the Design Templates and Color Schemes links shown in Figure 3.12) and sometimes to other resources on the Internet.

- Task panes include forward, back, and home buttons to navigate between the task panes that you have displayed during a work session.

Task panes are especially useful for applications with many features and options. They help a user find ways to carry out particular tasks without needing to learn everything about the application or to explore the entire user interface.

Property Sheets and Property Inspectors

Property sheets and property inspectors provide ways to view and manipulate the properties of an object. Many applications expose objects from code more-or-less directly to end users; spreadsheet cells, document paragraphs, or table rows might all be considered objects, depending on the application. It's often useful to give users a way to set the properties of these objects directly.

Figure 3.13 shows a property sheet from Internet Services Manager, which allows the user to manage websites based on Microsoft Internet Information Services (IIS).

Like many objects, IIS web applications have more properties than can conveniently be exposed in a single window. The tabbed interface provides a relatively natural way for users to select groups of related properties to work with. The buttons at the bottom of the property sheet stay active regardless of which tab is selected.

Property sheet conventions include the following:

- The border of a property sheet is not resizable.

- The property sheet is not modal.

- The title text of the property sheet is the name of the object plus the word "Properties." In some cases, you may choose to use the name of the object type instead of the specific object, such as "Form Properties" rather than the name of a particular form.

- If the user switches from one object to another within the application, the property sheet continues to show the properties of the original object.

- The OK button applies any changes to the object and then closes the property sheet. This is the default button on the property sheet and responds to the Enter key.

- The Cancel button discards any changes and then closes the property sheet. This button responds to the Escape key.

- The Apply button is disabled until the user has changed at least one property. When it is enabled, the Apply button applies any changes to the selected object, but does not close the property sheet. The Apply button disables itself until more changes are made.

- Property sheets almost always include What's This? help.

FIGURE 3.13
Property sheet for a
web application

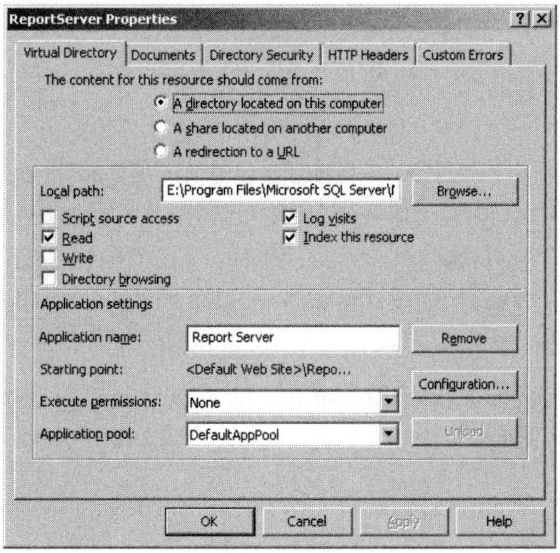

Most applications that implement property sheets allow you to have more than one property sheet open at the same time. This is useful when the user wants to compare the properties of multiple items.

Property inspectors also show the properties of an object, but there are some major differences between property inspectors and property sheets:

- Property inspectors always show the properties of the active object; if you switch objects, the inspector updates to show the properties of the new object.

- Property inspectors are typically implemented as toolbars or other dockable controls, rather than as separate windows.

- Changes made in a property inspector are applied to the selected object immediately.

Figure 3.14 shows some controls from the Formatting toolbar in Microsoft Excel, which act as a property inspector. When you change the selection, these controls update to show the font properties of the selection. If you change the controls, Excel updates the selection to match.

FIGURE 3.14
Property inspector in
Microsoft Excel

Bauhaus 93 ▾ 10 ▾ **B** *I* <u>U</u>

Floating Auxiliary Windows

The final common type of secondary window is the floating auxiliary window. These windows are sometimes called *toolboxes* or *palettes*. Figure 3.15 shows a typical example: the form design toolbox from Microsoft Access.

Floating auxiliary windows share these conventions:

- The title bar is only half the height of a normal title bar.

- The only title bar button is the close button.

- The window can be floating or docked. Some applications may allow the user to turn off docking, or disable docking entirely, for floating windows.

- Accessory windows can be resizable or fixed size. If they're resizable, the controls normally rearrange so as to remain visible as the window is resized.

- Accessory windows usually contain little if any text and many controls that perform actions.

- The size and position of the accessory window is preserved from one appearance to the next, even if the application is closed and reopened.

NOTE   Toolbars are a special case of floating auxiliary window. You'll learn more about toolbars in Chapter 8, "Common Windows UI Elements."

FIGURE 3.15
The Access form
design toolbox

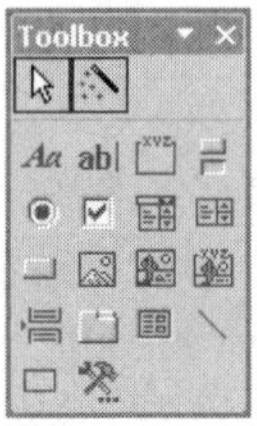

Irregular Windows

I said earlier that a window was a rectangular area on screen. In the last few years, there have been an increasing number of applications that violate that rule by using windows that are not rectangular. One good example is Windows Media Player, which can be customized with a variety of different skins. Figure 3.16 shows one of the ways Windows Media Player can look.

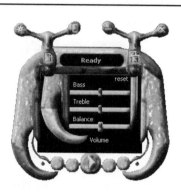

Although irregular windows have become more common, and tools for creating them have become more available, I have one simple piece of advice for most user interface designers when it comes to this trend: don't. All too often, developers seem to want their applications to look cool and modern without considering that this results in truly horrible usability.

Arranging Windows

Application developers have come up with a variety of ways to organize information. You can think of these concepts as visual patterns that your own application might be able to follow:

- No Document Interface
- Single-Document Interface
- Multiple-Document Interface
- Workbook
- Tabbed Documents
- Local Web

When developing an application, it's worth considering these patterns as starting points. You might well be able to develop an application that strikes users as instantly familiar by fitting into a category that they already understand.

No-Document Interface

Some applications (typically utilities) do not work with data files or allow the user to create new data. These applications typically implement a single window that contains controls for interacting with the application. For example, the Faber Toys (`http://www.faberbox.com/fabertoys .asp`) AutoRun application, shown in Figure 3.17, exists to display a list of the applications that Windows runs at startup.

FIGURE 3.17
An application with no
document windows

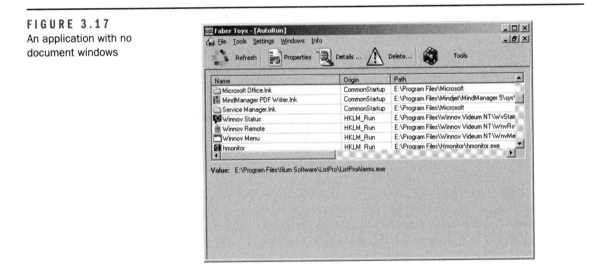

Single-Document Interface (SDI)

Applications designed to edit only one file at a time are referred to as single-document interface (SDI) applications. Notepad is a simple example of an SDI application. In an SDI application, the single document fills the entire primary window, as shown in Figure 3.18.

FIGURE 3.18
An application with
a single document
window

In Figure 3.18, I'm using Microsoft WordPad to edit a document. WordPad supplies the menu, toolbars, and ruler, as well as the status bar. The rest of the space is filled with the document, which can be saved as a separate data file. When you open a new file in WordPad, it automatically closes the one you're working on.

Multiple-Document Interface (MDI)

Some applications support viewing or editing more than one file at the same time, using multiple child windows within a single parent window. These are called multiple-document interface (MDI) applications. Figure 3.19 shows Microsoft Access, which uses a multiple-document interface.

As you can see from Figure 3.19, there's no requirement that every document within an MDI application must look the same. An application can choose to display different information and to use different styles for the various secondary document windows that it contains.

FIGURE 3.19
An application with multiple document windows

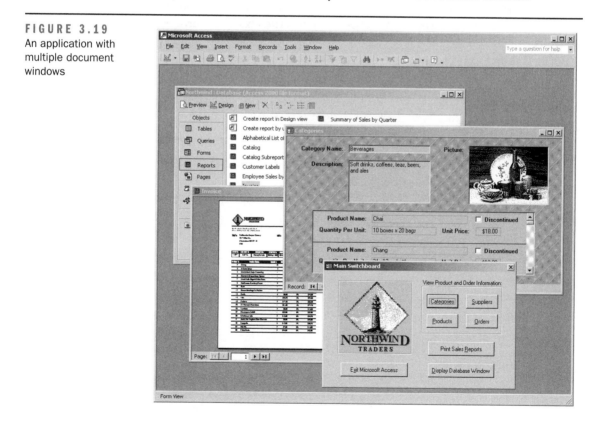

Workbook

In some cases, an application might let the user edit a series of closely interconnected documents. In this situation, a workbook user interface is appropriate. Figure 3.20 shows a workbook open in Microsoft Excel.

In this case, the workbook is divided into three worksheets (Sheet1, Sheet2, and Sheet3). Tabs at the bottom of the workbook provide a way for the user to switch between different worksheets in the same workbook. The entire workbook is saved as a single file.

TIP   Excel is both an MDI application and a workbook-based application. A single instance of Excel can load multiple workbooks at the same time.

The workbook interface is a solution to two problems. First, it allows storing and manipulating a group of documents as a single entity. Second, it provides a way to cram more information into the available real estate on the user's screen. Though you can see the contents of only one tab at a time, the workbook makes it easy to switch back and forth between tabs.

Tabbed Documents

Another way to deal with multiple documents within a single application that has become popular in recent years is the tabbed interface. Figure 3.21 shows a typical tabbed document interface (in this case, the CodeWright text editor).

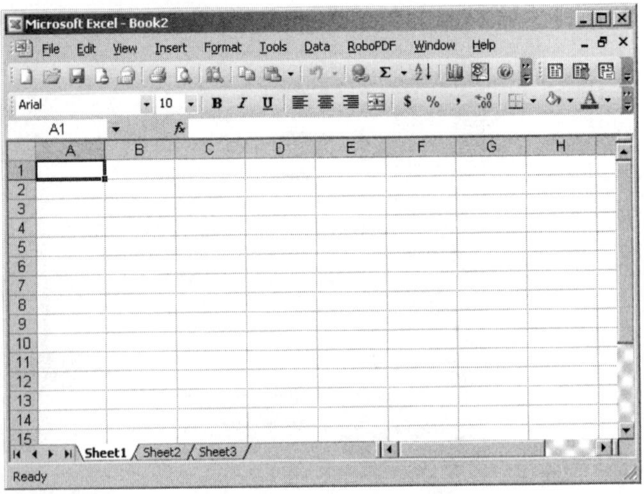

FIGURE 3.20
A workbook with three tabs open in Excel

Tabbed interfaces are a variant of MDI, with an important difference. When you're using an MDI application, you need to click on the Window menu to see the names of all open documents if you have one of them minimized. When you're using a tabbed interface, you can just scan the tabs to see which documents are open. The gain in document visibility is normally worth the loss of a little working area.

Local Web

Some applications bring an interface from the World Wide Web to your local computer. Consider the Microsoft SQL Server Best Practices Analyzer (`www.microsoft.com/downloads/ details.aspx?FamilyID=b352eb1f-d3ca-44ee-893e-9e07339c1f22&DisplayLang=en`), shown in Figure 3.22.

Although the Best Practices Analyzer is a Windows application, the designers have used interface standards from the Web as their reference. For instance, you move through the application by single-clicking on hyperlinks that are highlighted when the mouse passes over them.

If you're going to use Web interface standards in your Windows applications, I urge you to be restrained about it. Many web controls are more limited than their Windows counterparts, and you can end up constraining your users unnecessarily if you simply create HTML pages to use on their local computer. But careful use of web design can result in a more attractive application, and these days everyone understands Web conventions such as hyperlinks.

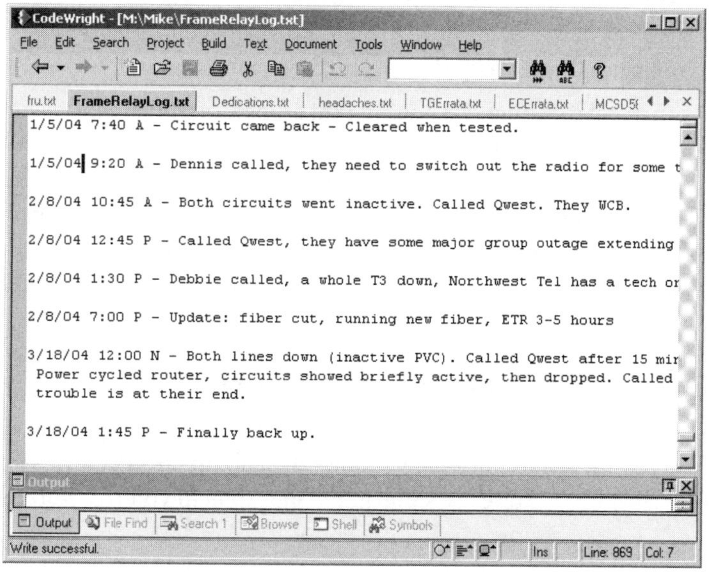

FIGURE 3.21
Using tabs to load multiple documents

FIGURE 3.22
A Windows application
with a Web interface

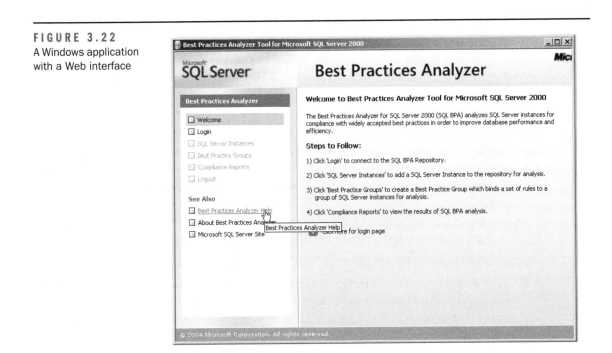

Using Multiple Main Windows

One more way of arranging Windows ought to be mentioned, although it's not one that I recommend. Figure 3.23 shows Visual Basic 6.0 running in its classic interface mode.

Yes, all those windows are part of a single application. Visual Basic was one of the handful of applications to take this approach of scattering multiple windows across the screen without providing an overall workspace to contain them. Although this does allow end users to arrange the windows just as they like, it ends up being terribly confusing. Imagine that you have four or five applications that use this approach all open at the same time—how can you ever tell which window belongs to which application?

Designing Your Window Strategy

One of the key decisions to make when you are developing an application is how to split up the application into multiple windows. Just about any Windows application involves more than one window. Here are some guidelines to help you structure your own applications:

- For a utility that runs in the background, consider minimizing it to a notification area icon.
- Implement a workbook or tabbed document interface if the user is expected to manage many documents at one time.

- Use the simplest set of windows that will possibly work for your application. There's no need to develop an MDI interface if the user never needs to work with more than one document at a time.

- Follow the Windows user interface guidelines closely. Dialog boxes, for example, should always be modal.

- Use modal dialog boxes for tasks that must be completed before the user can proceed with the application. For example, a modal dialog box is appropriate for selecting the name of a file after the user clicks the Save button.

- Use non-modal secondary windows such as task panes, property sheets, or property inspectors to prompt for information that does not need to be supplied immediately. For example, a task pane is appropriate for selecting fonts to apply to parts of a document.

- Use floating auxiliary windows to make selections of tools available to the user.

- Avoid irregular windows unless you're presenting an interface whose goal is to look different instead of one whose goal is to be usable.

- Use a web-like interface when you require more an innovative visual presentation.

FIGURE 3.23
Application without a
containing window

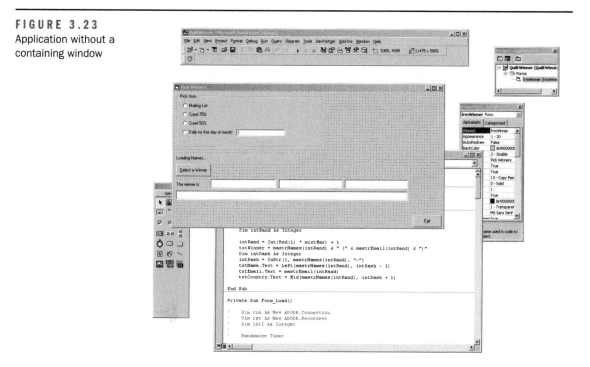

Summary

This chapter gave you a broad overview of Windows applications. You learned about the distinctions between primary and secondary windows, and about the user interface conventions that apply to both types. You also saw that secondary windows come in a variety of formats. Finally, you learned about various strategies for organizing the windows in your applications.

Now it's time to drill further into the details of a Windows application by understanding the details of individual controls. I'll start in the next chapter by examining button controls.

CHAPTER 4

Command Buttons

- The Look and Feel of Buttons

- Labeling Buttons

- Button Actions

'll start my examination of the common Windows control types with the common command button, usually just called a *button* (or sometimes, in older documentation, a *push button*). Buttons are controls that start actions or change properties. For example, a button might move the user from one panel of a wizard to the next, save a change to network properties, or close a dialog box.

NOTE   Not every button is a command button. See Chapter 6, "The Other Controls," for coverage of toggle buttons, and Chapter 8, "Common Windows User Interface Elements," for a discussion of toolbar buttons.

The Look and Feel of Buttons

You may think you already understand everything there is to know about command buttons: Click the left mouse button on them, and stuff happens. As it turns out, life isn't quite that simple under Windows. In this section, I'll review the finer points of button behavior under Windows and show you some of the applicable design standards.

How Buttons Function

A command button performs its associated action when it is pressed. Buttons can be pressed by either the mouse or the keyboard. I'll start with the mouse. Clicking the mouse's primary button anywhere on the command button and releasing it while it is still over the command button presses the command button.

Figure 4.1 shows a pair of buttons, with neither button having the input focus. The Cancel button has a normal button appearance, and the OK button has the default button appearance. The default button is the one that responds to the Enter key even if it doesn't have the focus. Any window can have at most one default button.

FIGURE 4.1
Normal and
default buttons

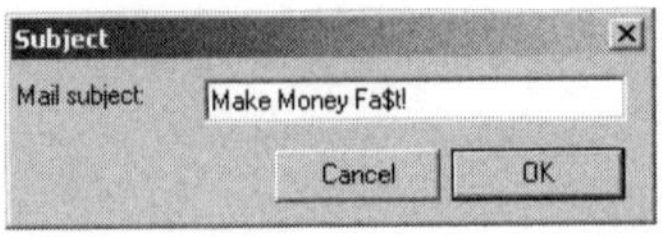

In Figure 4.2, I clicked the primary mouse button on the Cancel button, but haven't yet released it. The button takes on a pressed appearance, with the border redrawn to indicate that the button is sunken, and a dotted inner border indicating that this button has the focus. Note that the OK button is no longer drawn with the default button appearance as soon as I click the Cancel button.

FIGURE 4.2
Pressed button

Letting the mouse button up performs the button's action, and leaves the button with the input focus, as shown in Figure 4.3. However, just seeing a button drawn this way is no guarantee that it was pressed. If you click the mouse button on a button, move the cursor outside of the button's border, and then let go of the mouse button, the button will return to the input focus appearance, but its action will not be performed.

FIGURE 4.3
Button with the
input focus

As always, things look a bit different under the Microsoft Windows XP user interface. Figure 4.4 shows the normal and default button appearances, Figure 4.5 shows the pressed appearance, and Figure 4.6 shows a button with the input focus. Note that the pressed appearance is more subtle, and that the input focus and default appearances are identical for applications running under Windows XP.

FIGURE 4.4
Normal and default
buttons under
Windows XP

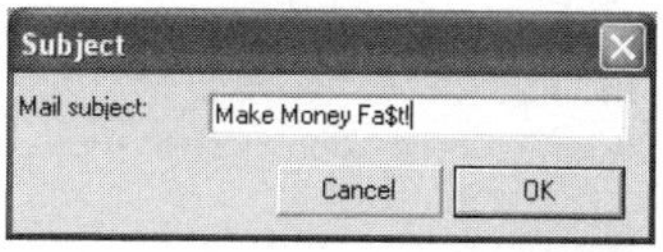

FIGURE 4.5
Pressed button
under Windows XP

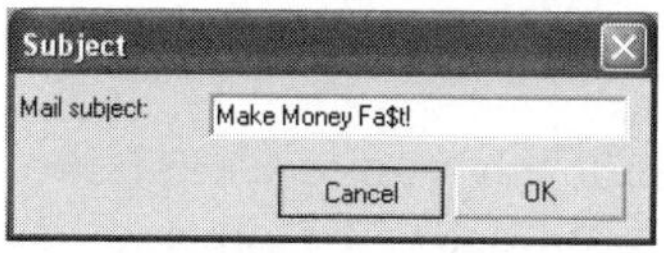

FIGURE 4.6
Button with the
input focus under
Windows XP

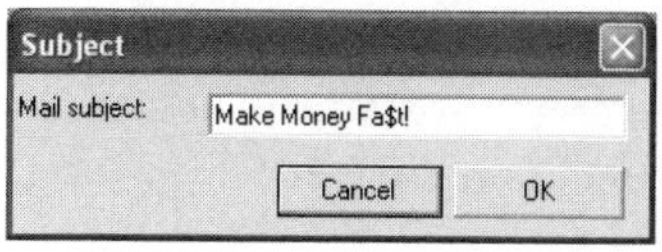

Distinguishing the Primary and Secondary Mouse Buttons

The primary mouse button is not necessarily the left mouse button. You can use the Mouse applet in Control Panel to switch the functions of the right and left mouse buttons, as shown in the following illustration:

Although swapping mouse buttons doesn't affect the functionality available from your application, it does change the way that documentation should be written. Referring to the *primary* and *secondary* mouse buttons is universal; referring to the *left* and *right* mouse buttons may be wrong depending on the user's preferences. In practice, though, this rule is often ignored in writing documentation because the precise terms are more cumbersome.

If you choose to experiment with the Mouse applet, remember that you need to use the right mouse button to uncheck the Switch Primary and Secondary Mouse Buttons check box if you use the left mouse button to check it.

In addition to using the mouse, you can also press a button with the keyboard. To do so, move the input focus to the button by using the Tab or Shift+Tab keys. Then press the spacebar. When you release the spacebar, the button's action will execute.

TIP   It's a general principle of Windows that every mouse action should have a keyboard alternative. If you ever find some functionality that requires a mouse, you should report it as a bug. Remember: Some people find using a mouse or other pointing device difficult or impossible.

Pressing a button with the spacebar can be cancelled, just as pressing a button with the mouse can. If you tab to a button, press the spacebar, and then (without letting go of the spacebar) press and release the Escape key, the button will return to its input focus appearance without carrying out its action.

There are three other ways for a button to be pressed with the keyboard:

- If a button is specified as the default button, pressing the Enter key presses the button if no other control is currently responding to the Enter key.

- If a button is specified as the cancel button, pressing the Escape key presses the button if no other control is currently responding to the Escape key.

- If a button has an accelerator key, pressing Alt together with that key presses the button. Accelerator keys are indicated with underline characters in most versions of the Windows user interface. For example, Alt+S presses the Select button, and Alt+H presses the Help button in the Character Map application shown in Figure 4.7.

TIP   Windows does not require you to assign every button an accelerator key. However, whether it's required or not, you should always do so. Leaving out accelerator keys makes your application much more difficult for users with special needs.

FIGURE 4.7
Buttons with
accelerator keys

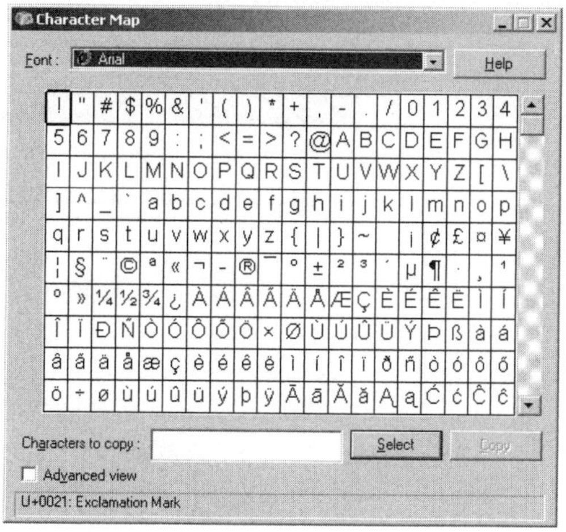

Laying Out Buttons

Although the functioning of buttons, such as the details of sensing mouse clicks and initiating button events in response, normally isn't under your direct control (most development tools these days make use of the underlying Windows controls, which behave in the proper way automatically), their arrangement is something that you can and should pay attention to. Placing buttons where the user expects to find them and laying them out neatly can make the difference between a professional user interface and one that looks slapdash.

When people in most locales scan a window, they tend to do so in the same way that they read a printed page: left to right and top to bottom, as shown in Figure 4.8. This is why it makes sense to put OK and Cancel buttons in the lower-right corner of the window, particularly when you are developing a dialog box. As the user moves through the controls of the window, making decisions and filling in information, she will naturally end up at these controls when she's ready to commit the information.

NOTE   There are exceptions to the left to right rule. For example, users of Hebrew or Arabic software scan right to left. If your software will be localized, you need to consider dynamically rearranging the user interface for these right to left locales. This is what Windows itself does.

But this doesn't mean that you should put all the buttons in a dialog box in a clump at the lower-right corner. In general, buttons should be closely associated with the controls that they operate on. Consider the Add and Remove buttons shown in Figure 4.9.

The Add button moves items from the Available Languages list box to the Enabled Languages list box. The Remove button moves items from the Enabled Languages list box to the Available Languages list box. That's why it makes sense to locate these two buttons between the list boxes.

FIGURE 4.8
Reading pattern
for a window

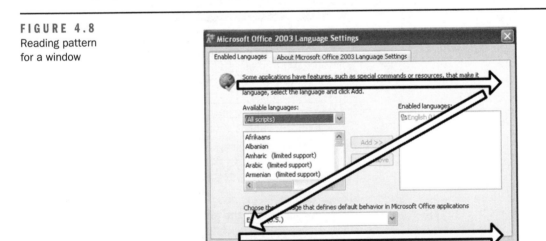

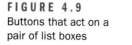

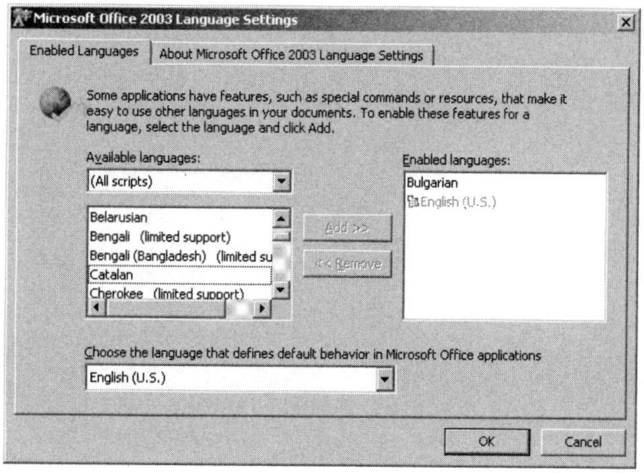

FIGURE 4.9
Buttons that act on a
pair of list boxes

The design of these buttons does not end with their location. The chevrons in the buttons' captions indicate the direction of movement. In addition, this particular dialog box selectively enables and disables the two buttons. The Add button is enabled only when the user has selected an item in the Available Languages list box. The Remove button is enabled only when the user has selected an item in the Enabled Languages list box. This provides an additional cue to the user as to which action makes sense at any given time.

When a window has multiple buttons that apply to the entire window, they should be arranged in a row along the bottom of the window. By convention, the OK button comes first, then the Cancel button (if there is one), and then any other buttons (as shown in Figure 4.10). If there is no OK button, place action-oriented buttons before the Cancel button. If there is a Help button, it normally comes last in the row.

Figure 4.11 shows another use for buttons: as a way to open further secondary windows. Each of the buttons whose name ends with an ellipsis opens another window that contains further options. In this case, buttons are serving as a way to pack more choices into a secondary window without increasing the size of the window.

NOTE   Between tabs and additional secondary windows—some up to four levels deep—the Outlook options dialog box probably holds a record for the number of choices that can be reached from a single menu item. Although providing flexibility for users is generally a good thing, a dialog box this complex can represent a substantial hurdle for users trying to find a particular setting.

FIGURE 4.10
Options dialog box
from Microsoft
Outlook 2003

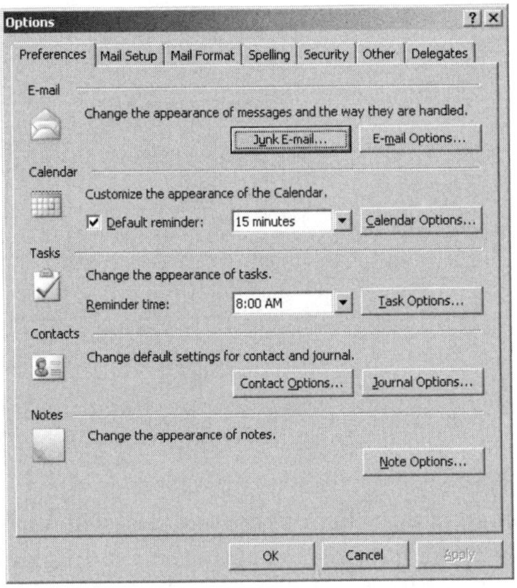

Figure 4.11 also shows the general rule for lining up buttons: They should be sized and arranged in neat rows and columns. The three buttons at the bottom of the dialog box are all the same size and are spaced evenly. The other buttons in the body of the dialog box are similarly a uniform size are and are laid out on a regular grid (along with several combo box controls that also fit the grid). Uniform sizing should take precedence over sizing buttons to fit their text.

Labeling Buttons

Nearly every button requires a text caption, but there are exceptions. Figure 4.11 shows some of the exceptions in standard Windows controls.

As you can see, there are no text captions for the button that shows the drop-down list of the combo box, the two buttons that change the value in the spin control, or the buttons that move to the previous and next months in the calendar control. There are two reasons for this. First, the presumption is that the user understands what these buttons do intuitively (though as you'll recall from Chapter 1, "The Big Picture," it's dangerous to depend on intuition in user interfaces). Second, there just isn't room for captions on these buttons. Despite the lack of text, they all have triangular bitmaps to give some hint of their functions.

TIP   Buttons with no caption text should still have a ToolTip to provide accessibility for screen readers.

FIGURE 4.11
Some buttons do not
require a caption

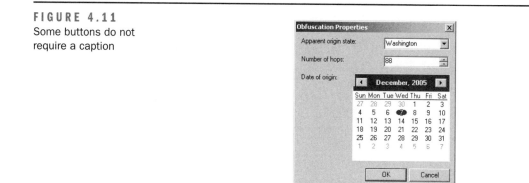

Most buttons, though, will require text. But what text? Here are some guidelines to follow when adding text to buttons:

- Use the shortest possible text that gets the point across. A single word is best.

- Because buttons normally trigger actions, verbs make the best captions. For example, Add, Move, Go, Remove, and Store are typical button captions.

- Use text that makes sense with as little context as possible. Some users (for example, those with visual disabilities) might read or hear only a single button's text or ToolTip at a time.

- Except for the OK and Cancel buttons, every button should have an appropriate shortcut key defined. Double-check the window to make sure that you haven't accidentally duplicated any shortcuts. By default, the OK key will respond to the Enter key and the Cancel button to the Escape key, which is why these buttons don't need shortcut keys.

- Use title-style capitalization for button text. That is, capitalize all words except for conjunctions of four letters or fewer.

- If the button will open an additional secondary window, add an ellipsis at the end of the text.

- Buttons that move or resize items generally benefit from having chevrons added to make text arrows. (You saw some buttons using this technique in Figure 4.10.)

It's also possible to label buttons with images instead of (or in addition to) text. You already saw some trivial examples in Figure 4.11, in which small bitmaps are used to make arrows on tiny buttons. But it's possible to go far beyond that when using images on buttons. For instance, Figure 4.12 shows a wizard from Microsoft MapPoint 2004.

Generally, buttons with images are found in two situations. First, they are used in applications in which the image makes up for a lack of space to display many words. For users who don't know what a sized pie chart looks like, Figure 4.13 provides a fast point of reference.

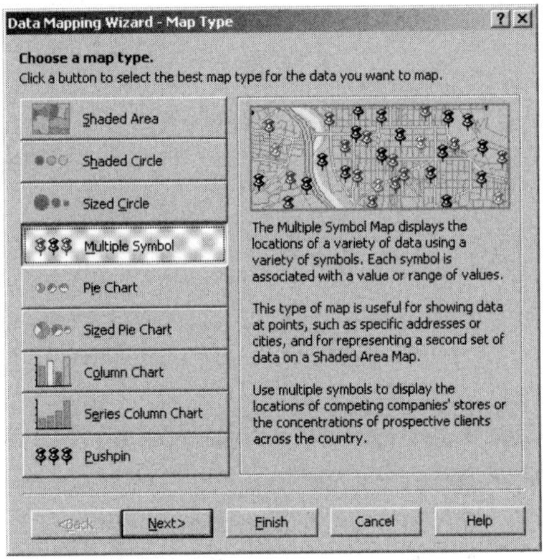

FIGURE 4.12
Buttons with images
and text

The other circumstance in which buttons with images can be useful is in consumer-oriented applications or those for inexperienced users. For example, Figure 4.13 shows the Backup Utility from Windows XP. The graphics on the buttons are apparently meant to indicate that the choices take users to easy wizards rather than to complex software that only an expert can understand. Although the buttons have only images on them, there is explanatory text next to each one. Text remains necessary in almost all cases because you can't expect users to guess what the images signify.

A few pictures can make an application seem friendlier or less threatening. Even here, buttons with pictures are much less common than they were a few years ago. There seems to have been a long-range trend toward using only text on buttons, and I recommend that you keep buttons with images to a minimum.

TIP One place where buttons with images are still the norm is on toolbars. I'll discuss toolbar buttons in Chapter 8.

Button Actions

The basic rule of thumb when it comes to making buttons actually do things is to adhere to what is sometimes called the *Principle of Least Surprise*: the result of doing something (whether in a user interface, a programming language, or the real world) should be unsurprising to the user. For instance, consider the five buttons on the Microsoft Utility Manager, shown in Figure 4.14.

FIGURE 4.13
Image-only buttons

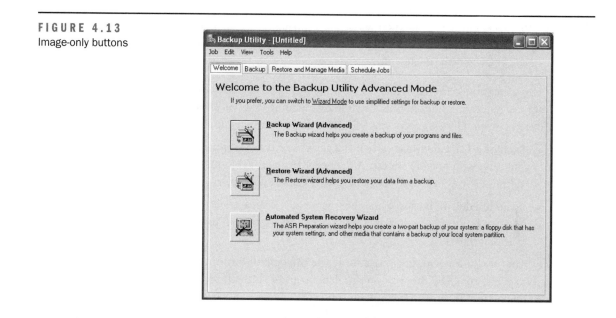

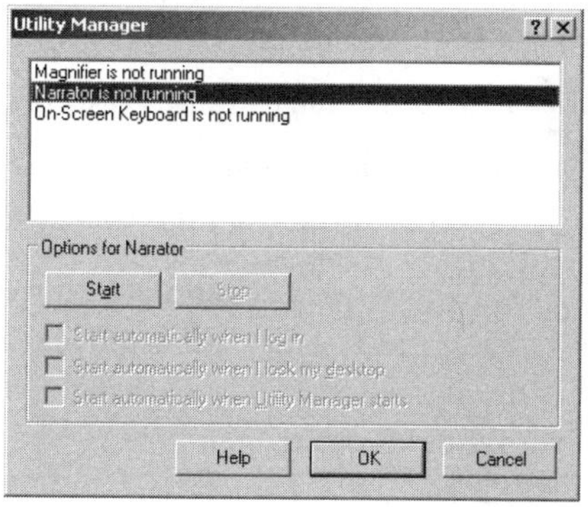

FIGURE 4.14
Microsoft Utility
Manager

Utility Manager is designed to help users turn on and off the various accessibility features of Windows. As you select different utilities in the list box, the label of the group just below the list box changes. In the figure, the label is Options for Narrator, making it clear that the Start and Stop buttons directly control the Narrator utility.

What about the OK button? If they have any experience with the various control panel applets, users will be expecting the OK button to commit changes made elsewhere in the dialog box—but not to make any changes itself. So, in line with the Principle of Least Surprise, the OK button should not change the state of the Narrator service (as indeed it does not).

NOTE   You might notice that the OK, Cancel, and Help buttons are not in the standard order in this dialog box. That just goes to show that not even Microsoft always applies the Windows design guidelines consistently.

As I mentioned earlier in this chapter, any dialog box can have at most one default button and at most one cancel button. But you shouldn't assume that you always need a default button and a cancel button. Here are some guidelines for deciding when it makes sense to set up these buttons:

- Include a Cancel button only if the actions of the rest of the window can be cancelled entirely, with no side effects. A Property Inspector that makes changes as you select options, for example, should not have a Cancel button.

- Include a default button when there is some overall action that the user expects the window to take. For example, it makes sense for the Save button to be the default button in a Save File dialog box.

- An OK button should almost always be the default button, if it exists at all. But if the changes made by the window are dangerous or difficult to undo, you might want to not make the OK button the default button (to make it more difficult to click by accident).

In addition to choosing whether to make a particular button the default button or cancel button, most development environments give you a choice of events for the button that you can respond to. Typically, buttons support at least three events:

- MouseDown when the primary mouse button is clicked on a command button.

- MouseUp when the primary mouse button is released over the command button.

- Click when Windows thinks the button has been clicked.

It should be clear from the discussion of standard button behavior at the start of the chapter that your code to perform an action when the button is clicked should almost always be attached to the Click event of the button. Using the MouseDown or MouseUp events lead to actions being out of synch with the rest of the Windows user interface, which is not a good idea.

Summary

Although they are generally straightforward controls, command buttons still have a few subtleties. When you're adding buttons to your application, you need to keep in mind basic principles of good design. These include respecting the user interface conventions for buttons, choosing appropriate text and images, and lining buttons up in standardized rows and columns.

In the next chapter, I'll tackle design issues for a slightly more complex control: the text box. When you let users type in whatever they like (instead of just clicking), things get more interesting.

CHAPTER 5

Using Text Input Controls

- The Basics of Text Entry

- Types of Text Controls

- Helping Users with Data Entry

- Choosing the Right Control

E ntering text is the core part of many applications. Depending on the way the application's user interface was designed, this can be an easy task or one that aggravates users. Allowing the user to tab into a disabled control, or setting the same accelerator key for multiple controls, can be annoying. A little care with the use of text input controls can go a long way in making your application's users happy.

The Basics of Text Entry

The absolute basic of text entry, of course, is simple: set the focus to a text control and start typing. As you do this, the characters you type will appear in the text control. But just as with other Windows controls, there is a lot of complexity lurking behind this simple story. I'll dig into these topics to start:

- Navigation between controls
- Working with text boxes
- Handling default values and passwords
- Problems with text boxes

Navigating Text Controls

From time to time, some company will decide that it needs to "modernize" its old mainframe applications. Generally speaking, this consists of bringing in a whole batch of consultants to rewrite everything from scratch using Windows on the client instead of old green-screen terminals. The new application usually looks much better, taking advantage of the Windows user interface. But, if it's not done right, the people who actually have to *use* the application end up fighting desperately to keep the old way—not because they can't stand change, but because the Windows version fails to meet their needs.

The problem, in the cases that I've witnessed, is that the whizbang new Windows version doesn't allow people to enter data as they did using the old mainframe version. When people have been doing data entry with a single application for a long time, they get it down to a science: type customer name, tab tab tab, type address, click spacebar, press down arrow, type account number, and so on. Watch a good data entry person some time—you'll see that their hands never leave the keyboard while they work (and they can converse with the person at the next terminal at the same time).

Can you imagine the effect on productivity when you replace this application with one that requires a mix of tabs, mouse clicks, and menu selections? It's not good. If you want to encourage people to use your Windows applications, you need to observe this rule:

RULE   Make sure that your applications are keyboard-friendly, even if your own style of working involves heavy use of the mouse.

To make data entry in your application keyboard-friendly, you need to take two steps. First, you need to make sure that the Tab key works to move from control to control in a sensible manner. Second, you need to define access keys for each control where the user can enter data.

The tab order for a dialog box or other window defines the order in which the Tab key moves the user between the various controls in the window. Figure 5.1 shows a Windows form developed in Visual Studio .NET. The top portion of the figure shows the form as the user works with it, whereas the bottom portion shows the tab order as the form is being designed.

When setting the tab order for the controls in a window, keep these points in mind:

- The tab order should proceed in "book order": left to right, top to bottom. If you're converting an existing application to Windows, though, you should consider maintaining the current tab order even if it's theoretically wrong to make migration easier.

- Every control that can receive the focus should be in the tab order.

- The only controls that cannot receive the focus that should be in the tab order are labels that directly precede controls that can get the focus.

- If a control is temporarily disabled, the tab order should skip that control.

Why include labels in the tab order at all, if they can't receive the focus? That has to do with the second part of making your application keyboard-friendly: access keys. An *access key* is a letter or number that can be used in conjunction with the Alt key to open a drop-down menu or to move the focus to a control. In most versions of Windows, access keys are indicated by underlined letters on the user interface. In Windows XP, the underlines are hidden until the user presses the Alt key, but the access keys still work.

FIGURE 5.1
Defining the tab order for a form

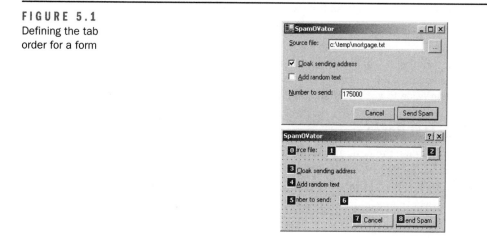

TIP You can change the way that Windows XP behaves in this regard through the Display control panel applet. Select the Appearance tab and click the Effects button; then uncheck the Hide Underlined Letters for Keyboard Navigation Until I Press the Alt Key check box.

Figure 5.2 shows a dialog box (in this case, the Add Criteria dialog box from Microsoft Query) displaying a number of access keys: A for And, O for Or, T for Total, and so on.

FIGURE 5.2
A dialog box with
access keys

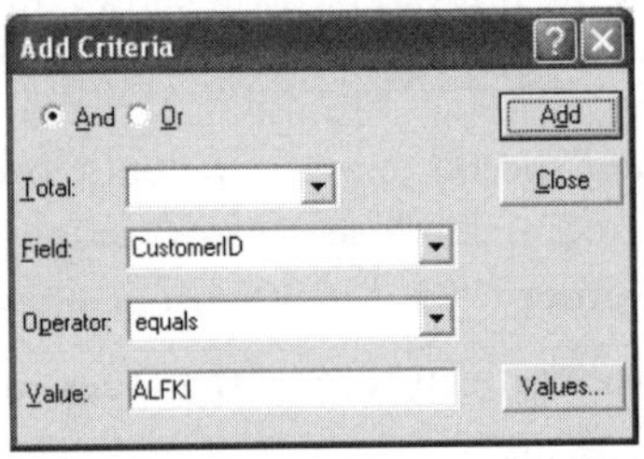

Some controls include their own text, so defining access keys for these controls is part of setting the properties for the controls. For instance, the radio buttons at the top of the Add Criteria dialog box and the buttons on the right side of the same dialog box all include their own text. But text box controls do not have their own text, which is where the associated labels come back into the picture. If you define an access control for a label and include that label in the tab order just before a text box control, Windows will use that access key as the access key for the text box control rather than for the label.

TIP Some screen readers look for a colon at the end of a label control's text to confirm that it is meant as the label for another control, so you should always include a colon when using this technique.

WARNING Be careful that you don't use the same letter for an access key on two different controls in the same dialog box. If you accidentally do this, the user will need to press the access key combination twice to get to the second of the controls.

Working with Text Boxes

Text boxes behave much the same across all Windows applications because the text box control itself is provided by the Windows Shell libraries, and most development environments just use this standard control. This is another area where standardization benefits users: After you learn how a text box works, you can depend on it to work that way everywhere.

You should be aware of the built-in text box features for two reasons. First, knowing what the control brings to your application will save you from reinventing the wheel. Second, you should avoid doing anything to disable or degrade the built-in features. For example, adding your own shortcut menu to a text box (and losing the standard shortcut menu) is usually a bad idea.

Built-in features of the standard text box control include the following:

- Selecting text with the mouse by clicking and dragging across the text that you want to select.

- Selecting text with the keyboard using the Shift and arrow keys.

- If you type when no text is selected, new characters are inserted at the cursor position.

- If you type when there is text selected, new characters overwrite the selection.

- A standard shortcut menu includes Undo, Cut, Copy, Paste, Delete, and Select All.

- Single-level undo (reversing the most recent operation).

The standard text box also supports the set of editing keys shown in Table 5.1.

TIP   The default text box doesn't support multiple fonts or text sizes. If you need these features, though, you can use a rich-text box, which I'll cover later in the chapter.

TABLE 5.1 Default editing keys for the text box control

Key or Combination	Effect
Home	Moves the cursor to the beginning of the line
End	Moves the cursor to the end of the line
Ctrl+A	Selects all text in the control
Ctrl+Right arrow	Moves the cursor to the start of the next word
Ctrl+Left arrow	Moves the cursor to the start of the previous word
Ctrl+Down arrow	Moves the cursor to the start of the next paragraph
Ctrl+Up arrow	Moves the cursor to the start of the previous paragraph
Ctrl+Home	Moves the cursor to the start of the text box
Ctrl+End	Moves the cursor to the end of the text box
Shift+Right arrow	Selects a character to the right
Shift+Left arrow	Selects a character to the left
Shift+Ctrl+Right arrow	Selects a full word to the right
Shift+Ctrl+Left arrow	Selects a full word to the left
Insert	Toggles between Insert mode and Overwrite mode

Supplying Default Values

One of your goals in text handling should be to make life as easy as possible for the users of your application. Carefully supplying default values for various controls can go a long way in this direction.

A *default value* is the value that a control has before the user interacts with the control. In the case of a text control, the default value might be no value at all, or it might be your best guess as to what the user would want to enter in that control. In general, you should only supply a non-blank default value if there is a good chance that the default will be correct. Otherwise, the user will have to replace the default with their own value, which can be distracting (and if the user prefers the mouse to the keyboard, she'll need to highlight the default value to replace it).

You can use several strategies to choose default values:

Fixed   The application always shows the same default value every time it is run.

Adaptive   The application attempts to adjust the default value to conform to the user's needs. For example, consider the Send In Batches Of text box shown in Figure 5.3. If the user replaces the original default of 500 with 200, an adaptive application would use 200 as the new default value. You can limit adaptation to a single session (in this case, it means starting over with 500 the next time the user runs the application) or store it across sessions (perhaps in the registry or .NET isolated storage) so that the application "remembers" the user's chosen defaults.

Derived   The default value of one control can be derived from the user's entry in another control. In Figure 5.3, the application updates the Last Mailing Date control to a value two weeks after the value of the First Mailing Date control when the user enters a first mailing date. If you take this strategy, be sure not to overwrite data that the user has actually entered. For example, if the user changed the last mailing date and then went back to change the first mailing date again, you shouldn't overwrite their choice for last mailing date.

User-Selected   Finally, you can allow the user to explicitly choose default values for himself. Consider the File Locations tab of the Options dialog box from Microsoft Word, shown in Figure 5.4. Here, the user can specify a location as the default for storing documents. That location is used as a starting value whenever Word displays a File Save dialog box.

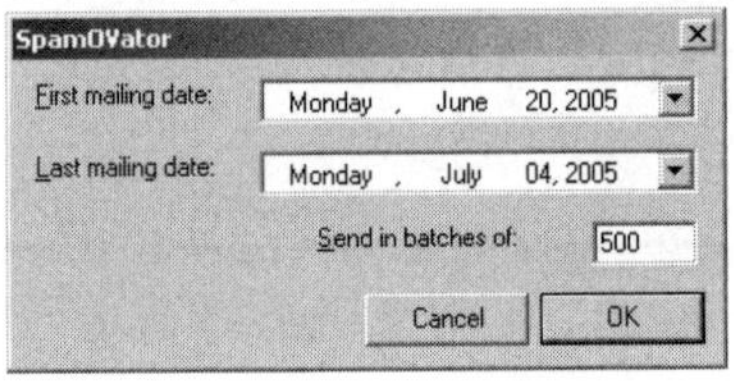

FIGURE 5.3
Default values in
a dialog box

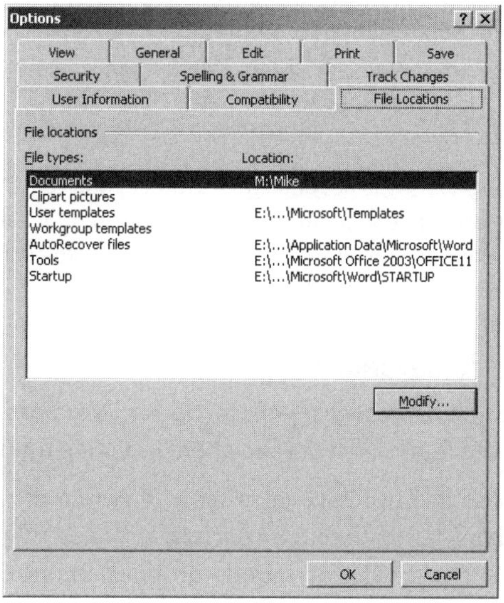

FIGURE 5.4
Setting default file
locations in Word

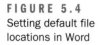

Handling Passwords

In these security-conscious times, you need to pay special attention to controls where
you ask the user to type in a password. Figure 5.5 shows a typical dialog box to prompt for
a password.

You need to ensure two things when prompting the user for a password. First, you need
to hide the password by masking the actual characters that the user types. In Figure 5.5, the
application does this by displaying an asterisk character for each character that the user types.
Second, you need to hide the password from other malicious applications. One way to do this
is by disabling cut and copy functionality on the text box.

Fortunately, Windows gives you both of these features "for free" by supplying an underlying password style for the text box control. Most development environments today expose this
functionality directly. If yours does not, you'll need to intercept keystrokes in the password
text box and filter them accordingly.

FIGURE 5.5
Prompting for a
password

TIP   Because you should not display passwords, even to the user who types them, changing a password requires special care. Typically, you should require a user to type any new password twice into two different controls. This protects them against accidentally making a typing mistake when entering a new password.

WARNING   Preventing copying is not enough to protect passwords against all malicious code. For example, some Trojan horse applications install software that allows them to monitor keystrokes straight from the keyboard. You should consider password-hiding as part of an overall security strategy, not as an ultimate protection.

Text Box Annoyances

There are some things that you can do with text boxes in your application—but shouldn't. Here are some things to watch out for when designing this portion of your application's user interface:

- Data should not disappear when you switch to another application. Users expect the state of an application to remain unchanged when they are not looking at it. This seems obvious, but it's a surprisingly common problem. Internet Explorer is the biggest culprit. If you're typing in a URL and switch to another application, the portion of the URL that you already typed will be selected when you switch back. This means that your next keystroke overwrites what you already typed.

- Text boxes should all be in the tab order, and should all be available via access keys. If you mess up on this rule, the application will work fine for mouse-centric users but will upset keyboard-centric users.

- Don't override the default editing behavior of text box controls without a very good reason and an explanation to your application's users.

Types of Text Controls

So far I've been concentrating on the classic text box control. But in fact there are five text input controls in common use:

- Single-line text box
- Multiline text box
- Rich-text box
- Masked edit control
- Spin box

Single-Line Text Box

As the name implies, a single-line text box is a text box that can hold a single line of characters. All the text boxes you've seen so far in this chapter (for example, the ones in Figure 5.1) are single-line text boxes. Although the single-line text box will not display multiple lines of text, it can still hold more text than it can display at one time. If there are more characters in the text box than will fit on the screen, the text automatically scrolls left and right as you reach the end of the available space. However, the single-line text box does not display a scroll bar.

Every text box you've seen in this chapter so far accepts input. But you can set a text box control to be disabled, as shown in Figure 5.6.

FIGURE 5.6
Enabled and disabled
text boxes and label

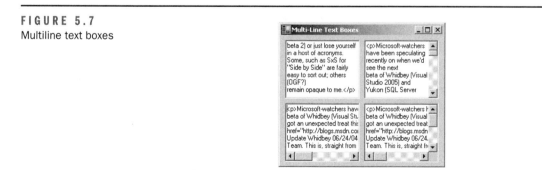

When a text box is disabled, it can't get the focus, and the user cannot interact with its contents. In other words, it behaves very much like a label control, but its appearance is close to that of a text box (it has the same sunken look but a different default background color). In general, a disabled text box control is appropriate for a control that sometimes interacts with the user, whereas a label control is more useful if the control never interacts with the user.

Multiline Text Box

As you can probably guess from the name, a multiline text box can hold more than one line of text. Such a text box can also be adorned with scroll bars, as shown in Figure 5.7, to allow you to read more text than can be displayed at one time.

A multiline text box can have a vertical scroll bar, a horizontal scroll bar, or both. In any case, you can use the standard movement keys to navigate the text within a multiline text box.

FIGURE 5.7
Multiline text boxes

TIP   In single-line text boxes, the Enter key normally moves the user to the next control in the tab order. In a multiline text box, the Enter key should start a new line in the text box.

Rich-Text Box

If the user needs to enter formatting information as well as text, the rich-text box is usually the best control to use on your user interface. Figure 5.8 shows WordPad in action. The entire area in which the user can edit text in WordPad is a single rich-text box.

The rich-text box supports a wide variety of operations, including the following:

- Text formatting
- Variable line spacing
- Paragraph formatting
- Bidirectional data entry
- Printing

Although not as full-featured as a dedicated word processor, the rich-text box can handle text-entry chores for most applications that require formatted text. The rich-text box can save its contents using Rich Text Format (RTF), a Microsoft standard for including formatting information with text.

NOTE   Microsoft has published the RTF standard at http://msdn.microsoft.com/library/en-us/dnrtfspec/html/rtfspec.asp. Many word processors, including Microsoft Word and WordPad, can import and edit RTF files.

FIGURE 5.8
Editing rich text
in WordPad

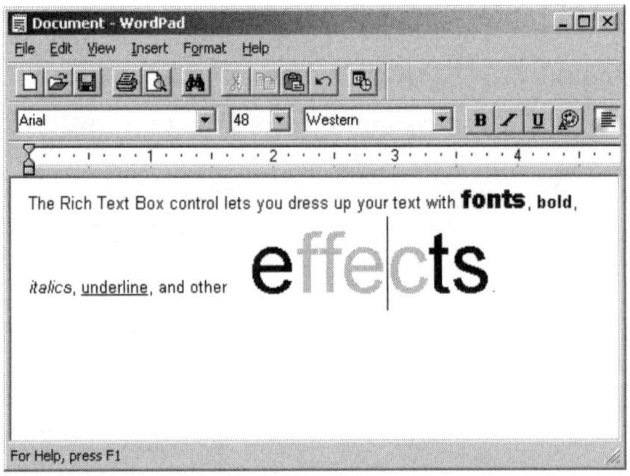

Masked Edit Control

A *masked edit control* is one in which the characters that the user can enter are constrained by position. For example, Figure 5.9 shows a masked edit control in Microsoft Access.

When the user tabs into the masked edit control, it displays the slashes (which it automatically adds to the data) and a set of underscore characters that the user will replace by typing. Although there is no visible clue as to the allowed values, in this case only numbers will be accepted to replace each underscore.

Typically, masked edit controls can specify one of the following for each character in the control:

- Literal character that the user doesn't type (such as the slashes in a date)
- Any alphabetic character
- Lower-case alphabetic character
- Upper-case alphabetic character
- Any digit

    Characters in a masked edit control can be required or optional.

Masked edit controls are not widely used because they do not offer good cues for the user who doesn't know what you're expecting them to type. If the control is expecting an uppercase alphabetic character, and the user types anything else, nothing happens. The user must notice that the character wasn't accepted by the control and hunt around for some other character that it's happier with. This can be a frustrating experience. For anything other than standard formats such as dates and times, you're better off letting the user fill in the entire control and then displaying a friendly error message if necessary.

Spin Box

A final text entry control is the *spin box* which is a text box coupled with a pair of buttons known as an up-down control, as shown in Figure 5.10.

FIGURE 5.10
Dialog box including
two spin boxes

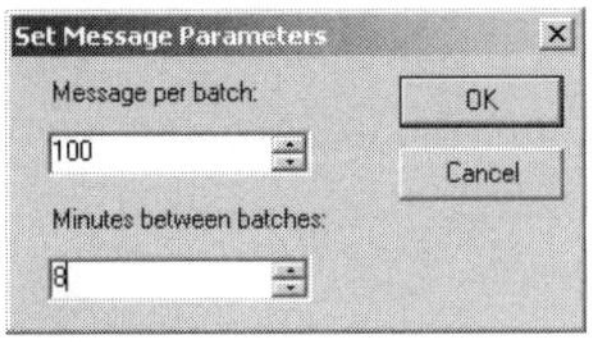

Spin boxes are useful when you're expecting the user to enter a value from an ordered set of numbers: quantities, times, dates, and so on. With a spin box, the user can either type in a value or use the up-down control to move to adjacent values. That is, if the box currently displays the value 80, clicking the up button changes the value to 81, whereas clicking the down button changes the value to 79. If the user holds one of the buttons down, the value continues to change, and the rate of change accelerates.

When designing a spin box, you should attempt to set a default value close to the value that the user will most likely want. That minimizes the number of clicks on the up-down control that will be required to set the user's preferred value.

Figure 5.11 shows another dialog box with spin box controls: the Date and Time Properties dialog box from Windows Server 2003. There are two spin box controls in this dialog box, one for the year and one for the time. The one for the time is actually a sort of three-in-one control, with the up-down control applying only to the currently selected portion of the time. For example, when the focus is on the minutes section of the time, the associated up-down control changes only the minutes—not the hours or seconds.

NOTE   In addition to the text controls that I introduced in this chapter, other controls can include a text box portion. The most important of these, the combo box, is covered in Chapter 6, "The Other Controls."

FIGURE 5.11
Date and Time
Properties dialog box

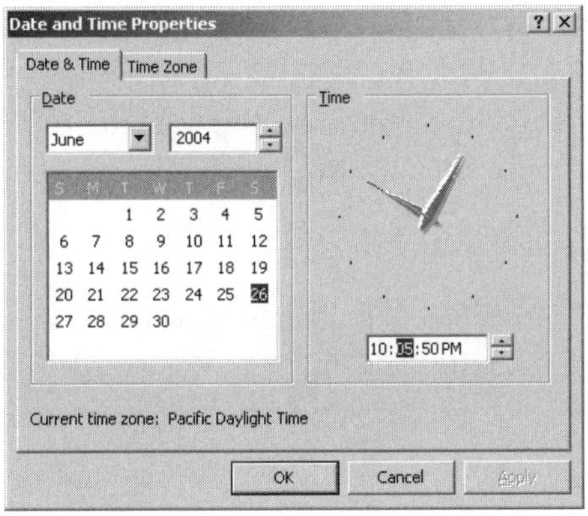

Helping Users with Data Entry

One of the goals of a good user interface is to make it easy for the user to interact with the application. This involves more than just making the application look pretty or making sure that everything on the screen is laid out in a sensible and straightforward manner. The best applications go further to actually help the user do things correctly. Here are some things that you can do to help the user enter data in your application:

- Check data entry immediately and provide feedback close to the location of any error. Feedback should be close in both physical location and time. If there's a mistake in a text box, the time to notify the user is as soon as he leaves that text box—not later, when he clicks the OK button. The feedback should also make it clear exactly what data is incorrect and how it can be corrected. This feedback might involve displaying a balloon tip with an error message, or changing the color of the text box containing bad data, as well as playing the system error beep to alert the user to the problem.

- If a text box can accept input from only a restricted set of possible values (for example, if only numerals are appropriate), you should refuse to accept invalid characters at all, and play the system error beep if the user types an invalid character.

- When there is more than one way to enter correct data, be forgiving. For example, a credit card number can contain dashes to separate parts of the overall number, but the dashes are not required. In such a case, you should accept input with or without the dashes.

- If you can't be forgiving, be clear. For example, instead of using the label "Credit Card Number:" use the label "Credit Card Number (without dashes or spaces)" if your application expects the user to type only numbers in a text box.

Choosing the Right Control

There are quite a few different controls that allow the user to enter text. Each one has its own strengths and weaknesses in particular situations. Here are some guidelines for choosing between them:

- For short pieces of text that are not constrained in any way, use a single-line text box.

- For longer pieces of text that won't fit across the dialog box, use a multiline text box, which allows the user to see the entire piece of text at one time, without having to scroll from side to side.

- For short or long pieces of text that require fonts, alignment, or other formatting, use a rich-text box.

- For numeric values that may need a slight adjustment, use a spin box.
- For values constrained according to a well-known scheme (such as dates or times) use a masked edit control.

There's one case in which text controls are sometimes inappropriately used: when the data comes from a fixed set of choices. For example, you might expect the user to choose one of the values red, green, or blue to set a color. Or an address input might expect the user to input one of the valid two-letter state abbreviations.

In these cases, you're better off not using a text control because there are too many possibilities for errors. Instead, use a control that explicitly limits the user's choices. For a small number of choices, radio buttons or toggle buttons are usually appropriate. For a larger number of choices, a list box or combo box works well. You'll read about all of these controls in Chapter 6.

Summary

Text controls are one of the most important tools to allow users to interact with your application. In this chapter, you learned many of the conventions that surround these controls, including standard navigation and editing procedures, and were introduced to a variety of different text controls. By using these controls properly, you can make it easy for users to enter data in your application.

But there are many other controls besides text controls available for specialized situations. In the next chapter, I'll survey some of these other controls to show you the possibilities.

CHAPTER 6

The Other Controls

- Presenting Choices

- Handling Lists

- Space Management with Tabs

- ListViews and TreeViews

- Grid Controls

- Miscellaneous Controls

Labels, buttons, and text controls make up a large part of the user interface of most applications. But there are dozens of other controls available to user interface designers. Some of these controls are a standard part of Windows, whereas others are supplied by special libraries from independent software vendors (ISVs) such as ComponentOne (`www.componentone.com/`) and Developer Express (`www.devexpress.com`). In this chapter, you'll learn about some of these other controls and see how to use them effectively.

Presenting Choices

Sometimes you'll need to have the user choose one or more of a small set of alternatives. For example, you might be accepting data from a COM port and need the user to select one of the COM ports that actually exists on the computer. In such a situation, you should present the users with only the acceptable choices. Windows includes several controls for this purpose:

- Radio buttons (also called option buttons)
- Check boxes
- Toggle buttons

These controls can be grouped together to make their relationship clear by using the standard group box control.

Radio Buttons

Radio buttons are the best way to let the user select from a group of two or more mutually exclusive choices. How many more? There's no fixed upper limit, but if you need to present more than seven or eight choices, you should consider a list control instead (see "Handling Lists" later in this chapter).

Figure 6.1 shows a typical use of radio buttons.

Here, the Windows XP System control panel applet presents the user with three choices for handling user notification of automatic updates. These three choices are mutually exclusive; that is, only one of them can be active at a time. This makes radio buttons a good choice. The radio buttons themselves are the three circles in the Notification Settings area of the user interface. The current setting is indicated by a dot in one of the circles; the other two circles are empty. If you click a radio button, that button becomes the current setting, and the other radio buttons in the group are cleared.

TIP   Radio buttons do not toggle. That is, if you click a radio button that is already set as the current setting, it is not cleared. It remains set until you click another radio button in the same group of buttons.

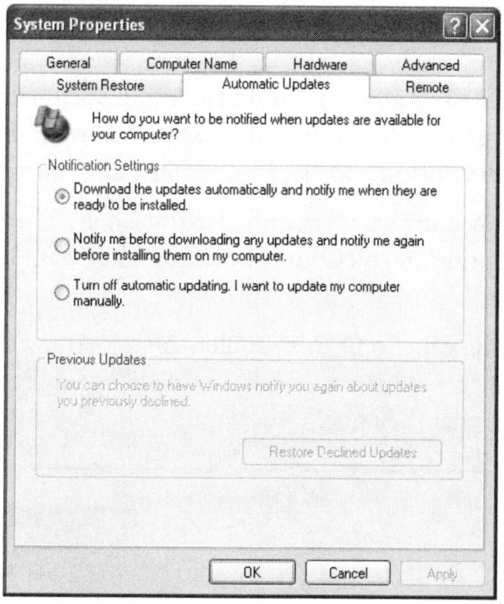

FIGURE 6.1
Selecting notification
settings with radio
buttons

Radio buttons come with an associated label that represents the value or effect of this particular button. These labels should include shortcut keys to support using the keyboard to choose an option. If you can describe the choices with only short bits of text, you should use phrases with sentence-style capitalization. If more text is needed to make the option clear, use full sentences, as shown in Figure 6.1. Ideally, the length of the descriptive text for each option within a group should be about the same.

Sometimes a radio button leads to further choices when it is selected. For example, consider the dialog box shown in Figure 6.2. When the user selects Other, the combo box that lists countries becomes available. In such a case, the label for the appropriate radio button should end in a colon to indicate that the user can make a further selection.

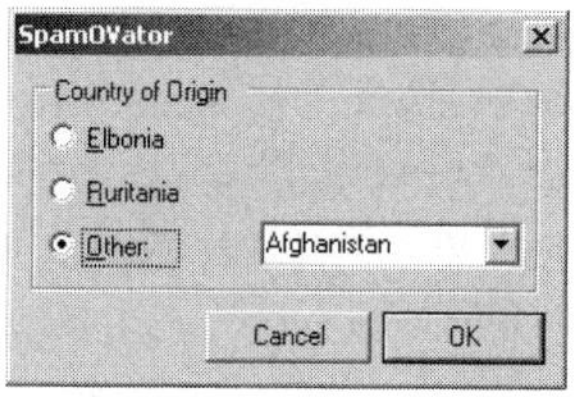

FIGURE 6.2
Radio button
leading to
additional
information

Radio buttons always use text labels. If you want to use graphic labels for a group of mutually exclusive choices, you should use toggle buttons, which I'll cover a bit later in this chapter.

If you use the Tab key to move to a radio button, the button's state is not changed, but it will be highlighted as the control that has the focus. In this case, pressing the spacebar sets that particular radio button and clears all other radio buttons in the group.

Avoid repeating words in radio button labels. This can make it difficult for the user to quickly scan the option and pick out the one that they want to select. Figure 6.3 shows a dialog box that has this problem.

Normally, you can fix this problem by rewording the dialog box to pull out the common text. Figure 6.4 shows a rewrite of the same dialog box designed to make it easier for users to choose the option that they like.

FIGURE 6.3
Poorly labeled
radio buttons

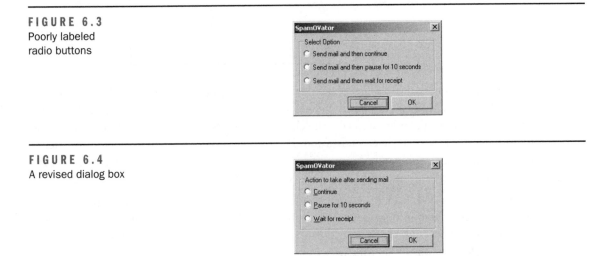

FIGURE 6.4
A revised dialog box

Check Boxes

Occasionally, new developers confuse check boxes with radio buttons, but there's an important difference in their usage. Check boxes are used for options that are *not* mutually exclusive. Figure 6.5 shows a good example of check box use, from the Edit tab of the Options dialog box in Microsoft Excel 2003.

This particular dialog box lets you choose numerous options related to editing. You can turn these options on or off, independently of one another. For example, Allow Cell Drag and Drop can be either on or off, regardless of the setting for Extend List Formats and Formulas. Radio buttons don't work for lists like this because they allow only a single option to be selected at a time.

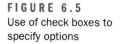
FIGURE 6.5
Use of check boxes to
specify options

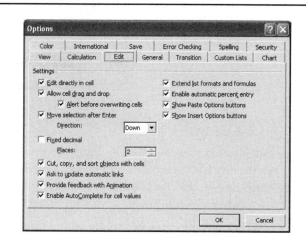

Check boxes should be used only for settings that are either distinctly on or off. For example, a reasonable check box label could be "Save backup files" if the application offers a choice between saving backup files or not saving any backup files at all. But "Save backup files to C:" would not be a good check box label because it's not clear what it would mean to leave the box unchecked.

A check box is displayed as a square with an accompanying label. If the option represented by the check box is set, Windows displays an X in the check box. Otherwise, the check box will be empty.

NOTE   Some applications also support a third, indeterminate setting for check boxes. In this case, the indeterminate setting is represented by a gray square. This is often used when a check box shows the state of a selection. If the check box option is set for some but not all of the selection, the check box will be displayed with the indeterminate appearance.

A user can toggle the state of a check box in three different ways:

1. Click the primary mouse button on the check box itself.
2. Click the primary mouse button on the label that accompanies the check box.
3. Press the spacebar when the check box has the focus.

The label for a check box should include an access key to allow keyboard access to the check box. Pressing the access key moves the focus to the check box, but it does not toggle the state of the check box.

Generally, check boxes toggle from checked to unchecked. But this behavior changes when the check box starts in its indeterminate state. For example, consider the check box shown in Figure 6.6.

FIGURE 6.6
A check box in the
indeterminate state

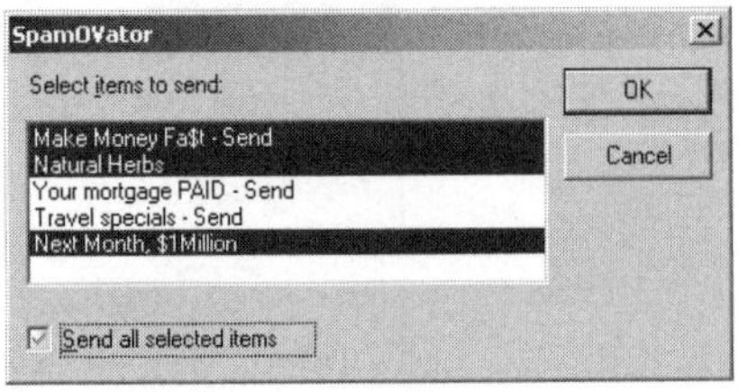

In this user interface, the check box indicates whether the selected items in the list should be sent. When the user has selected a mix of items, some of which are currently set to be sent and some of which are not, the check box has the indeterminate appearance. In this case, toggling the check box (whether with the mouse or with the spacebar) cycles through three states:

1. The first click sets the check box to the selected state and sets the property for every selected item.

2. The second click sets the check box to the unselected state and removes the property for every selected item.

3. The third click sets the check box to the indeterminate state and returns all selected items to their original state.

Each check box includes an associated label that represents the value or effect of this particular button. These labels should include shortcut keys to support using the keyboard to choose an option. If you can describe the choices with only short bits of text, you should use phrases with sentence-style capitalization. If more text is needed to make the option clear, use full sentences. Ideally, the length of the descriptive text for each option within a group should be about the same.

Sometimes a check box leads to further choices when it is selected. For example, consider the Options dialog box from Microsoft Word 2003, shown in Figure 6.7. The Recently Used File List and Measurement Units check boxes enable other controls for more detailed information. The labels for these check boxes end in a colon to indicate that the user can make a further selection.

Toggle Buttons

Toggle buttons are a less common (but still useful) way to handle choices. In functionality, they are very similar to radio buttons: A group of toggle buttons should be used for a set of mutually exclusive choices. But visually, toggle buttons are very different from radio buttons. Figure 6.8 shows a typical set of toggle buttons.

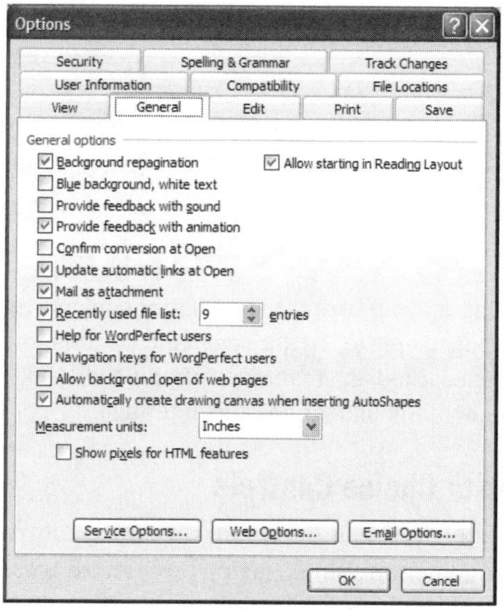

FIGURE 6.7
Check boxes leading
to other controls

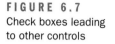

FIGURE 6.8
Using toggle buttons
for exclusive choices

Toggle buttons function like the tuning buttons on older car radios: When you press one toggle button in, all the other buttons in the group "pop out." Thus, at most one toggle button in a group will have the depressed look at any time. In Figure 6.8, the 4–6 years option is selected, so that particular button is depressed.

Within a group of toggle buttons, you can move the focus with the arrow keys. As you move the focus, the button that has the focus is always the selected one. Alternatively, you can select a toggle button by clicking it. If you click a toggle button that's already selected, nothing happens.

One advantage of toggle buttons over radio buttons in some situations is that you can display images on toggle buttons, either in conjunction with text or instead of text. This lets you design more flexible and attractive user interfaces in some cases. Figure 6.9 shows a set of graphical toggle buttons.

FIGURE 6.9
Toggle buttons with
graphics

> **WARNING**   Depending on your users, toggle buttons might represent a training issue. If users have
> been exposed only to regular command buttons, they'll be expecting a button to do some-
> thing when clicked and to release after it's clicked. You need to provide help and guidance
> so new users will understand this interface.

Issues with Choice Controls

You'll usually need to group multiple choice controls (radio buttons, check boxes, or toggle buttons) together on a single dialog box. There are several tools that you can use to provide this grouping.

The first and most obvious way to group these controls is to line them up with one another and to space them evenly. Not only does this help the user tell which controls are associated with one another, but it also makes your user interface more pleasant. Compare the two versions of the dialog box shown in Figures 6.10 and 6.11. They might have the same functionality, but the second version will be much easier to work with than the first.

FIGURE 6.10
Dialog box with
haphazard control
grouping

FIGURE 6.11
Dialog box with careful
control grouping

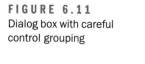

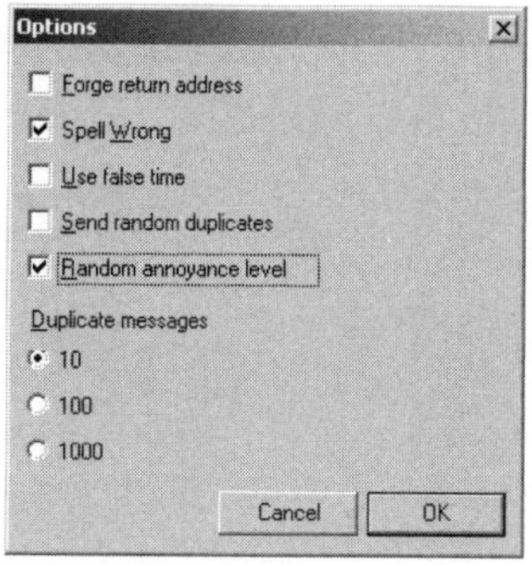

Windows also provides the group box control specifically to group choice controls together. The group box is a frame with its own label that can hold radio buttons, check boxes, or toggle buttons. If you have more than one set of radio buttons on the same dialog box, group boxes are the best way to keep them from interfering with one another. Otherwise, selecting an option in one group would deselect all options in the other groups. Figure 6.12 shows group boxes in action.

In some cases, you may want to use an invisible group box to get the grouping effect and develop your own user interface to indicate which choice controls are part of a group. The Excel options dialog box, shown in Figure 6.13, is a good example of this technique. The Comments and Objects section of the View tab are two distinct sets of radio buttons, even if the corresponding group boxes are invisible.

As Figure 6.13 shows, you can also use grouping with check boxes. But in this case, the grouping is purely for visual effect. The check boxes remain independent, and you can check or uncheck any one of them without affecting the others.

FIGURE 6.12
A dialog box with
two group boxes

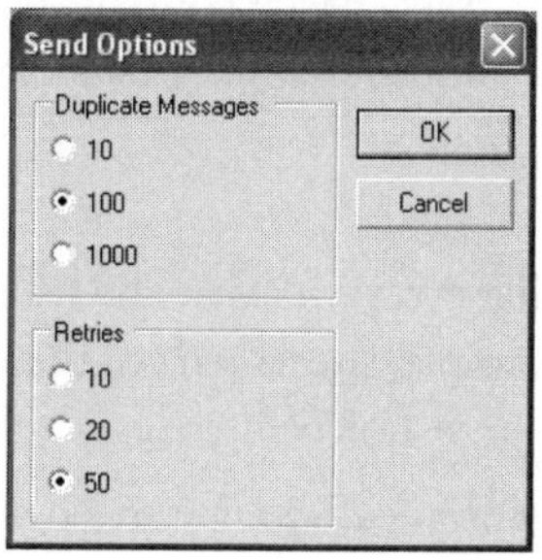

FIGURE 6.13
Options dialog box
from Microsoft Excel

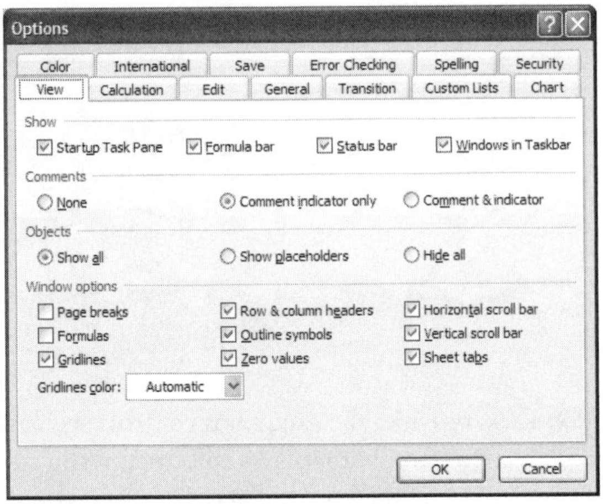

The biggest problem to watch out for with choice controls is simply to make sure that you select the appropriate control for the situation. In general, you can rely on these rules of thumb:

RULE   (1) If you are presenting a set of mutually exclusive choices with text labels, use *radio buttons*. (2) If you are presenting a set of mutually exclusive choices with graphical labels, use *toggle buttons*. (3) If you are presenting a set of independent choices, use *check boxes*.

Handling Lists

Choice controls are useful as long as you don't have too many choices. After you get more than five to seven choices, radio buttons or check boxes start to become cumbersome. In these cases, you should move to a list-based control such as the list box or combo box. Both of these controls are suited for choosing among lists of dozens or even hundreds of items.

List Boxes

The purpose of a list box is to allow the user to select one or more items from a list of choices. Figure 6.14, for example, shows part of the interface for setting network card properties under Windows 2003. The list of properties for the current network card is presented in a list box.

This particular example demonstrates two of the strengths of the list box control. First, it can comfortably display more options that you can provide radio buttons for in the same space. Second, it's not limited to a fixed list of options. For network card configuration, Windows builds the list of properties dynamically. Although the list may change, the same control can always be used to select an item from it.

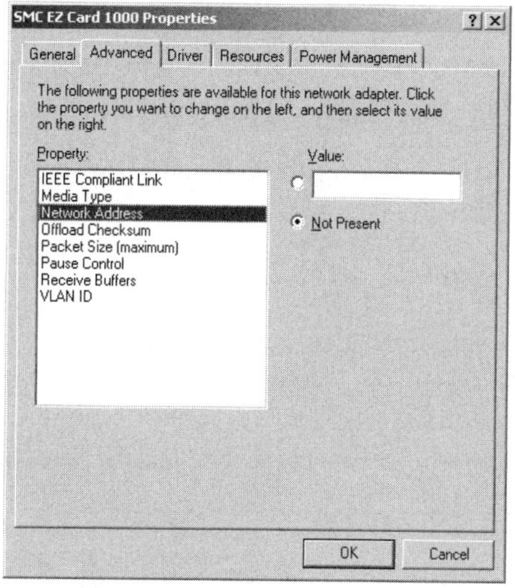

FIGURE 6.14
Selecting from a
list box

The entries in this particular list box are arranged in alphabetical order. You should generally order the entries to make it easy for the user to browse them. For numeric items, this means increasing or decreasing order; for dates, you'd use chronological order. Alphabetical order is a good default when there's no other natural order to use for a particular list. But don't feel that you always have to employ one of these lexical orders. For example, if you're offering a choice of countries for the user, and most of your users reside in the United States, you should make it the first entry so that it's easy for them to find without scrolling through the entire list.

Most list boxes are *simple list boxes*. User interaction with a simple list box is straightforward:

- Clicking a list entry selects that entry and deselects any currently selected entry.

- The arrow keys move the selection up or down in the list one entry at a time.

- The Page Up and Page Down keys move the selection up or down an entire page at a time.

- The Home and End keys move the selection to the start or end of the list.

- Typing a letter or number selects the next item beginning with that letter or number.

The simple list box supports only a single selected item at a time. Two other list box styles allow the user to select multiple items: the *multiselection list box* and the *extended-selection list box*.

A multiselection list box works like a simple list box with one exception: Selecting an item does not automatically deselect the currently selected item. Instead, to deselect an item that's already selected, you click it again. Thus, you can select as many items as you like in a multiselection list box by running down the list and clicking each one.

An extended-selection list box returns to the behavior of the simple list box for single clicks. However, it also implements two additional selection tools:

- Ctrl+Click selects an item without deselecting any other item.
- Shift+Click selects all items from the currently selected item to the item just clicked in the list.

Multiselection list boxes are well-suited for scrolling down a list and picking individual items. Extended-selection list boxes are well-suited for selecting a range of items from a list.

Combo Boxes

A *combo box* is a control that is a combination of a text control and a list control. The list control is normally hidden, but it drops down from the text control when the user clicks an arrow at the end of the text control. Figure 6.15 shows the Task Information dialog box from Microsoft Project 2003, which displays several combo box controls.

FIGURE 6.15
A dialog box with several combo box controls

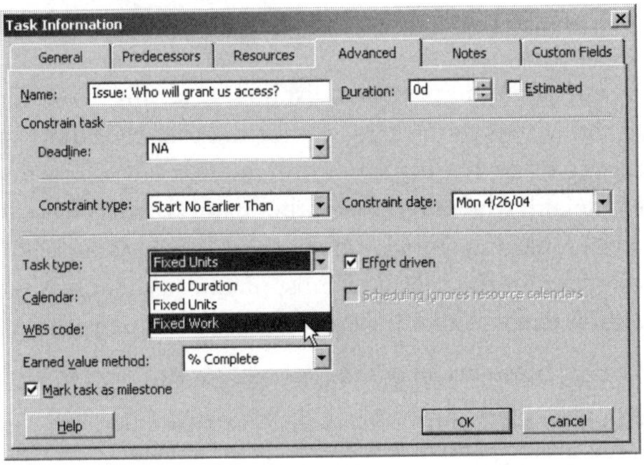

In the figure, the Task Type combo box list has been dropped down by clicking the arrow. As you can see, moving the cursor over an item in the list selects that item. If the user clicks on an item in the list, that item becomes the new value for the text portion of the combo box, and the list vanishes.

The combo box control also supports selecting items with the keyboard. To do so, you can type Alt+Down Arrow to display the list, and then type characters to march items on the list.

Combo boxes might or might not allow the user to enter items in the text portion that do not appear on the list. Whether you should allow this depends on what you're doing with the control. For example, a combo box that displays the states of the United States generally should not allow arbitrary entries; the list in the combo box is complete. But a combo box used for selecting a sales tax rate might need to allow arbitrary data entry for cases in which the developer did not anticipate a particular rate. In such a case, you can make the combo box more useful by making it adaptive. When the user enters a value that isn't in the list, persist that value so that it can be added to the list the next time that particular combo box is used.

NOTE   Combo boxes that do not allow arbitrary text entry are sometimes called *drop-down list boxes*.

General List Control Techniques

List boxes and combo boxes do not include a label control by default. But as with other controls that lack built-in labels, you should add a label to provide keyboard access to the control. Use sentence capitalization and an access key in the label, and end the label with a colon.

Ideally, a list box or the list portion of a combo box should display somewhere between three and eight items, and be wide enough to display all of the entries in the list. If it's not feasible to make the list wide enough for the text that it has to hold, consider these options:

- Make sure that the list is wide enough that the visible portions of the items are distinct.

- Use an ellipsis to remove common parts of the items to compress them. For example, if all the items are files on the user's computer, you might be able to replace part of the path with an ellipsis.

- Add a horizontal scroll bar to the list.

- Add a tooltip to the list, so that when the user hovers the mouse over an entry, all of the text displays in the tooltip, possibly spread over several lines.

Depending on your development environment, you may be able to add check boxes, icons, or multiple columns to your list box or combo box controls. However, if you need this level of complexity, you should consider using a ListView control (discussed later in this chapter) instead. The ListView is more flexible and offers a more modern-looking appearance.

Space Management with Tabs

The tab control will be familiar to most users of Windows from many Control Panel applets, such as the Power Options Properties dialog box shown in Figure 6.16.

The tabs at the top of the dialog box are meant to resemble those on dividers in a physical file cabinet. At any given time, one tab is selected, and the rest of the dialog box displays controls that are associated with that tab. If the user clicks a different tab, that tab is selected and the constituent controls change correspondingly.

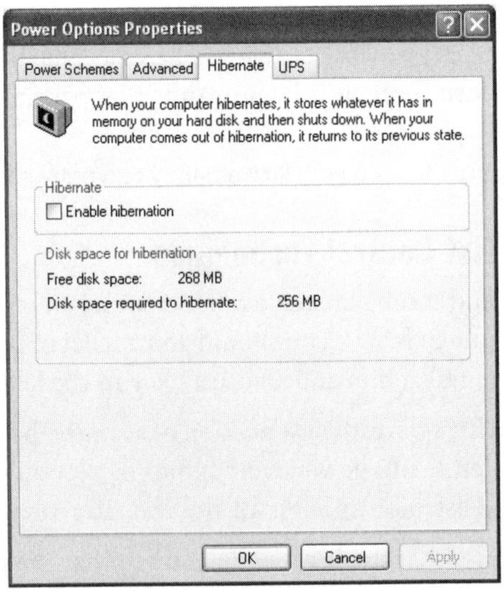

FIGURE 6.16
A tabbed dialog box

In addition to the mouse, the user can navigate between tabs using the Ctrl key plus appropriate other keys. Ctrl+Tab and Ctrl+Shift+Tab move to the next tab and previous tab, respectively. Ctrl+Page Up and Ctrl+Page Down move in larger increments. If the dialog box displays only a single row of tabs, these keys move to the first or last tab. But if a control has more than a single row of tabs, these keys move the next or previous row.

It's easy to go overboard with tabs. Figure 6.17 shows the properties of a Windows user on a network using Active Directory and Exchange. As you can see, there are four rows of tabs at the top of this dialog box. Really, this is 17 dialog boxes condensed into one, which makes it hard for anyone to remember where everything is.

The behavior of multiple rows of tabs is also confusing to some users. Figure 6.18 shows what happens when you click the COM+ tab in the dialog box shown in Figure 6.17. The act of bringing the tab to the fore also rearranges the rows of tabs, destroying any spatial memory of their location.

Another way to handle more tabs than can fit in a single row is to use a scrolling row of tabs. Figure 6.19 shows the Options dialog box from eMbedded Visual C++ 4.0.

See the two small arrows to the right of the tabs? Those indicate that there are more tabs to the left and right of those that you can see. Clicking the small arrows causes the entire set of tabs to shift to the left or right. This style of tab control has largely fallen out of fashion now, primarily because it is far too easy for the user to not even notice the extra tabs.

FIGURE 6.17
Multiplying tabs

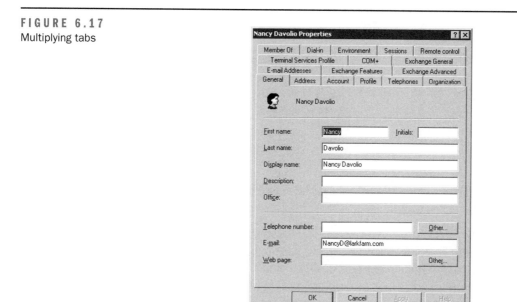

FIGURE 6.18
Rearranging tabs

FIGURE 6.19
Options dialog box
with scrollable tabs

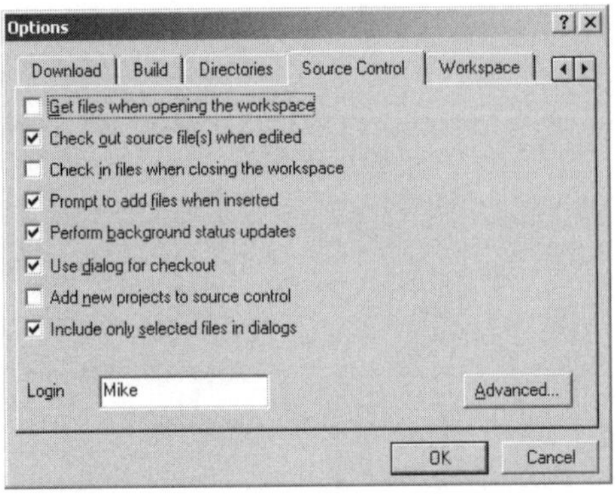

Generally, you should keep the text on tabs short, so that tabs will fit without scrolling or multiple rows. Keeping the text about the same length on each tab helps make the control look more balanced as well. Sometimes you'll see tabs to the left, right, or bottom of a dialog box; but for the most part Windows developers seem to have standardized on tabs at the top.

Tabbed dialog boxes necessarily hide controls from the user, so you need to work extra hard to make all the controls in such a dialog box easy to find. The best way to ensure this is to take the time to think about a logical division of controls into tabs. For example, consider the Options dialog box from Microsoft FrontPage 2003, shown in Figure 6.20.

Note that the tab labels are selected to as to be quite distinct; if you're looking for a .NET-related setting, it's clear that the ASP.NET tab is the place to go. This dialog box uses a General tab to hold options that don't fit elsewhere; some dialog boxes have a Miscellaneous tab for that purpose. The important thing is to make sure that the different tabs give the user a good idea of what they'll find.

FIGURE 6.20
Tabbed dialog box
from FrontPage

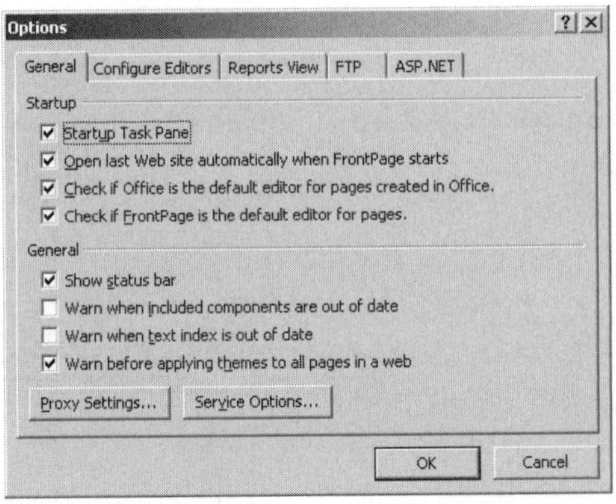

Figure 6.20 also shows a strategy for keeping the number of tabs to a minimum. The FrontPage developers apparently decided that proxy settings and service options would not need to be changed often, so those settings are removed to their own dialog boxes (accessible via command buttons) rather than having their own tabs in the main dialog box.

If at all possible, try to avoid making the user visit all the tabs in a dialog box. The user should be able to navigate to the particular tab that they care about, make their changes, and get out. This means that the other tabs in the dialog box should have sensible defaults, and that your code should be designed to only apply changes from controls that the user actually visited.

ListViews and TreeViews

Microsoft introduced the ListView and TreeView controls in Windows 95; in the decade since then, these two controls have become staples of Windows user interfaces. Figure 6.21 shows them in their original habitat: Windows Explorer.

The left panel of Explorer is a TreeView control that displays hierarchical information (in this case, the folders of the Windows file system). The TreeView indicates the levels of the hierarchy by indentation and (optionally) by drawing lines between nodes and their siblings. The + and – signs to the left of nodes allow the user to expand and contract the hierarchy by clicking with the mouse.

FIGURE 6.21
ListView and Tree-
View in Windows
Explorer

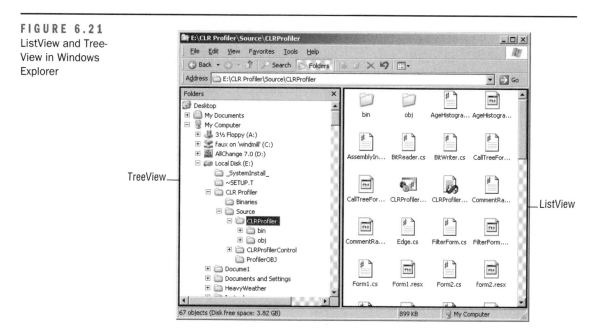

Each node in the TreeView has a text label and an optional icon. As you can see in Figure 6.21, different nodes can have different icons. A node can also have different icons depending on its state. For example, the open folder icon for the selected folder is subtly different from the closed folder icon used for other folders in the Explorer hierarchy.

As with other standard Windows controls, the TreeView can be manipulated with the keyboard:

- The up arrow moves to the next visible node above the currently selected node. It won't expand nodes.

- The down arrow moves to the next visible node below the currently selected node. It won't expand nodes.

- The right arrow moves along a particular branch of the hierarchy to the right. If a branch is not currently expanded, the right arrow will expand it.

- The left arrow moves along a particular branch of the hierarchy to the left. If a branch is currently expanded, the left arrow will collapse it.

- The * on the numeric keyboard expands the current node and all of its subbranches.

- Typing a letter or a number will move the focus to the next node in the TreeView that starts with the character typed.

The right pane of the Explorer window is a ListView control. The ListView provides a flexible way to display a list of items. By default, the ListView enables four different ways to view the list: small icons, large icons, list, and details. Figure 6.21 shows the small icon view. Figure 6.22 shows the same ListView in large icon view. There are fewer icons visible at a time, but Windows uses the higher-resolution icons to draw them. There's also room for additional information with each icon.

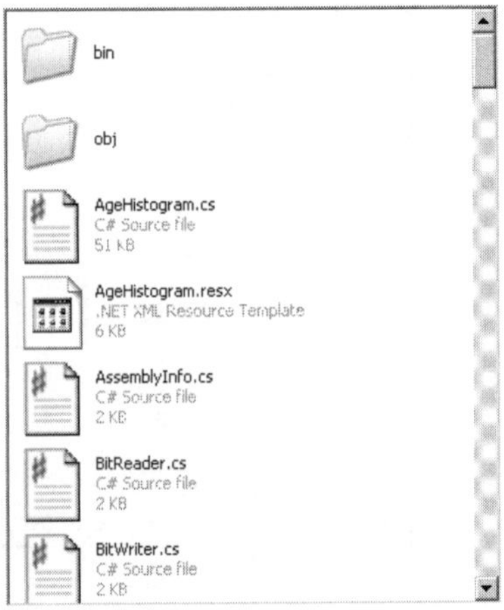

FIGURE 6.22
ListView in large
icon view

In list view, the list is shown as a simple, multiple-column list of items. Figure 6.23 shows the ListView in list view.

Finally, details view lets you define additional columns of information to be displayed for each item in the list. A ListView in details view, as shown in Figure 6.24, is ideal when you need to display multiple pieces of information for many objects simultaneously.

The most recent versions of Windows add a fifth view: thumbnail view. Thumbnail view is designed to be used with folders containing images. In thumbnail view, each image file is displayed as a reduced version, as shown in Figure 6.25.

ListView controls normally display the same selection behavior as extended-selection list box controls. You can use the Ctrl+Click and Shift+Click shortcuts to select multiple items in a ListView. You can also select multiple items by drawing a bounding box with the mouse: Click the primary mouse button, drag a rectangle that encloses the items that you want to select, and release the button to select them all.

You can also use the keyboard to perform selection operations in the ListView. First, use the navigation keys (up and down arrows, Page Up, Page Down, Home, or End) to navigate to an item that you want to select. Then, press the spacebar to select the item. To select a range of contiguous items, hold down the Shift key and use the navigation keys; all items from the initial selection to the final selection will end up selected. To select noncontiguous items, first select one item, and then hold down the Ctrl key and use the navigation keys to move to the next item that you want to select. Press the spacebar to select the second item, and repeat for as many items as you like.

FIGURE 6.23
ListView in list view

FIGURE 6.24
ListView in details view

Name ▲	Size	Type	Date Moc ▲
bin		File Folder	8/24/200
obj		File Folder	8/24/200
AgeHistogram.cs	51 KB	C# Source file	10/23/20
AgeHistogram.resx	6 KB	.NET XML Resource …	12/17/20
AssemblyInfo.cs	2 KB	C# Source file	10/23/20
BitReader.cs	2 KB	C# Source file	10/23/20
BitWriter.cs	2 KB	C# Source file	10/23/20
CallTreeForm.cs	72 KB	C# Source file	10/24/20
CallTreeForm.resx	15 KB	.NET XML Resource …	8/18/200
CLRProfiler.csproj	15 KB	C# Project file	8/8/2003
CLRProfiler.csproj.user	2 KB	Visual Studio Projec…	8/20/200
CommentRangeForm.cs	8 KB	C# Source file	10/23/20
CommentRangeForm.resx	5 KB	.NET XML Resource …	12/17/20
Edge.cs	2 KB	C# Source file	10/23/20
FilterForm.cs	13 KB	C# Source file	10/23/20
FilterForm.resx	6 KB	.NET XML Resource …	8/18/200
Form1.cs	76 KB	C# Source file	10/24/20
Form1.resx	25 KB	.NET XML Resource …	12/17/20
Form2.cs	3 KB	C# Source file	10/23/20
form2.resx	5 KB	.NET XML Resource …	12/17/20
form3.cs	6 KB	C# Source file	10/23/20
form3.resx	6 KB	.NET XML Resource …	12/17/20
form5.cs	6 KB	C# Source file	10/23/20
form5.resx	6 KB	.NET XML Resource …	12/17/20
FunctionFilter.cs	12 KB	C# Source file	10/23/20
FunctionFilter.resx	2 KB	.NET XML Resource …	9/20/200
FunctionFind.cs	7 KB	C# Source file	10/23/20

FIGURE 6.25
ListView in
thumbnail view

ListViews support column operations when in details view:

- To sort by a column, click the header at the top of the column. To sort the column in the opposite direction, click the header a second time.

- To resize a column, grab the right side of the column header with the mouse and drag it to the left or right.

- To move a column, grab the middle of the column header with the mouse and drag it to its new position.

TIP   Pressing Ctrl plus the + key on the numeric keyboard adjusts the width of all columns in the ListView to fit their contents.

RULE   For consistency with the way that most ListView controls work, you should define context menus (shortcut menus) for each item in the ListView. Different items can have different context menus.

Grid Controls

A *grid control* displays information in rows and columns. Windows itself does not supply a standard grid control, which seems odd considering how frequently such controls are useful. But most development environments contain a grid control. For example, Visual Studio .NET supplies the flexible DataGrid control. Figure 6.26 shows a DataGrid control in action.

As Figure 6.26 suggests, grid controls are well-suited to displaying information from a database. The rows and columns of a grid control map well to the rows and columns of a database table or view.

Because grids are so useful for displaying database information, and because Microsoft doesn't have one built into the operating system, they have been an especially attractive target for independent software vendors (ISVs). Figure 6.27 shows one of the many such grid controls, in this case the XtraGrid control from Developer Express (http://www.devexpress.com).

The features of commercial grid controls vary widely. If you're considering buying such a control for your own applications, here are some things to keep in mind:

- Is the price in line with your budget? Be sure to check both the price for developers and the cost to redistribute copies of the control in your application.

- Does the control offer connectivity to the source of data that you're planning to use?

- Does the control offer the display options you require? For example, can it handle graphics, Unicode characters, or alpha blending?

- Does the control support the operations you need for end users? Check out the navigation, editing, filtering, resizing, and export capabilities.

- Can the control be customized to fit in with the look and feel of your application?

FIGURE 6.26
SQL Server data
displayed on a grid

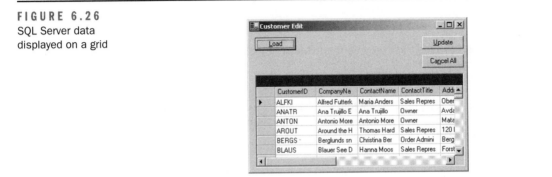

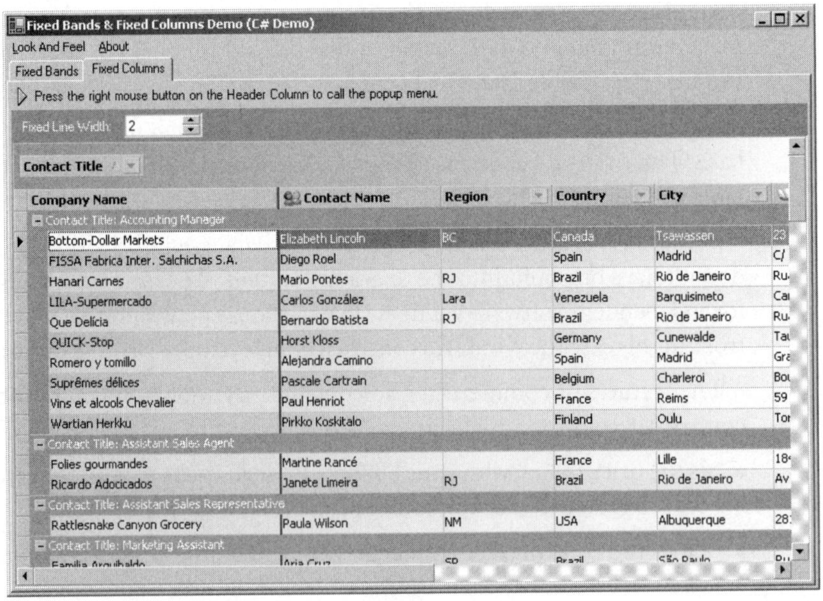

FIGURE 6.27
A commercial grid
control in action

Miscellaneous Controls

In addition to the major classes of controls that I covered previously, there are some that don't fit in elsewhere. In this section, I demonstrate two of these miscellaneous controls that I consider important for good user interfaces:

- ProgressBar
- Outlook Bar

ProgressBar

Figure 6.28 shows a typical ProgressBar control in action. The ProgressBar is the sunken control in the middle of the dialog box containing the filled-in rectangles.

The ProgressBar is used as an indicator to the user that their computer hasn't frozen, crashed, or otherwise become nonfunctional during a lengthy operation. As a first step, of course, you can change the cursor to the hourglass if the application is busy. But over the course of their Windows experience, most users have become accustomed to applications getting stuck in this state and appearing to be busy when they're actually crashed.

The ProgressBar gets around this problem by combining a visual indication that the application is busy with a visual indication that it hasn't died completely. As the application carries out a time-consuming operation, it periodically updates the ProgressBar control, adding additional filled-in blocks to the hollow rectangle.

For a ProgressBar to be effective, it must behave in a predictable manner:

- The control should start with no blocks displayed when the operation begins, but it should quickly display the first block.
- The control should display the final block just as the operation ends.
- The control should never go in the wrong direction—that is, you should never remove a block that's already been drawn (unless of course the process is really moving in reverse).
- The progress should be uniform—that is, the blocks should appear at roughly equal time intervals.

FIGURE 6.28
Using a ProgressBar control to indicate progress

The last point is perhaps the most important and the most difficult to achieve. Depending on your application's architecture, it may be difficult to estimate how long a lengthy operation will take or to come up with a way to send regular updates to the ProgressBar control. In this case, you should remember that users would rather have a pleasant surprise than an unpleasant one. It's much better to have a ProgressBar that takes forever to get through the first half and then rushes through the rest (because you overestimated the time for the operation) than to have one that gets to 95 percent complete and stays there for an agonizingly long time.

Outlook Bar

Microsoft introduced the Outlook Bar control with Outlook 97, and although it's no longer used in the Outlook user interface as of Outlook 2003, the name stuck. Figure 6.29 shows an Outlook Bar in an open file dialog box.

Usually Outlook Bar controls are used to provide gross navigation features. In the case of the open file dialog box, for example, the icons on the Outlook Bar allow the user to quickly jump to particular folders. In other cases, an Outlook Bar control might be used to move the user between functional areas of an application.

For the most part, Outlook Bar controls are "eye candy": nice to look at, but not offering a great deal of functionality. The shortcut menu on the control allows the user to choose between large and small icons, and to reorder the icons on the bar. Although Microsoft does not provide a standard Outlook Bar control for applications to use, such controls are available from many independent software vendors.

FIGURE 6.29
Using an Outlook Bar
as a navigation aid

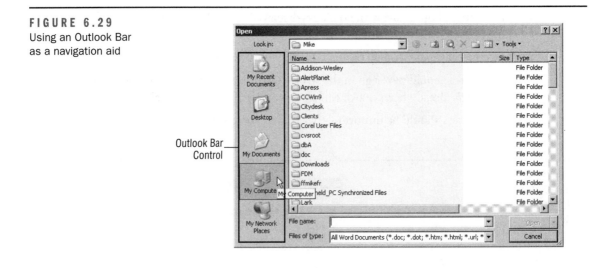

What's Left?

There are many other controls available for specific purposes. For example, choosing a calendar date is a common operation; most data-input applications need this functionality. Surprisingly enough, Windows doesn't include a standard date-picking control. But most development environments have remedied this lack by now. Figure 6.30 shows a form created with Visual Studio .NET that contains two DateTimePicker controls.

The DateTimePicker control shown here functions similarly to a combo box. Normally, it displays a date in the text portion of the control, but the user can click the drop-down arrow at the end of the control to display a pageable calendar. Selecting a date from the calendar places that date into the text portion of the control and hides the calendar again.

The DateTimePicker is only one of many, many custom controls that are available, either as part of development tools or as separate controls. You can find controls designed to display Gantt charts (similar to Microsoft Project), charting controls, controls that bring a Web look to the desktop, and many more. In general, you should reserve these exotic controls for cases in which they actually add value to your application. It's all too common to see an application dressed up with the latest and most innovative controls just so that it will look modern. The key question is whether these controls actually make things any easier for the user. Remember, any extra power that they bring to your application is balanced by the additional training that users need to go through to use the controls effectively. When in doubt, err on the side of the simple and boring user interface that uses only standard controls.

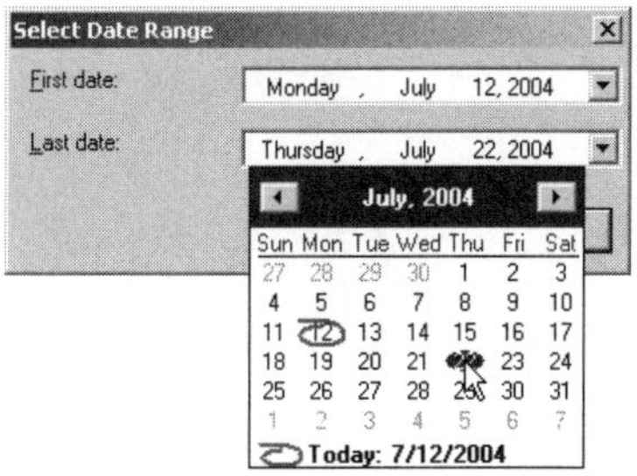

FIGURE 6.30
Choosing dates with
a DateTimePicker
control

Summary

In this chapter, you learned about the uses and capabilities of many of the common Windows controls. These controls include choice controls (radio buttons, check boxes, and toggle buttons) for choosing between a small number of alternatives, and list controls (list boxes and combo boxes) for selecting items from longer lists. You also saw tab controls, ListViews, and TreeViews, as well as other miscellaneous controls that are useful in specific situations.

By now, you've seen most of the pieces that go into building the user interface for a Windows application. Now it's time to take a more holistic view of the world: How do these pieces fit together in an actual user interface? I'll start answering that question in the next chapter, which deals with the basic design and use of dialog boxes.

CHAPTER 7

Dialog Boxes

- Overview of Dialog Boxes

- Dialog Box Layout

- Cascading Dialog Boxes

- Preventing Dialog Box Problems

- Using the Common Dialog Boxes

D ialog boxes—secondary windows with which the user can interact to perform a function, or which deliver information to the user—are an important part of many applications. Indeed, some applications feature so many dialog boxes that it seems as if the entire application consists of dialog boxes. In this chapter, I'll discuss some of the variations of dialog boxes and show you how to construct effective and useful dialog boxes.

Overview of Dialog Boxes

I'll start with a few overarching issues. When designing an application's user interface, it helps to have some sense of what dialog boxes are good for (and what they're not good for). In this section, I'll present several different ways to think about the taxonomy of dialog boxes.

The Uses of Dialog Boxes

Dialog boxes interrupt the flow of an application to a greater or lesser extent. Most dialog boxes require you to deal with them before you can resume interacting with the rest of the application (but see the discussion of modeless dialog boxes later in this chapter for an exception to that rule). As a result, the best uses of dialog boxes are for tasks that interrupt your normal flow in the first place.

One good use for a dialog box is to hide some of the complexity of a complex application. An application that has been extended and refined over several versions often contains many functions that the casual or everyday user won't need to access. Figure 7.1 shows the Resource Leveling dialog box from Microsoft Project 2003. Resource leveling is an important capability of the program, but it's not one that novice users are likely to need. Even advanced users use resource leveling infrequently. Thus, it makes sense to push these controls off to a dialog box instead of cluttering the main user interface with them.

Another good use of a dialog box is to manage an operation that requires the user's full attention or that cannot be performed while the application is doing some other task. A good example is the ubiquitous File Save dialog box. Most applications require their internal files to be in some sort of consistent state before they can be saved. If the user could change things while the save was going on, the most likely result would be a corrupted (and useless) file. By placing the Save function into a separate dialog box, developers can ensure that no changes are being made to the file at the same time that it's being saved.

Sometimes a dialog box is an organizational device, pulling together information that is otherwise scattered across an application. For example, an accounting application could use a dialog box to show all the information about a customer: address, current account balance, past orders, and so on. Even if all this information might be available elsewhere in the application, it can be useful to have a single place to visit to retrieve it from.

FIGURE 7.1
Dialog box for
uncommon use

FIGURE 7.1
Dialog box for
uncommon use

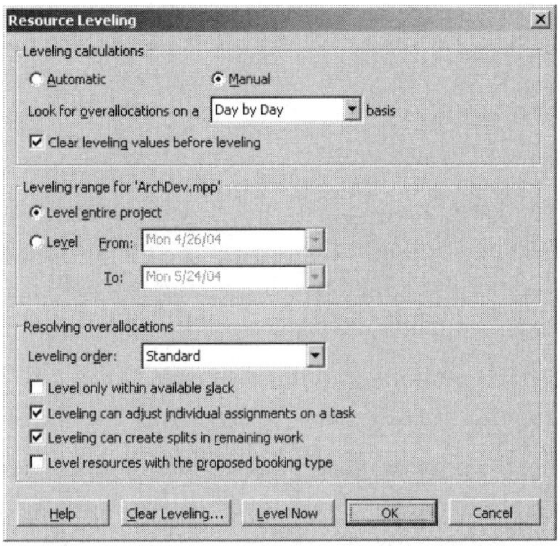

Finally, some things just plain take up too much space to be included on an application's main user interface. Consider the dialog box from Microsoft Office InfoPath 2003 shown in Figure 7.2.

If the controls on this dialog box were part of the application's main user interface, there would be little room left over to edit anything else on a screen with an 800×600 resolution. Thus, pulling the controls off to a dialog box is a reasonable solution. An alternative solution is to try to redesign your controls so that they take up less screen real estate.

Given those reasons for putting things into dialog boxes, it's worth asking what *doesn't* belong in a dialog box. The easiest rule of thumb is to avoid interrupting the user unnecessarily. Figure 7.3 shows a portion of the Microsoft Excel user interface.

FIGURE 7.2
InfoPath Data
Validation
dialog box

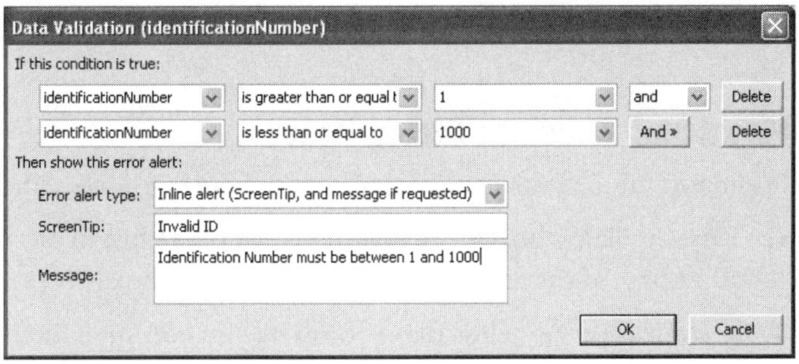

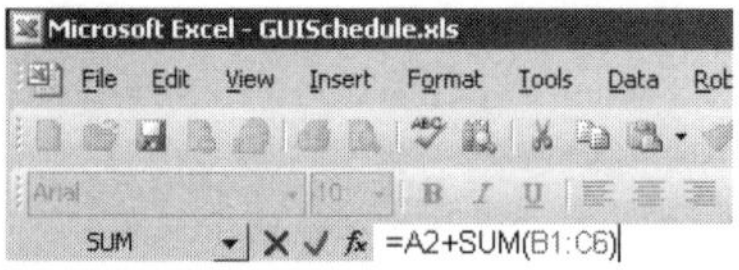

FIGURE 7.3
Entering a formula
in Excel

With the Excel formula bar, a user can enter a formula simply by selecting a cell on the spreadsheet and typing. Thus, entering a formula doesn't require any interruption to the user's workflow at all. Imagine how distracting it would be to have to open a separate dialog box to enter every formula in a complex worksheet!

It's worth mentioning, though, that even in this case Excel offers a dialog box-based alternative for entering formulas. Figure 7.4 shows the Excel Insert Function dialog box.

The Insert Function dialog box provides an alternative user interface for less-experienced users to build formulas. The Excel developers opted to cater to different users with different interfaces. Novices can use the Insert Function dialog box, whereas experienced users might prefer to type formulas directly into the formula bar.

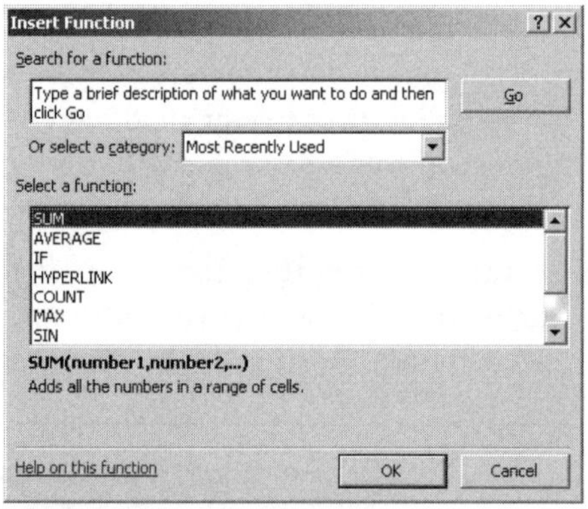

FIGURE 7.4
Inserting a function
in Excel

Modal and Modeless Dialog Boxes

It's important to understand the difference between a *modal* dialog box and a *modeless* dialog box:

- A modal dialog box is one that demands the focus; in fact, it doesn't let you work with any other part of the application while the dialog box is on screen.

- In contrast, a modeless dialog box lets you continue interacting with the rest of the application while it's displayed.

Most dialog boxes are modal, probably because the underlying Windows API makes it easy to create modal dialog boxes, and because the original Windows user interface design guidelines called for modal dialog boxes. It's also undeniably easier for developers to work with a modal dialog box. If the dialog box is modal, you can be sure that the selection or other state within the rest of the application isn't changing while the user is working in the dialog box.

Modeless dialog boxes are typically used to bring in chunks of functionality to an application. Figure 7.5 shows a good example of this technique: the Sorting and Grouping dialog box from Microsoft Access 2002.

The Sorting and Grouping dialog box works in conjunction with other features of the Access report designer to determine how records will be ordered and grouped on the final report. Typically, a user needs to adjust settings in this dialog box while also working with controls on the report. Thus, making it a modal dialog box would be a nuisance; making it a modeless dialog box allows the user full access to the report even while the dialog box is open. The tradeoff is that the Access developers needed to write code to hide the dialog box if the user moves to some other Access object where sorting and grouping doesn't make sense.

Modeless dialog boxes seem to be largely out of fashion, though. Often, it's difficult to tell visually whether a particular dialog box is modeless (although the dialog box shown in Figure 7.5 offers a clue: It doesn't include OK or Cancel buttons). In many cases, toolbars and floating accessory windows are used instead of modeless dialog boxes. They have the same advantage of being modeless, but are also clearly visually distinct from modal dialog boxes. My advice is to stick to modal dialog boxes, and to use these other user interface elements when you need modeless functionality.

NOTE   You can read more about floating accessory windows in Chapter 3, "Managing Windows," and more about toolbars in Chapter 8, "Common Windows UI Elements."

FIGURE 7.5
Sorting and Grouping
in Access

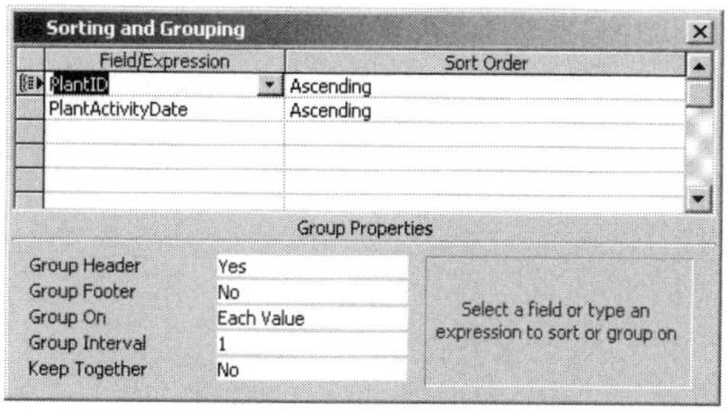

Four Types of Dialog Boxes

Alan Cooper, in his book *About Face 2.0* (Wiley, 2003) offers another way to think about dialog boxes, classifying them into four types according to their goals:

- Property
- Function
- Process
- Bulletin

Splitting your own application's dialog boxes into these categories can help you confirm that each dialog box has a distinct function to benefit the user. The first two of these categories are user-initiated dialog boxes; the last two are application-initiated dialog boxes. After briefly describing all four types, I'll focus on user-initiated dialog boxes for the remainder of this chapter.

Property Dialog Boxes

A *property* dialog box is used to set the properties of an object or of the application itself. With most property dialog boxes, the user selects an object within the application and then uses a menu item, toolbar button, or shortcut key to open a dialog box that affects the properties of the selected object. For example, Figure 7.6 shows the Virtual Machine Control Panel from VMware.

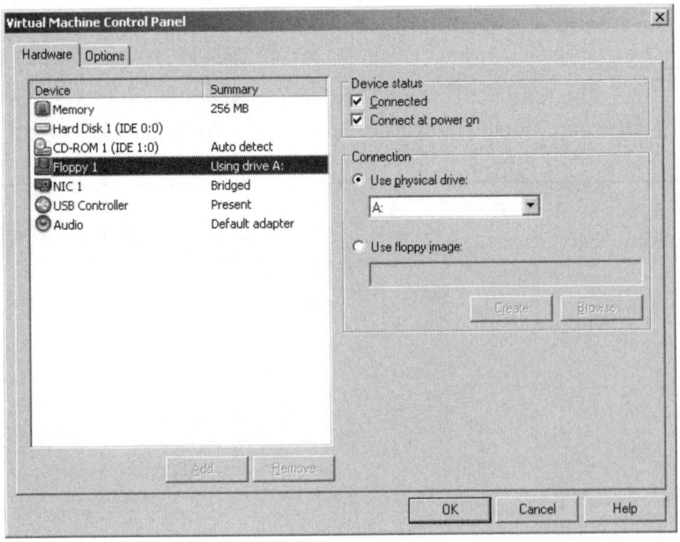

FIGURE 7.6
Setting properties of a VMware virtual machine

VMware allows the user to load more than one virtual machine at the same time. After selecting a virtual machine to work with, the user can open the Virtual Machine Control Panel to fine-tune the settings for the selected virtual machine. The OK button closes the dialog box and applies any changes to the settings.

Function Dialog Boxes

Most *function* dialog boxes do two things: they allow the user to configure the parameters for a function and then invoke that function. A good example is the Print dialog box (Figure 7.7 shows the Microsoft Word version of this dialog box).

The Print dialog box is pretty complicated, especially when you realize that several of the buttons on it open subsidiary dialog boxes (I'll discuss this technique of cascading dialog boxes later in this chapter). But it fits clearly into the three-step pattern of the function dialog box:

1. The user chooses a function to perform, which opens the dialog box.

2. The user uses the controls in the dialog box to configure the function.

3. The user clicks OK to perform the function, which closes the dialog box.

Function dialog boxes are useful, but you should keep two points in mind. First, if at all possible, the default choices should all be correct for the user when they invoke the dialog box. This simplifies their job by removing step 2 from the process. Second, provide a shortcut to perform the function with no configuration at all. In Word, for example, there's a Print toolbar button that prints the current document using the current defaults without requiring any further user interaction.

FIGURE 7.7
The Print dialog box

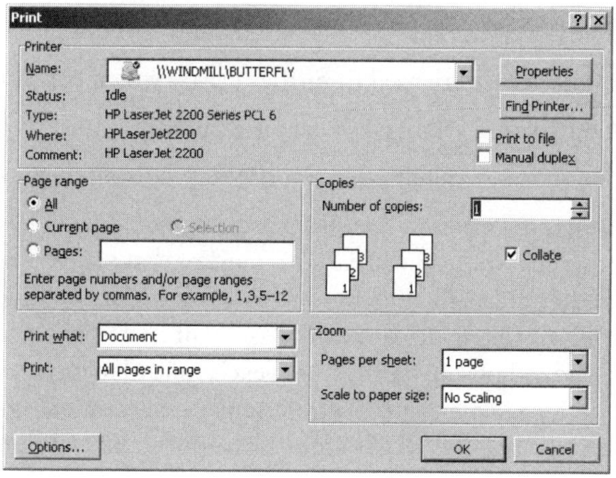

Process Dialog Boxes

Process dialog boxes are those that the application displays to indicate to the user that some long-running operation is in progress. I discussed these dialog boxes in the "Progress Bar" section of Chapter 6, "The Other Controls." I won't be further concerned with such dialog boxes in this chapter.

Bulletin Dialog Boxes

Cooper's classification of bulletin dialog boxes refers to what are usually called message boxes: modal dialog boxes used by the application to present a specific message to the user. See Chapter 2, "Putting Words on the Screen," for a discussion of this type of dialog box.

Dialog Box Layout

When you're designing a dialog box, you need to keep the user in mind. It's not enough to just get the necessary controls onto the dialog box; you need to arrange them in some sort of logical order and make their use apparent. I offered advice on individual controls in the last several chapters. Now it's time to look at how all these controls can be put together to build coherent dialog boxes.

Arranging Controls

People tend to appreciate order. Take a look at the Paragraph dialog box from Microsoft Publisher 2003, shown in Figure 7.8.

You can see several techniques used here to keep the controls on the dialog box orderly:

- The developer split the dialog box into two tabs, each with a specific function.
- Group boxes are used to further clarify which controls work with each other.
- Controls are arranged in neat rows and columns.
- The command buttons are at the very bottom of the dialog box.

The natural order of reading this dialog box is from left to right and top to bottom, and the controls are arranged to take advantage of that order. The first choice the user needs to make is whether to use the Indents and Spacing tab or the Line and Paragraph Breaks tab, and the tabs are the first controls that the user will encounter. They can then move down through the dialog box, choosing settings from each control in turn. After making all their choices, they can look at the Sample control to get a sense of how the selection will change if they click OK. The final controls at the very bottom of the dialog box let the user choose whether to apply or discard these changes.

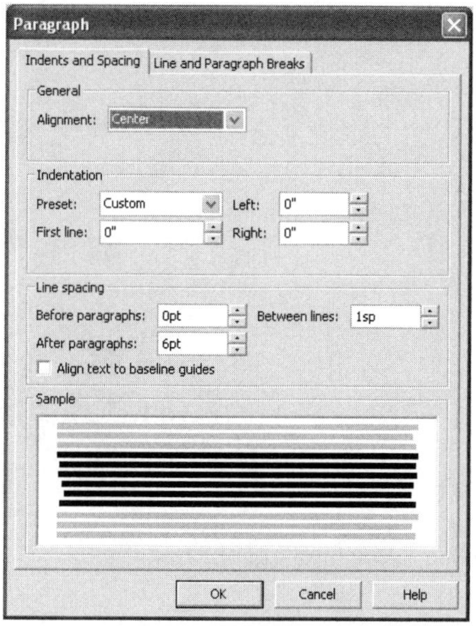

FIGURE 7.8
A moderately complex
dialog box

Adding More Controls

It seems to be nearly inevitable that dialog boxes gain more controls and options with each new release of an application. This can present a problem because there's a limit (set by the minimum screen resolution that you care to support) to how large you can make a dialog box. At some point, making controls smaller and setting them closer together will no longer do the job. Designers have come up with several solutions to this problem.

NOTE   I'm not necessarily recommending feature bloat, just trying to point out ways to deal with it. If you can improve your application without adding new controls, by all means do so.

One possibility is to add tabs to the dialog box, with each tab holding additional controls. This metaphor is readily understandable to most users, and works well up to a point. Figure 7.9 shows the Microsoft Excel Options dialog box, which probably goes beyond that point.

The problem with dialog boxes such as this one is that some actions can produce results that the user doesn't expect. Clicking on any tab in the second row brings that entire row of tabs to the front. The problem gets worse when there are three or four rows of tabs. Users tend to feel that things are moving around at random in such a dialog box.

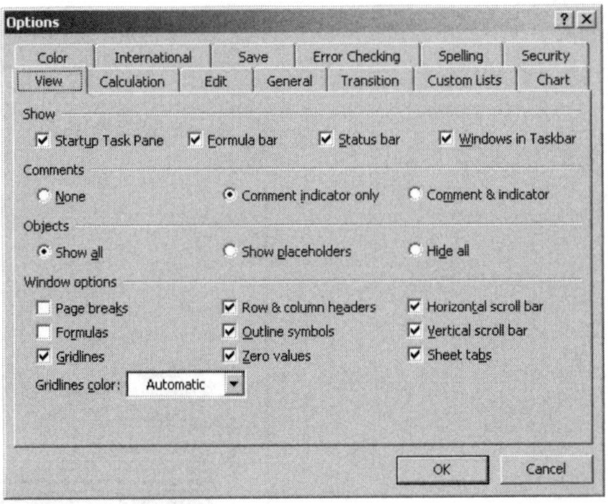

FIGURE 7.9
Dialog box with two
rows of tabs

RULE   Limit tabbed dialog boxes to one row of tabs.

Another strategy is to design dialog boxes that mutate depending on user selections. For example, Figure 7.10 shows the initial state of the standard Insert Object dialog box.

If the user selects the Create From File radio button, though, the other controls in the dialog box change, as shown in Figure 7.11.

Although this technique does allow you to put more controls into a dialog box without using more space, it can also be confusing to the user because there's no clue in the initial state of the dialog box that the other controls are lurking there. A better way to handle this might be to have all the controls visible, but to have them enabled by the radio buttons, as shown in Figure 7.12.

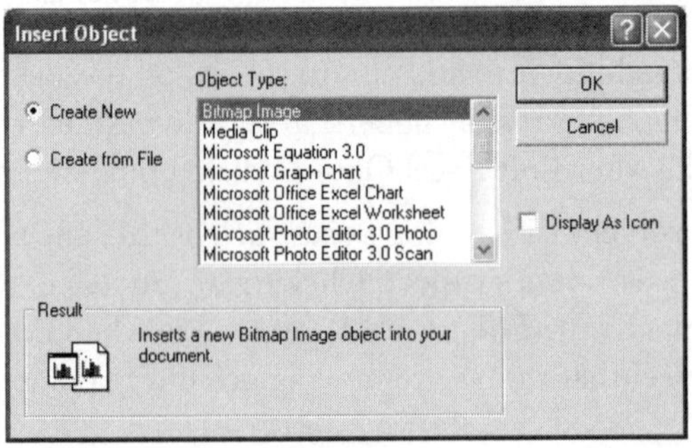

FIGURE 7.10
The Insert Object
dialog box

FIGURE 7.11
The Insert Object
dialog box revisited

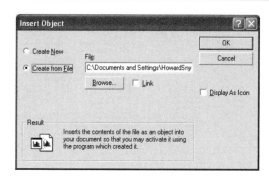

FIGURE 7.12
The Insert Object
dialog box redesigned

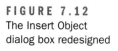

Some applications play games with using non-standard controls (or by using standard controls in non-standard ways) to cram more functionality into a limited space. For instance, Microsoft invented the drop-down command button, shown in Figure 7.13, for Office applications.

By now, you should be able to guess that I'm no great fan of this particular piece of innovation. As with the mutating dialog box, this command button does not give the user any good hint of the particular extra functionality that it hides (although the arrow does at least imply the presence of extra functionality). With a little redesign, this dialog box could host a set of radio buttons to pick the open mode, which would be much easier for novice users to understand.

Finally, don't overlook the obvious way to handle a dialog box that's getting too unwieldy: break it up into two or more dialog boxes. Often, this is the best choice. If you can find a natural way to split the functionality that you're trying to put into a single dialog box, users will appreciate two simple dialog boxes in place of one overly complex one.

FIGURE 7.13
A dialog box with a
drop-down command
button

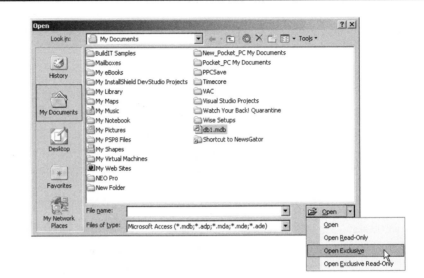

Dealing with Buttons

Buttons on dialog boxes should serve one of two distinct functions:

- To dismiss the dialog box
- To open another dialog box

I'll discuss the second type of button in the section "Cascading Dialog Boxes," later in this chapter. But first, a few rules of thumb for dealing with the other type of button, which I refer to as an *action button*.

Every dialog box needs at least one action button; otherwise it may not be clear to the user how to get rid of the dialog box. The close button (in the upper-right corner of the dialog box) closes the dialog box, but it's unfortunately ambiguous: does just closing a function dialog box execute the function or not?

Typically, a property dialog box has two action buttons:

- OK commits any changes to properties made within the dialog box and closes the dialog box.
- Cancel discards any changes to properties made within the dialog box and closes the dialog box.

The typical function dialog box also has two action buttons:

- OK performs the function and closes the dialog box.
- Cancel closes the dialog box without performing any function.

The pattern here is that action buttons close the dialog box. By convention, such buttons provide the user with a way out of the dialog box. There are two exceptions to this rule:

- If the dialog box has an Apply button (see Figure 7.14), this button commits any changes to properties made within the dialog box without closing the dialog box.

- If the dialog box has a Help button, this button opens a help window without closing the dialog box.

FIGURE 7.14
Dialog box with an
Apply button

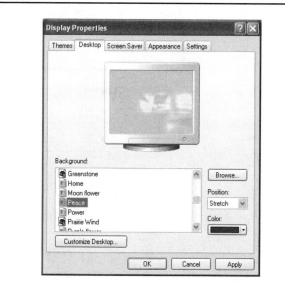

If there is only one action button that actually performs the function or commits changes, it should be labeled OK for consistency with other dialog boxes—even if another verb seems to make more sense. For example, refer to the Print dialog box shown in Figure 7.7. Even if Print would make sense as a caption for the action button that prints the object of the dialog box, it's labeled OK. The title bar of the dialog box is where the more specific verb, Print, appears.

On some occasions, a dialog box might have more than one action button. Figure 7.15 shows an example.

FIGURE 7.15
Find and Replace
dialog box

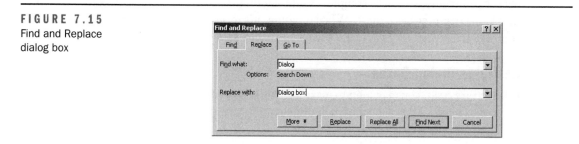

This figure shows the Find and Replace dialog box from Microsoft Word. This dialog box offers three distinct actions (Replace, Replace All, and Find Next), each with its own action button. If your dialog box can perform multiple actions, make sure that you also include a Cancel action button for times when the user decides that they'd rather back out of the dialog box without doing anything.

Unfolding Dialog Boxes

Figure 7.15 also shows another technique for hiding some complexity in dialog boxes: the *unfolding dialog box*. Clicking the More button in the Find and Replace dialog box transforms it, as shown in Figure 7.16.

FIGURE 7.16
Find and Replace
dialog box expanded

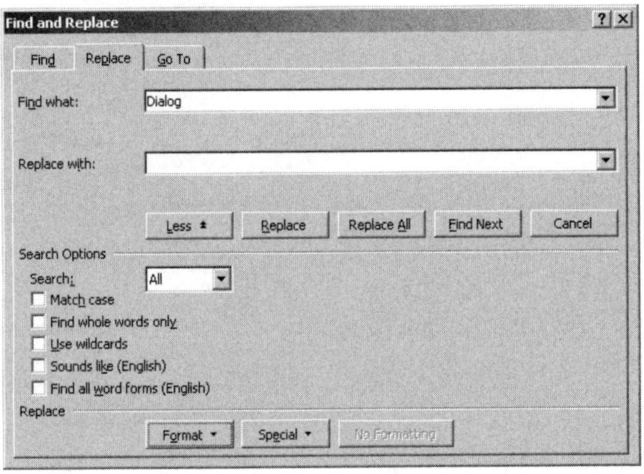

There are a few things to note about this unfolding technique. First, the control that actually does the unfolding has a visual cue in the form of a tiny double arrowhead (which you can create with a graphics program; it's not part of any of the standard fonts). Second, the control changes its caption, and the arrowhead is reversed when the dialog box has been unfolded. The same control can then hide the additional controls.

If you choose to implement this technique, do so carefully. You need to strike a balance between hiding unnecessary complexity and burying controls that the user would use if only they knew that they were there. When in doubt, it's probably better not to hide the advanced controls. Discoverability is usually a worse problem than confusion.

Resizable Dialog Boxes

In some rare cases, you may want to make a dialog box resizable to help deal with a cluttered layout. For example, if the dialog box includes a listview control with several columns, you can start out with a size that will fit on any screen and let the user make the dialog box (and therefore the listview) wider to see more information. This isn't a good technique for revealing extra controls, though, because there's no visual cue to tell the user that more controls are available.

In general, I recommend trying other solutions before moving to a resizable dialog box. Having the dialog box look cramped by default isn't very attractive, and if there's room for all the controls you need not make it resizable in the first place. If you do allow the user to resize a dialog box, you should store the new size so that you can display it at their preferred size the next time they display the same dialog box.

Cascading Dialog Boxes

Sometimes a single dialog box leads to a whole tree of choices. That is, the user might open a dialog box that offers a button for additional customization, and the button in turn opens another dialog box. This progression can continue, with the second dialog box opening a third, the third dialog box opening a fourth, and so on. Figure 7.17 shows a three-level example from Microsoft Office InfoPath 2003.

FIGURE 7.17
Cascading dialog boxes

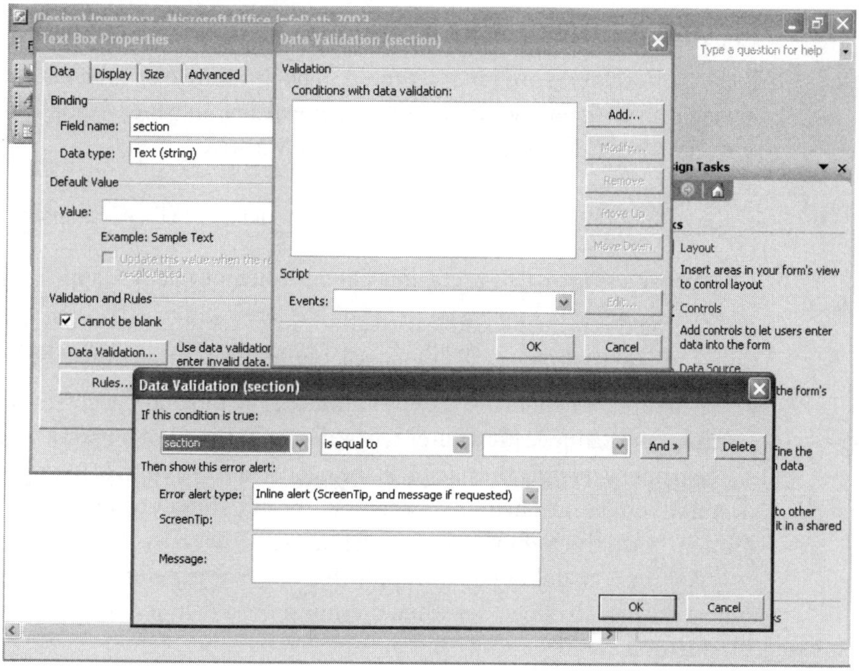

In this case, the user started by right-clicking on a control and selecting Properties from the shortcut menu to display the Text Box Properties dialog box. Then they clicked on Data Validation to display the Data Validation dialog box. Then they clicked on Add to display the second Data Validation dialog box. The result is a stack of three dialog boxes on top of the application. At any given time, the user can interact only with the dialog box on top of the stack; its modality prevents changing anything further down.

Cascading dialog boxes provide an excellent way to allow users to do as much or as little customization as they require. By using the initial dialog box for the most commonly adjusted options, and pushing less frequent options off to later dialog boxes in the series, you can help control the complexity of the situation.

The major problem I've seen with cascading dialog boxes is that users can get confused about just which dialog box is active. With a three-box cascade on screen, there are three different OK buttons and three different Cancel buttons. Even if only one set is active, people will still attempt to click the wrong ones and get frustrated. The user can also get frustrated trying to remember how to get back to a particular option if they have to drill down three or four levels to find it.

Preventing Dialog Box Problems

Software developers are often tempted to be innovative or even cute when they should be following standards and doing what the user expects. In general, applications should adhere to what has been called the Principle of Least Surprise:

RULE	The result of performing some operation should be obvious, consistent, and predictable.

To put it less formally, users don't like it when developers appear to be practical jokers.

Violating this principle can lead to all sorts of user interface issues. I already mentioned some things to watch out for in dialog boxes, but here are some others to be aware of:

- It's tempting to help the user by automatically moving the cursor when they fill an edit control. For example, after a user types all of a Zip code or a phone number, some applications help out by moving the cursor to the next data entry control in the tab order. Unfortunately, this doesn't really help the user. First, they might not be done with the edit control, even if they typed the right number of characters. What if the last character they typed was a mistake? Second, unless you can apply this rule to every edit control on a dialog box, you're asking the user to remember when they must press Tab and when they must not—a maddening situation.

- Sometimes developers omit the OK and Cancel action buttons on a property dialog box, reasoning that nothing can be changed in the dialog box and that the Close button will suffice. Although that's technically true, the result is that the user must figure out what's going on instead of following a common idiom. Making the user figure out what your application is doing is usually a bad idea.

- Don't assume that the user can see their application behind the dialog box, particularly if the dialog box is large. They may be running on a small screen (such as on a laptop) or have arranged their open windows in some fashion that you did not anticipate. The most important consequence is that dialog boxes should provide the user with context, either through their title bar or through some other text control. For example, instead of titling a dialog box "Customer Properties," you should title it "Customer 1278 Properties," so that the user will know which customer they're working with, even if they get interrupted and need to come back to your application later.

Using the Common Dialog Boxes

You don't need to build every dialog box from scratch. In fact, you should not do so. Windows provides a set of common dialog boxes built right into the system that you can use from your applications. Using these dialog boxes has several advantages:

- They are already familiar to the user.
- They're designed to fit in with the way that Windows does things.
- They have the benefit of Microsoft's own large-scale usability studies behind them.

In the remainder of this chapter, I'll show you the common dialog boxes that Windows supplies:

- Open dialog box
- Save As dialog box
- Browse for Folder dialog box
- Find dialog box
- Replace dialog box
- Print dialog box
- Page Setup dialog box
- Font dialog box
- Color dialog box

You should not feel compelled to use the common dialog boxes if you need additional functionality. For example, Word uses its own Print dialog box rather than the common Print dialog box because Word's version supplies additional customization choices for the user. Even in these cases, though, the common dialog boxes supply a good starting point for designing your own alternatives.

Open Dialog Box

The Open dialog box allows the user to select a file for the application to open. Figure 7.18 shows this dialog box.

The Open dialog box packs in quite a bit of functionality that you might find hard to duplicate if you were coding a similar interface from scratch:

- It properly handles both long and short filenames.

- Icons within the dialog box have the same shortcut menus that they would in Windows Explorer.

- The file area acts as both a drag-and-drop source and a drag-and-drop target.

- Double-clicking a file opens the file (although clicking twice slowly puts the file into rename mode, just as it does in Explorer).

- Shortcuts are automatically dereferenced to the files that they refer to.

- The File Name text box supports directly entering HTTP or FTP addresses for files.

- It supports selecting multiple files.

FIGURE 7.18
The Open dialog box

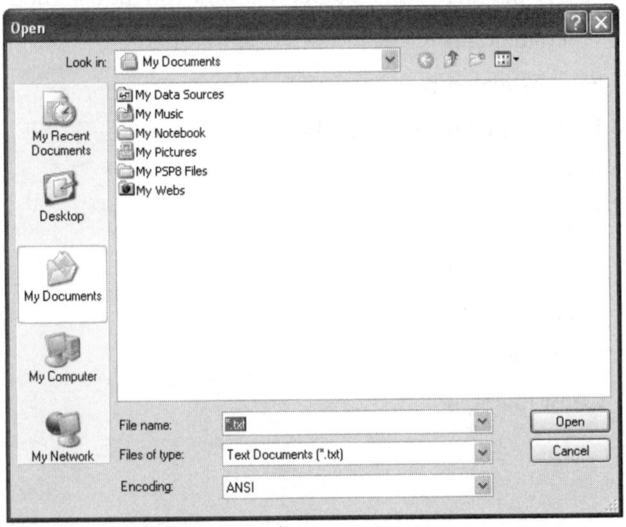

The Open dialog box returns the name of a file (or of multiple files, if you choose to enable that capability) to your application. It's up to your own code to act on that filename.

Save As Dialog Box

The Save As dialog box, shown in Figure 7.19, is the preferred interface for an application that needs to prompt the user for a filename and then save a file to that name.

The Save As dialog box is very similar to the Open dialog box. But it does supply some additional functionality. First, it will automatically add the extension to the filename if the user supplies a filename with no extension. Second, it will warn the user if the name they're trying to use is already in use.

The end result of the Save As dialog box is to inform your application of the filename that should be used for the save. It's up to your code to do the saving.

Browse for Folder Dialog Box

The Browse for Folder dialog box, shown in Figure 7.20, is the standard way for the user to locate a folder (rather than a file) on their computer.

The Browse for Folder dialog box displays a TreeView with all the folders that the user has access to, including special folders (such as the desktop or My Documents) and network drives. It can also be used to create new folders by directing the dialog box to display the New Folder button, which is built in to the dialog box but normally hidden.

FIGURE 7.19
The Save As dialog box

FIGURE 7.20
The Browse for Folder
dialog box

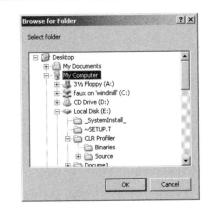

> **NOTE**   The Browse for Folder dialog box seems to be falling out of fashion. It is often replaced by the Open dialog box running in its no-files mode, which displays only folders.

Find Dialog Box

Figure 7.21 displays the system standard Find dialog box.

The Find dialog box supports the bare minimum functionality that you'd expect to find here: searching up or down in a file, matching or ignoring case, and finding the next match. If you need something more advanced, you'll need to code it yourself.

FIGURE 7.21
Find dialog box

Replace Dialog Box

The Replace dialog box is a companion to the Find dialog box. Figure 7.22 shows the Replace dialog box.

The Replace dialog box supports replacing a single instance, replacing all instances in the file, or skipping an instance and finding the next one. It does not, however, let you choose the direction of search.

FIGURE 7.22
The Replace dialog box

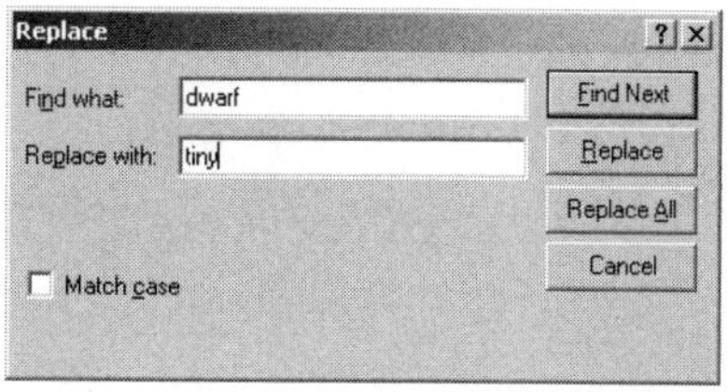

NOTE   The Find and Replace dialog boxes are simple enough that you should code your own rather than use the common dialog boxes, especially if you don't make use of any other functionality from the common dialog box library.

Print Dialog Box

The Print dialog box, shown in Figure 7.23, provides the user with an interface to the system's printing services.

FIGURE 7.23
The Print dialog box

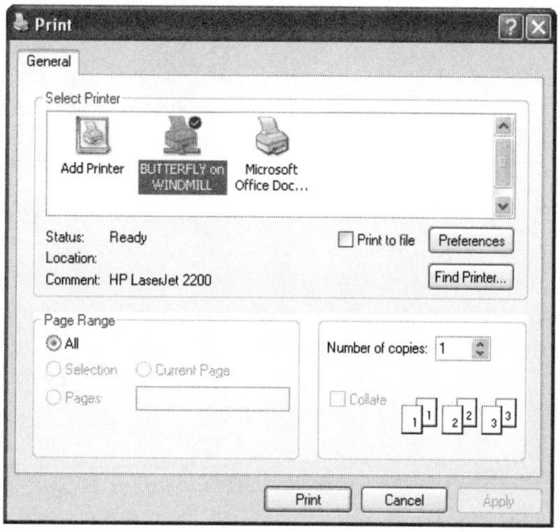

The Print dialog box packs in quite a bit of functionality:

- You can define new printers.

- You can select any existing printer.

- You can use the Preferences button to configure a printer.

- You can print to a file instead of directly to the printer.

- You can choose which portion of the document to print.

- You can choose how many copies to print and whether the copies should be collated.

Most applications will probably find this dialog box adequate for their printing needs.

Page Setup Dialog Box

The Page Setup dialog box works in conjunction with the Print dialog box to let the user dictate the formatting for your document. Figure 7.24 shows this dialog box.

The goal of the Page Setup dialog box is to let users set the details of the way their files should print. These details include the margins, orientation, and paper size and source.

Font Dialog Box

The Font dialog box, shown in Figure 7.25, is the easiest interface to use when you need to let a user select a font for use in your application.

FIGURE 7.25
The Font dialog box

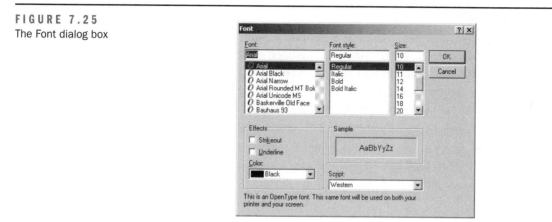

The Font dialog box shows all the fonts on the system and lets the user specify other parameters such as style and size. It also displays a preview sample of the font, which helps the user pick an appropriate font without false starts. When the user clicks OK, the Font dialog box makes the properties of the selected font available to your application. You'll typically use these properties to set the properties of a selection.

Color Dialog Box

Finally, the system provides the Color dialog box, as shown in Figure 7.26.

The Color dialog box lets the user pick from a predefined set of basic colors or use a set of extended controls to define custom colors. It can save custom colors for the future so that the user can easily refer to them after defining them once.

FIGURE 7.26
The Color dialog box

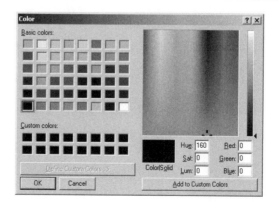

Summary

Dialog boxes are one of the most important means of communication between your application and your users. In this chapter, I provided several different ways to classify dialog boxes, and showed you some tips for creating and using effective dialog boxes. I also discussed topics such as unfolding dialog boxes and cascading dialog boxes, as well as the importance of not surprising your users. One good way to avoid surprises is to use the common dialog boxes for common tasks.

Besides dialog boxes, Windows applications have many other elements in common, including splitter bars, toolbars, menus, and so on. I'll discuss a number of these common elements in the next chapter.

CHAPTER 8

Common Windows User Interface Elements

- Toolbars

- Floating Auxiliary Windows

- Status Bars

- Splitters

- Menus

- Wizards

I n this chapter, I'll continue digging into some of the common interface elements that users
have come to expect from Windows applications. Most of these—toolbars, floating accessory
windows, status bars, splitters, and menus—are used as parts of an application's primary window. As you build up applications from these pieces, you'll also find yourself needing specialized
secondary windows. I'll also look at the design and use of one type of secondary window, the
wizard, in this chapter. Wizards are specialized secondary windows that help a user perform a
particular task.

Toolbars

If we all had computer monitors of unlimited size, toolbars might never have been invented.
Like many other parts of the user interface, toolbars are designed to help with a compromise:
They pack a lot of functionality into a limited amount of space. Figure 8.1 shows a typical tool-
bar from a recent application; in this case, Microsoft Outlook 2003.

FIGURE 8.1
The parts of a
toolbar

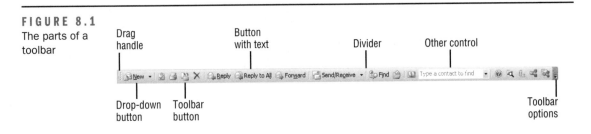

A toolbar is more than just a collection of buttons. As the figure shows, a modern toolbar can
have these components:

Drag handle   The drag handle allows users to move the toolbar around from one position
on screen to another.

Drop-down button   Drop-down buttons provide access to a menu of additional functionality.

Toolbar button   Toolbar buttons enable the toolbar's functionality. Clicking a button
normally performs some action.

Button with text   Originally, toolbar buttons displayed only an icon. These days, most
development environments let you put an icon, text, or both on a toolbar button.

Divider   Dividers are small vertical lines on the toolbar that are used to group buttons
together.

Other control   Controls such as combo boxes and toggle buttons can also be placed on toolbars, as well as on toolbar buttons. In Figure 8.1, the toolbar includes a combo box control.

Toolbar options   The right end of many toolbars has a toolbar options control, which provides a shortcut to customization functions for the toolbar. When a toolbar doesn't have enough room to display all its controls (due to being too close to the edge of the screen), the options control also provides access to hidden buttons).

Not every toolbar has all these components, of course.

Almost every application now lets you pull toolbars loose and lets them float, as shown in Figure 8.2. You can tell this toolbar is independent of the menu area because it has its own border and title bar.

FIGURE 8.2
A toolbar in floating
mode

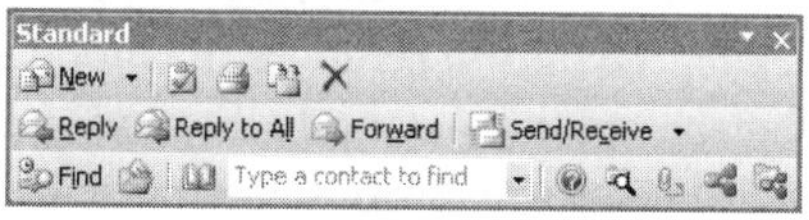

NOTE   I'll discuss docking and floating toolbars in Chapter 11, "User Choice, Customization, and Confusion."

Broadly speaking, toolbar buttons provide one of three types of functionality:

- Triggering actions
- Setting modes
- Displaying further options

Most toolbar buttons trigger an action. When the user clicks the primary mouse button on such a button, the application performs the requested action. If possible, this should be done without further user interaction. For example, clicking the Save toolbar button in Microsoft Word saves the current document. If the document has never been saved (and so does not have a filename), clicking the Save toolbar button opens the Save As dialog box to collect the necessary information, but otherwise it simply saves the document quietly.

Some toolbar buttons are used to display and set modes. For example, the bold, underline, and italic toolbar buttons in Microsoft Word fit into this category. Figure 8.3 shows how these toolbar buttons react to the selected text.

In Figure 8.3, the entire selection is in italics, so Word displays the italics toolbar button in its pushed state. Contrast this with Figure 8.4.

FIGURE 8.3
Mode-setting toolbar
buttons

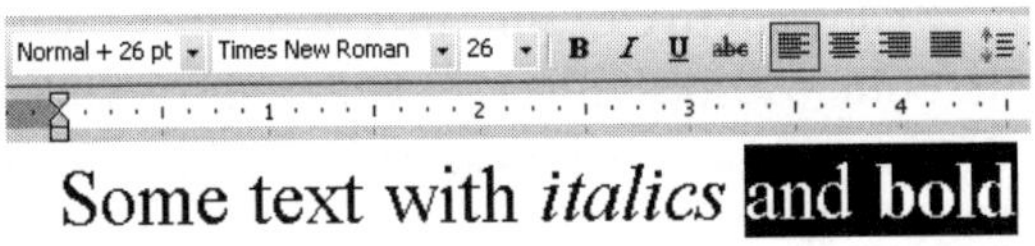

FIGURE 8.4
Mode-setting toolbar
buttons

In Figure 8.4, only part of the selection is in bold, so Word does not display the bold toolbar button in its pushed state.

Mode-setting toolbar buttons also act to affect the selection. If the mode does not already apply to the selection, clicking the button applies the mode. If the mode already applies to the selection, clicking the button removes the mode. If the mode partially applies to the selection, clicking the button applies the mode. For example, clicking the bold toolbar button shown in Figure 8.4 would make the entire selection bold.

Drop-down buttons have two different modes of operation. If you click the main part of the button, it performs the default action for the button. But if you click the drop-down arrow instead, the button displays a selection of alternative actions, as shown in Figure 8.5.

With the drop-down list of buttons displayed, you can select any action by moving the cursor down to it and then releasing the primary mouse button.

There are two slightly different situations in which drop-down toolbar buttons are a good solution. In the first, there is a set of closely related actions (such as the various new object actions that Microsoft Outlook can perform) of which one is always the most likely action. In this case, the default function of the drop-down toolbar button should remain the same, even if another action is selected from the drop-down list.

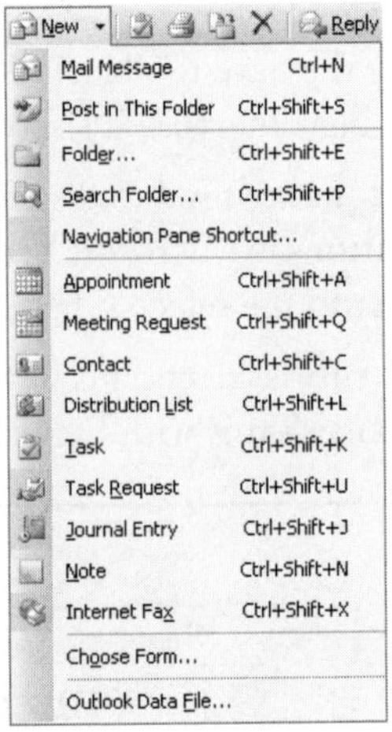

FIGURE 8.5
Drop-down toolbar
button in action

In the second situation, the toolbar button is used for grouping a set of actions, but none of those actions is clearly the most likely. In this case, selecting an action from the drop-down list should make that action the default action for the toolbar button, changing the image on the toolbar accordingly. This assumes, of course, that a user is most likely to repeat an action that they've just performed, rather than wanting to perform a new action.

Even if toolbar buttons are only 16 pixels high in the most common format, the images on these buttons can be quite complex. As Figure 8.6 shows, in many applications toolbar button images use anti-aliasing (lighter color pixels designed to make lines less jagged) and 3D effects for a professional look.

FIGURE 8.6
Some toolbar buttons

Professional-looking toolbar buttons can make a big difference to the way your application is viewed by users. Depending on the audience and your own artistic skills, you may want to invest in buying toolbar images from a company such as glyFX (http://www.glyfx.com/).

Because toolbar buttons can be inscrutable for the user, you should take steps to make their use more evident:

- Use care in selecting icons. When there is a standard icon for an action (such as open or save) you should use that icon.

- Group related toolbar buttons together, using drop-down buttons or dividers.

- Add a ToolTip to every toolbar button, so the user can get an additional hint by hovering the cursor over the button. This will also make your application more accessible to disabled users.

- Disable toolbar buttons that are not currently applicable.

- Use toolbars to display buttons for the most common operations by default, but allow users to add other actions to reflect their own usage patterns.

Floating Auxiliary Windows

Another useful way of organizing the user interface for some applications is to create *floating auxiliary windows*, sometimes called *palettes*. Figure 8.7 shows the drawing program Paint Shop Pro with several palettes open.

FIGURE 8.7
Using palettes for
functionality

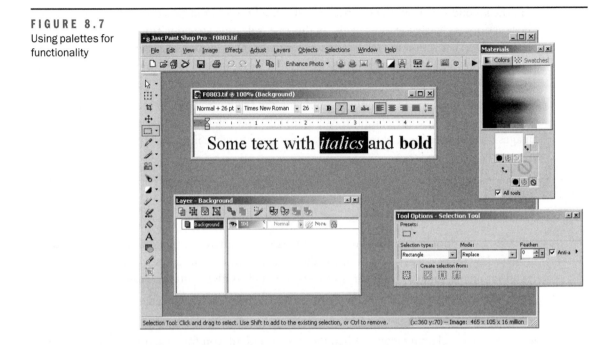

Palettes are frequently used in image-manipulation programs and integrated development environments. In these types of applications, there are many functions available to users, but groups of functions tend to be used together. For example, in an image-manipulation application, the user might need to adjust the size, shape, color, and texture of a drawing tool to achieve the desired effect. It makes sense to put the controls for those operations together into a palette so that they can be hidden or shown as a unit.

Palettes are an excellent choice when your application's functionality is "chunky"—that is, when there are groups of related actions that are generally performed together. They also work well when you can identify more advanced functions that can be hidden away on their own palette until the user is ready to learn about them.

Designers have tried a variety of visual approaches with palettes, including windows that slide out from the edge of the screen, windows that drop down from toolbars, and windows with half-height caption bars (like an undocked toolbar). The easiest and most standard way to implement such windows is simply as an undocked toolbar. Indeed, in many applications, there really isn't a difference between a toolbar and a palette other than the fact that one is docked and the other is not.

Status Bars

Another common user interface convention is the *status bar*. Figure 8.8 shows a typical status bar, this one from Visual Studio .NET.

The status bar, which is always located at the bottom of the application's primary window, contains information that the user might want but does not warrant interrupting the user with a modal message box. In this particular case, there's a message about a recent system action, information on the location of the cursor in the current code-editing window, and the status of the Insert key.

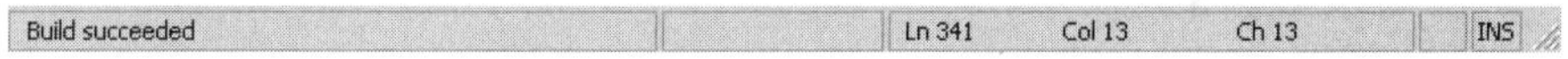

FIGURE 8.8
Visual Studio .NET
status bar

| Build succeeded | | Ln 341 | Col 13 | Ch 13 | INS |

As the name suggests, status bars are best used for status information. This should be information that the user might want to refer to, but is not readily available elsewhere in the user interface and is not critical. Developers seem to feel the need to fill the status bar with information, which leads to two distinct misuses of this tool:

- Displaying excess information on the status bar
- Displaying critical information on the status bar

As an example of the first problem, you'll often find status bars displaying the system date and time. In most cases, this is simply visual clutter. Do you really care what time it is when you're using a word processor? Even if you do, that information is already readily at hand on the Windows Taskbar.

An example of the second problem is displaying error messages that prevent the application from functioning properly on the status bar and nowhere else. Suppose that you're writing an XML editor that can save only well-formed XML files. If the user attempts to save a file that's not well formed, you should inform them of this error with a message box, not with a message on the status bar. It's easy to overlook information on the status bar, and the user might falsely assume that the file had been saved.

On the other hand, you could enhance this hypothetical application by using both a message box and the status bar by displaying an icon on the status bar whenever a file was not well formed, and using the message box only when the user tries to save a file that is not well formed. That way, the user could tell at a glance whether there was a problem, without trying to actually save the file.

RULE   Status bars are most useful as an outward reflection of an application's inner state. If your application uses modes that are not immediately obvious to the user (for example, Insert versus Overwrite for text entry), showing the current mode on the status bar can be very helpful to the user.

You can also use the status bar as a data entry device. For example, clicking the line number on the Visual Studio .NET status bar opens a dialog box that lets you enter a different line number to jump to.

Splitters

Splitters allow you to turn a window into multiple panes. Depending on the application, splitters are used in a variety of ways. Figure 8.9 shows a splitter in Windows Explorer, where it divides the folder list from the file list.

The vertical splitter bar in this case provides a way for the user to adjust the relative amount of space devoted to each of the two panes (the folder list and the file list). When the user moves the cursor over the splitter bar, it displays a two-headed arrow as a visual cue that this piece of the user interface can be dragged by holding down the primary mouse button and moving the mouse. Dragging the splitter to the left gives the file list pane more space at the expense of the folder list pane; dragging the splitter to the right gives more space to the folder list pane at the expense of the file list pane. No matter how far you drag the splitter, the total amount of space taken up on screen by the application never changes; the splitter just adjusts space allocation within the application.

FIGURE 8.9
A vertical splitter bar in Explorer

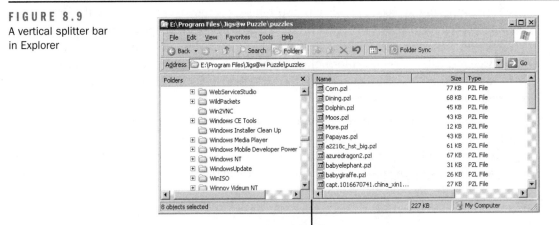

Splitter bar

Editing applications such as Word or Visual Studio use splitters in a different way. By default, these applications do not display a splitter, but they provide a handle that allows you to create one, as shown in Figure 8.10.

At any time, the user can grab the splitter handle with the mouse and drag it downward to form a pair of panes separated by a splitter bar, as shown in Figure 8.11.

FIGURE 8.10
Visual Studio .NET editing window

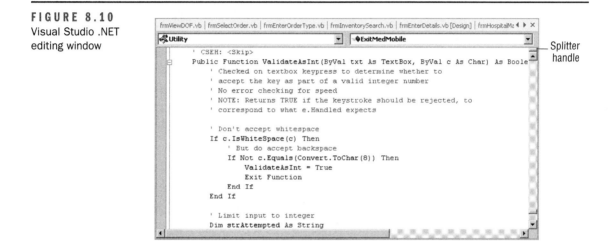

FIGURE 8.11
Visual Studio .NET editing window with split

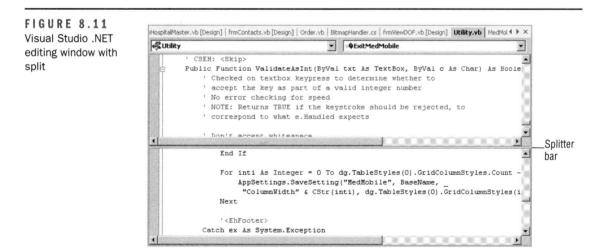

By using the splitter bar to split the single editing window into two panes, users can work in two different parts of the same source file, even if they are separated by many lines of code. The two panes can be scrolled independently, either horizontally or vertically. The splitter bar can be dragged up and down to alter the relative screen real estate allocated to the two panes. If the user drags the splitter bar all the way to the top of the window, Visual Studio .NET removes the splitter bar and displays just the splitter handle again.

Microsoft Excel takes this convention one step further by placing two splitter handles in its main window, as you can see in Figure 8.12.

By providing two different splitter handles, the Excel designers made it possible for the user to split the window horizontally, vertically, or both. Figure 8.13 shows Excel with both horizontal and vertical splitter bars displayed at the same time.

The user can move either splitter independently or both together (by grabbing the place where the two splitters cross). Although there's no reason why you couldn't allow multiple vertical or horizontal splitters in the same application, I recommend against it. The pair of splitters in Excel is already confusing enough.

FIGURE 8.12
Splitter handles in
Microsoft Excel

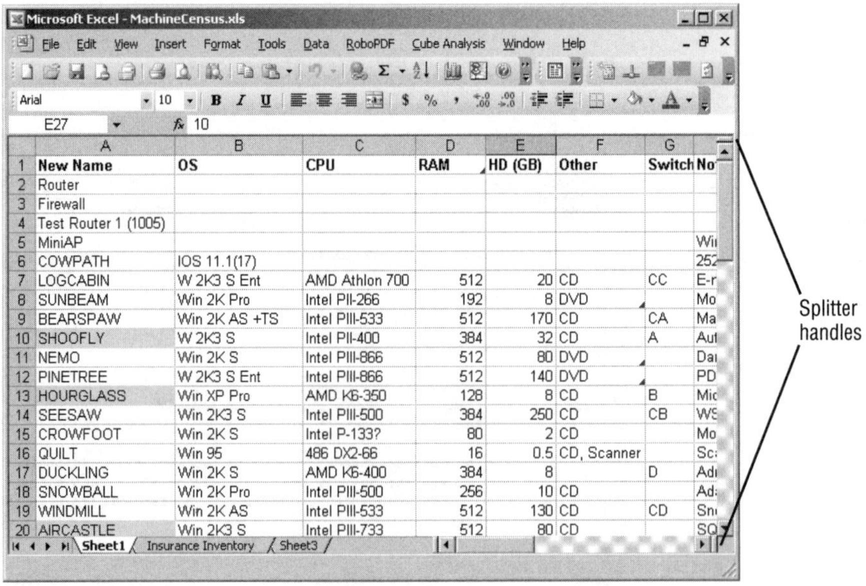

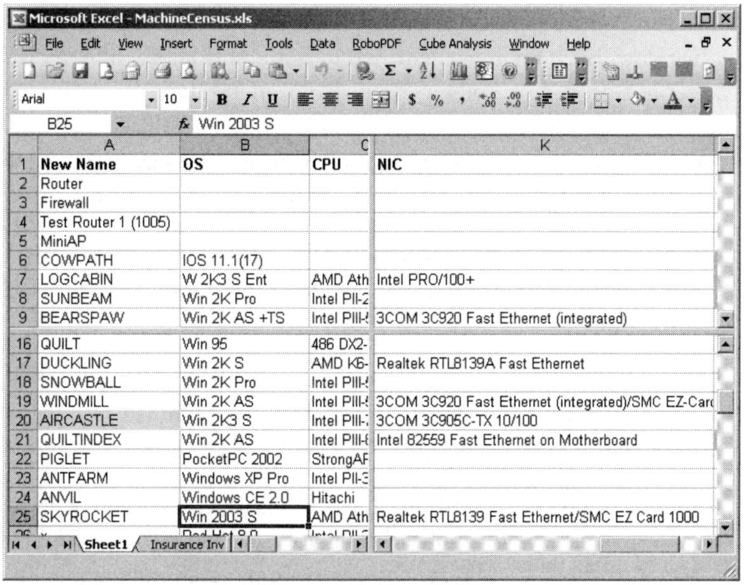

FIGURE 8.13
Excel window split into
four panes

Menus

Many applications don't have splitters or status bars, and even toolbars are not necessary for simple applications. But just about every Windows application has one or more *menus*. In this section, I'll discuss some of the basic principles of organizing menus in Windows applications and look at some of the design issues surrounding them.

Menu Mechanics

You've undoubtedly used menus in Windows applications. But you may not have consciously absorbed all the fine points of menu operation, so I'll review the subject here and offer some tips along the way. As with standard window behavior (which I discussed in Chapter 3, "Managing Windows"), these mechanics should be taken care of by any reasonable development tool—but it doesn't hurt to know what you should expect.

Menus and Menu Items

Menus are available from the menu bar, which is an area directly beneath the caption bar of the window. Each menu is identified by a menu title. Each menu title provides you with a way to get to a drop-down menu composed of menu items.

NOTE   If an application allows a large amount of customization, the menu bar might be located anywhere, rather than directly below the caption bar. I'll discuss this further in Chapter 11.

A drop-down menu generally displays a list of menu items in a single column. There are three ways in which applications handle menus with too many items to display at the current screen resolution:

- Display only as many items as will fit, and let the rest be cut off by the bottom of the screen.
- Display the menu items in two or more columns.
- Display the menu items in a scrolling column.

You can see the second and third of these choices in the behavior of the Windows Start menu when you have many applications involved. For your own applications, though, there is a much better solution: don't place that many items on a single menu. Split the items between multiple menus and, if necessary, use cascading menus (discussed later in this chapter) to add an additional level of hierarchy.

Using the Mouse with Menus

When you roll the mouse cursor over a menu title, that menu title is highlighted in some fashion. Exactly how it's highlighted depends on the operating system and the library used to construct the application. Figure 8.14 shows some of the ways that a highlighted menu title can appear.

FIGURE 8.14
Highlighted
menu titles

From top to bottom, Figure 8.14 shows these menu styles:

- System standard on Windows 2003

- Office 2003 on Windows 2003

- System standard on Windows XP

- Office 2003 on Windows XP

Regardless of the exact combination of software and operating system, the menu highlighting is meant to indicate to users that this is a place that they can click. Clicking the menu title displays the drop-down menu descending from that menu title, as shown in Figure 8.15.

With a drop-down menu displayed, the user has several options:

- Moving the mouse from side to side opens each menu in turn as the cursor passes over its menu title.

- Moving the mouse down highlights each menu item in the current drop-down menu as the cursor passes over it.

- Moving the mouse entirely outside of the menu area leaves the most recent highlighting in place.

To activate a menu item, the user points the cursor to that menu item and clicks the primary mouse button. This triggers the menu item's action without further confirmation (just as clicking a toolbar button does). There's also a shortcut method for triggering a menu action: Click the menu title, and without releasing the mouse button, move the mouse down to the desired menu item. Then release the mouse button to trigger the action. In either case, after the user triggers a menu action, Windows closes the menu.

FIGURE 8.15
Drop-down menu
in action

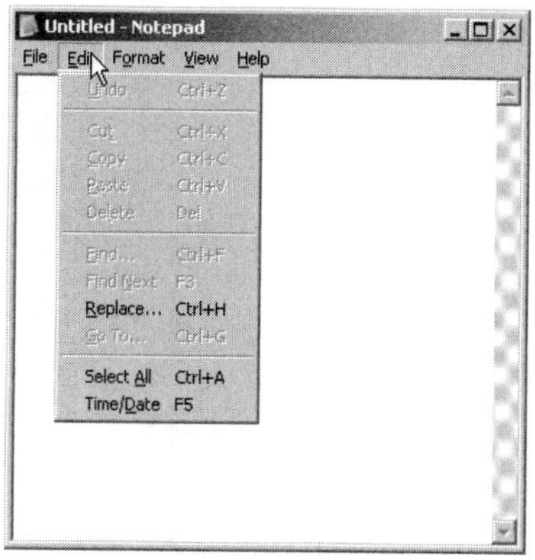

If you click a menu item and move the mouse off the menu before releasing the button, the menu will vanish but the associated action will not be triggered. If you click a menu item and move the mouse to a different menu item before releasing the mouse button, the last menu item will be the one that is executed.

Using the Keyboard with Menus

Of course, there's also a complete interface for using menus with the keyboard rather than the mouse. To start with, pressing and releasing either the Alt key or the F10 key will activate the first menu, just as if you had passed the mouse cursor over it. From here, you can move between menus by using the left and right arrow keys, or by pressing the alphanumeric key that corresponds to the accelerator key of the menu title.

With a menu highlighted, press either the up arrow or the down arrow to display the associated drop-down menu. You can at this point still navigate between menus with the left and right arrow keys, or between menu items using the up and down arrows. With a particular menu item highlighted, the Enter key will activate the menu item to trigger the corresponding action.

With a drop-down menu open, the user can press the Esc key to close the menu. This will leave the menu title highlighted. To completely deactivate the menus, click Esc a second time.

There are also two different ways to speed up keyboard access to menu commands. The first is through the use of *accelerator keys*. For example, the File menu is generally assigned F as an accelerator key and contains an Exit menu item that is assigned X as an accelerator key. With these assignments, a user can trigger the Exit menu item by pressing Alt+F and then X; or by pressing Alt+F,X (that is, holding down the Alt key and pressing F, followed by X without releasing the Alt key).

FIGURE 8.16
Menu items with direct
shortcut keys

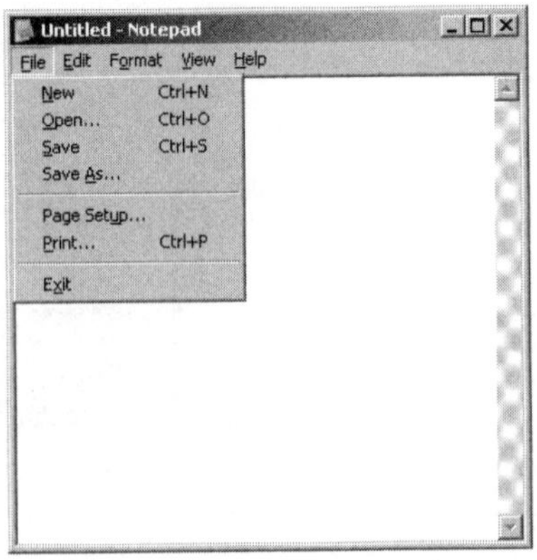

The second way to speed up keyboard access is to assign shortcuts directly to menu items. For example, the Open menu item on the File menu is often assigned Ctrl+O as a shortcut key. In this case, pressing Ctrl+O triggers the same action as selecting Open from the File menu, without actually displaying the menu. By convention, these direct shortcut keys should be displayed directly to the right of the corresponding menu item, as shown in Figure 8.16.

Although some shortcut keys are quite common (for example, Ctrl+O for open or Ctrl+F for find), they are by no means standard across every application ever written. They can't be, of course, because every application has its own functionality. That's why it's so useful to display the direct shortcuts on your application's menus: It provides an easy way for users to learn how to most efficiently use your application.

Types of Menu Items

Menu items perform one of three distinct operations:

- Triggering actions
- Setting modes
- Opening further menus

Most menu items trigger an action. When the user selects the menu item, the application performs the requested action. If possible, this should be done without further user interaction. For example, selecting the Save menu item on the File menu in Microsoft Word saves the current document. If the document has never been saved (and so does not have a filename), selecting the Save menu item will open the Save As dialog box to collect the necessary information, but otherwise it simply saves the document quietly.

Some menu items, though, always require user input. A good example is the AutoFormat menu item in Microsoft Excel. The user can select this menu item to apply an AutoFormat, but they'll always need to select the actual AutoFormat from the AutoFormat dialog box. To indicate this on the menu, follow the menu item with *ellipsis points* (...), as shown in Figure 8.17.

FIGURE 8.17
Indicating that a menu item requires more input

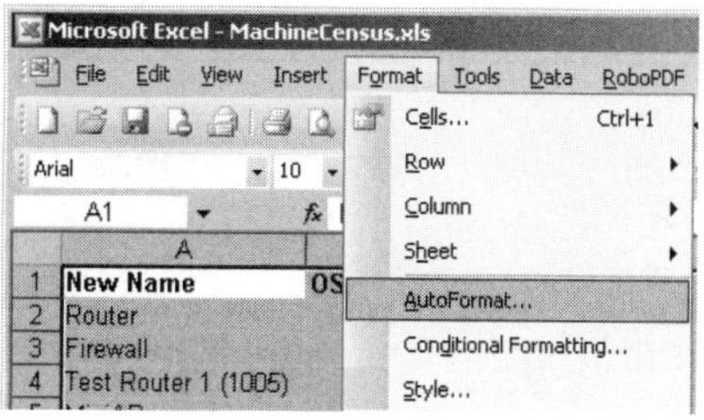

Most applications have some limit on the particular actions that are allowed at any given time. You should be sure to give visual cues on menus by disabling menu items that are not currently allowed.

Some menu items are used to set modes in an application. These menu items operate similarly to check box controls, and the application can display a check to the left of them. Figure 8.18 shows the View menu of WordPad, which has four such menu items. This menu lets you turn various parts of the user interface on or off. If a particular part is currently displayed, the menu item is displayed with a check to the left; if the menu item has no check, that piece of user interface is currently hidden. Selecting one of these menu items toggles the state from displayed to hidden or back.

FIGURE 8.18
Menu items with
checkmarks

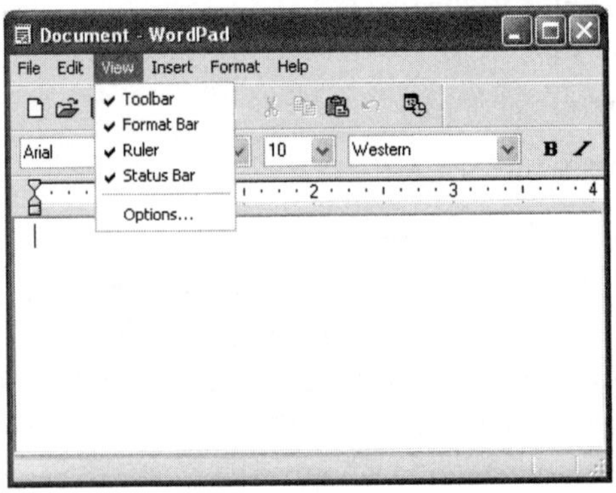

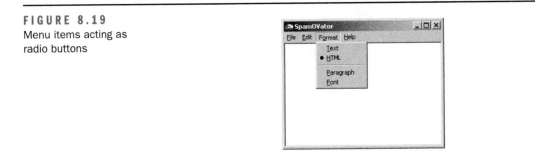

Checked menu items have the same semantics as check box controls: any number can be checked or unchecked independently. In some cases, you might also see menu items that are the equivalent of radio buttons, so that selecting one deselects any others. Figure 8.19 shows that such items are rendered with a dot to the left if they are selected.

Finally, menu items can open additional menus that are subsidiary to the main menu. I'll discuss these *cascading menus* later in the chapter.

FIGURE 8.19
Menu items acting as
radio buttons

Organizing and Naming Menu Commands

With so many menu commands in the average application, it pays to put some thought into their organization. Ideally, you want users to find your menu arrangement so obvious that they can go straight to the functionality they want without any thought. Although you're unlikely to reach that ideal, there are some things that you can do to make life easier. I'll discuss four topics in this section:

- Common menus
- Naming menu items
- Cascading menus
- Using dividers

Common Menus

If your application uses functionality that is the same as (or very similar to) that used by other applications, you can benefit by using the common menu structures that many applications agree on.

File menu   The File menu is generally the first menu on the menu bar. It contains commands that operate directly on a file (assuming that your application is file-based). Typical menu items for the File menu include New, Open, Save, Save As, Send To, Print, and Properties. The File menu also often contains a most-recently used (MRU) list of files that you have worked with in the application. The final item in the File menu should be the Exit menu item.

Edit menu   The Edit menu provides a home for general-purpose editing commands, which include Cut, Copy, Paste, Undo, Redo, Find, Replace, Select All, Go To, and Delete.

View menu   The View menu is a place for commands that change the user's view of data. Typical commands for the View menu include Full Screen and Zoom. If you allow showing or hiding particular parts of the user interface, these menu items should also be placed on the View menu.

Tools menu   The Tools menu provides access to actions that open up additional functionality. Typical entries here include Options, Customize, Add-Ins, and Macros. Any large chunk of functionality is a candidate for the Tools menu. For example, launching wizards or processes such as a spell-check is usually done from this menu.

Window menu   If your application allows multiple child windows, the Window menu provides access to functions for managing these windows. These entries include Arrange All, Next Window, Previous Window, Hide, Unhide, and any commands relating to panes. You should also provide dynamic menu items on this menu for each currently open window.

Help menu   The Help menu is the main interface to your application's help system. The menu items on this menu can include Contents, Index, About, and Online Feedback.

In addition to these standard menus, you should also feel free to commandeer any other menu that matches your own application's functionality. For example, if you allow the user to insert a variety of different objects into documents, you'll probably want to include an Insert menu modeled after Excel's Insert menu.

Naming Menu Items

Naming menu items is mainly a matter of common sense. But common sense is often quite uncommon, especially when you've been writing code for 22 hours straight. In that light, here are some guidelines to help you choose effective and useful names for menu titles and menu items.

- Every menu title (and its accelerator key) should be unique in the application. That is, you can't have two Format menus in the same application.

- Every menu item on a single menu (and its accelerator key) should be unique on that menu. Menu items can, however, repeat across menus. For example, both the Edit and Format menus could include a Picture menu item without causing confusion.

- Every menu title and menu item should have an accelerator key.

- Commonly used menu items should have direct shortcut keys.

- Menu title names should be a single word.

- Both menu title names and item names should be brief and clear. Strive for the shortest text that captures the functionality.

- Use only real words, or terms that your application uses consistently, in menu text. Don't use made-up words such as HomeRow unless those terms are used elsewhere in your application.

- If a menu item consists of more than one word (such as Task Pane or Reveal Formatting) use book title capitalization.

- Don't format menu items with fonts, bold, italics, or other non-standard formatting. Use the system menu font.

- Use verbs or phrases consisting of a verb and a noun for action-oriented menu items. Use nouns for state-oriented menu items. For example, a menu item to set the background color should be Set Background, not Background Set. A checked menu item that controls whether a selection is in italics should be captioned Italics.

- If a common application (such as Internet Explorer or one of the Microsoft Office programs) provides similar functionality to your application, use the same menu items that that application does for the similar functionality.

Using Cascading Menus

Cascading menus (also called *submenus*) are a way of adding additional functionality to a menu without merely adding more menu items to the menu. Figure 8.20 shows a cascading menu in action.

FIGURE 8.20
Cascading menu in
Microsoft Excel

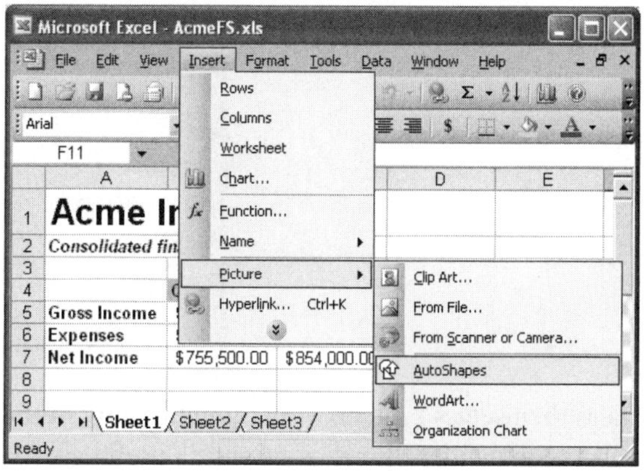

In this particular case, the Picture menu item on the Insert menu in turn leads to an entire menu of different types of pictures that the user can insert in a spreadsheet. Rather than including each of these menu items individually in the main Insert menu, the Excel developers chose to use a cascading menu to group them together.

Cascading menus are distinguished visually by the small triangle at the right side of the menu. In Figure 8.20, the Name menu item also leads to a cascading menu.

If you're using the mouse to navigate menus, there is a small delay before the cascading menu is delayed. To avoid this delay, you can click the cascading menu item. When navigating with the keyboard, there's no delay; selecting the cascading menu item immediately displays the submenu.

Cascading menus are a useful device for hiding complexity and grouping functionality. But there's a trade-off here: The more functionality you place on a cascading menu, the more time users will spend navigating to get to those menu items. You can also place cascading menus on cascading menus, but you should use this technique sparingly, if at all. Such sub-submenus are very hard for the user to discover.

Using Dividers

Menu *dividers* provide a device for grouping menu items together. Figure 8.21 shows a menu with several dividers.

Dividers on a menu

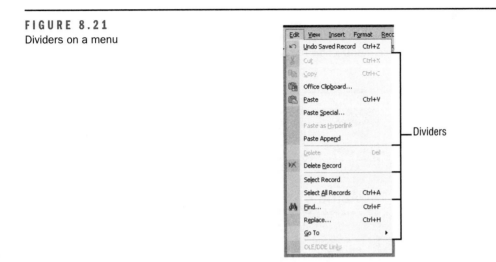

Dividers themselves have no direct functionality in the application. You can't highlight or click on a menu divider. But they provide a useful visual cue for the user in a hurry who's scanning the menu, looking for desired functionality. In Figure 8.21, for example, all the menu items having to do with Clipboard operations are in one section of the menu, and those having to do with deletions are in another section, walled off from one another by dividers.

RULE   Dividers don't take up much space, and they enhance the look of most menus by introducing some much-needed empty space into the menu. You use them whenever you have a group of related menu items that you can group using this technique.

Shortcut Menus

Shortcut menus (also called *context menus* or *pop-up menus*) are a way to attach a menu directly to an object or a portion of the user interface of your application, rather than having the menu be a part of the main menu bar. Shortcut menus provide a useful place to show frequently used actions.

WARNING   Sometimes you'll see shortcut menus referred to as *right-click menus*, but this is not technically correct because they are left-click menus if the user chooses to swap their mouse buttons.

Shortcut menus have several advantages in most applications:

- Because they include only functions that apply to the current object, they are typically shorter and easier to navigate than regular menus.

- Because they're displayed at the point where the user clicks the mouse, they remove the need for the user to move the mouse across the screen to select a menu item.

- Because they're displayed only on demand, they don't take up screen real estate or contribute to visual busyness in your application.

Shortcut menus are displayed when the user clicks the secondary mouse button somewhere in the application, or when they click Shift+F10 or the Application key (on keyboards that are equipped with such a key). The user can then select an item on the shortcut menu with the primary mouse button. Alternatively, they can click outside of the menu with either mouse button (clicking elsewhere with the secondary mouse button displays the shortcut menu appropriate to the new location) or press the Esc key to dismiss the shortcut menu without selecting an item.

Follow these guidelines when designing shortcut menus:

- Keep shortcut menus short. As a rule of thumb, limit them to a dozen items or fewer.

- Make shortcut menus as sensitive to context as possible. If the user clicks part of the user interface (such as a toolbar or status bar), the shortcut menu should contain commands that act on that piece of the user interface. If they click on an object, include actions that can be performed on that object.

- Place the most important and common actions at the top of the shortcut menu to further minimize mouse movement.

- Don't display direct shortcut keys on shortcut menus. You know the user already has their hand on the mouse when they see a shortcut menu, so you don't need to provide keyboard cues.

- The shortcut menu shouldn't contain any surprises. That is, every action on the shortcut menu should also be available elsewhere in the user interface, so that the user is never forced to use a shortcut menu.

- By convention, the Properties command should be the last command on a shortcut menu (when it is present at all).

Menu Styles

Most of the menus that you've seen in this chapter (and indeed, most of the menus that you'll see on screen) are simple gray panels with black text. But there are applications that do fancier things with menus, and you should be aware of those style innovations. Microsoft Office appears to be the leading source of such innovations, and I'll admit that I'm not at all sure that they're a good thing. On the one hand, Microsoft invests a lot of time and money in usability testing, which means they should know something about what works. On the other, it seems like many of these innovations are just a way to make Microsoft's own applications look different and memorable. My advice is to adapt these new styles if you can do so easily, but don't waste an enormous amount of time trying to mimic Microsoft (especially considering that they'll change things again with their next release).

One such innovation is the menu icon. Figure 8.22 shows the Edit menu from Excel 2003.

The menu items with icons are those that match toolbar buttons with the same icon. If the user knows their toolbars well, this can provide a visual cue for quickly finding an item on the menu. On the other hand, I also suspect that this was done mainly to fill up unused space (which needed to be reserved for check marks on menu items that reflect state). There's nothing wrong with this from the standpoint of eye candy, but I doubt that it really helps anyone very much.

Something that I'm sure doesn't help is the continuing search for new visual styles for menus. Figure 8.23 shows the same menu in two different versions of Office.

The menu on the left comes from Excel 2002, and the menu on the right comes from Excel 2003. In the intervening year, the Excel designers opted for a more shaded approach to the left margin of the menu and different default colors. To me, this change is in the same category as slapping "New and Improved" on the front of a box of laundry detergent.

Finally, Office is the original home of the *adaptive menu*, sometimes called the *IntelliMenu*. Adaptive menus have a small downward-pointing arrow at the bottom. When you hover over this arrow with the mouse cursor for a moment, the menu expands to show additional items, as shown in Figure 8.24.

FIGURE 8.22
A menu with icons

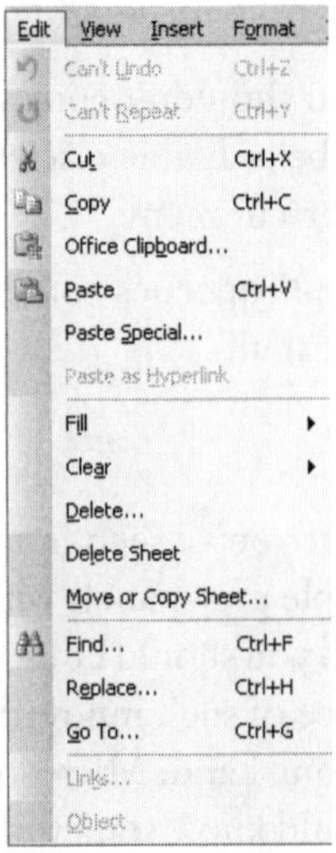

FIGURE 8.23
Menu changes
from Office XP to
Office 2003

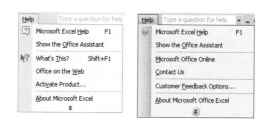

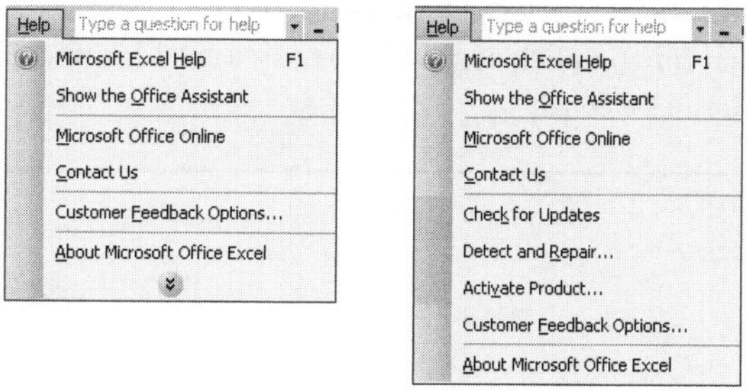

FIGURE 8.24
Adaptive menu in
action

Adaptive menus are designed to help make life easier for new users by showing only the most common menu items by default. Unfortunately, new users are also the ones least likely to understand that there are more menu items lurking, whereas advanced users tend to get annoyed by having to go hunting for the advanced menu items. I suggest you avoid this technique unless you have a truly overwhelming number of menu items in your application. Even then, you should provide users with a way to turn off the adaptive behavior and simply display all of the menu items at all times.

TIP   If you do decide that you want to adapt one of the fancy menu styles, several ISVs sell complete menu design packages for popular development environments. A good place to start is with a component reseller such as Xtras.NET (http://xtras.net/).

Wizards

The user interface pieces I've looked at so far in this chapter are all designed to be a part of your application's primary window (though they also apply to some secondary windows). Wizards, in contrast, are always secondary windows. A *wizard* offers a step-by-step interface to help a user perform a particular task. Wizards don't replace other ways to perform tasks, but they're often the most accessible way for a new user to get started with an application.

Wizards vary a good deal in design, but the most common way to build a wizard is as a secondary window (usually modal) that displays a series of pages. The first page provides an introduction to the wizard, explaining its purpose. After that comes one or more pages in which the user interacts with the wizard. Finally, there's a completion page that confirms the user's choices and tells the wizard to actually perform its work.

If you have a computer science background, you may recognize a wizard as a *state machine*. In a state machine, work is divided into a series of states that are connected by transitions. In a wizard, each button click serves as a transition. Figure 8.25 shows a state machine diagram of a hypothetical wizard.

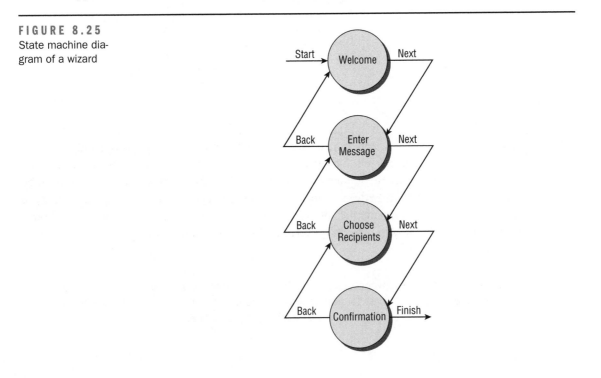

FIGURE 8.25
State machine diagram of a wizard

This particular wizard starts with a welcome page. It then contains two functional pages, followed by a confirmation page. Each page has Next and Back buttons to allow the user to move through the wizard. You should design wizards so that the user can move back and change their mind at any time; a wizard should not make any permanent changes before the user confirms their choices on the final page of the wizard. In addition to Back and Next, there are three other standard buttons that you may find in a wizard:

- The Cancel button discards all the user's choices and closes the wizard without performing any actions.

- The Finish button completes the wizard and performs the specified actions. You can include the Finish button on pages before the confirmation page if it makes sense to finish the wizard with default choices for the other pages.

- The Help button opens context-sensitive help specific to the wizard.

Figure 8.26 shows a typical wizard welcome page.

FIGURE 8.26
First page of a
wizard

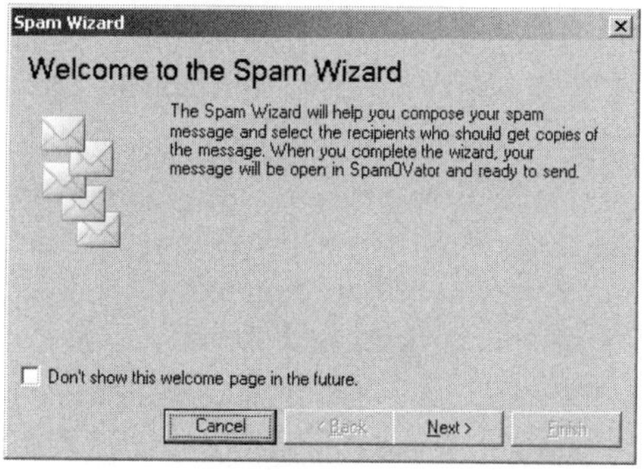

The welcome page contains a graphic identifying the theme of the wizard, a title, and some explanatory text. It also has all the buttons that will be used throughout the wizard, even if some of them don't apply on this page. The buttons that do not apply are disabled. This way, the buttons won't appear to change or jump around as the user moves from page to page. It's also useful to include a check box that allows experienced users to suppress the welcome message after they've read it a few times.

Figure 8.27 shows an interior page from the wizard.

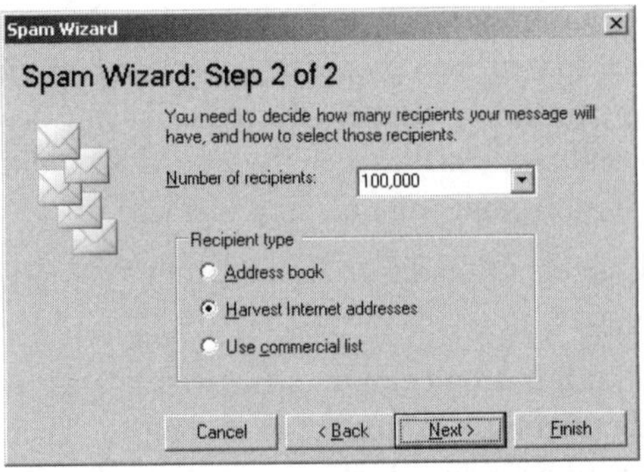

FIGURE 8.27
An interior page of a wizard

The interior pages of a wizard should repeat the thematic graphic from the welcome page. If you need additional space for other controls, consider using a reduced-size or cropped version of the graphic. Group controls together into pages with cohesive functionality, and provide the user with an explanation of the page. Each page should also contain a title indicating where the user is in the process.

Figure 8.28 shows the confirmation page of a wizard.

Once again, the confirmation page repeats the visual theme of the rest of the wizard. The text on this page should make it clear to the user exactly what will happen when they click the Finish button. You might also want to provide ways to help the user proceed with likely next steps, which can take the form of offering to open a help page or giving the user a choice of modes in which to open a newly created object.

In general, user interface text on a wizard should be friendly and informal. This part of your application's user interface will be most useful for novice users; advanced users should be able to work with objects and perform tasks directly, without the handholding.

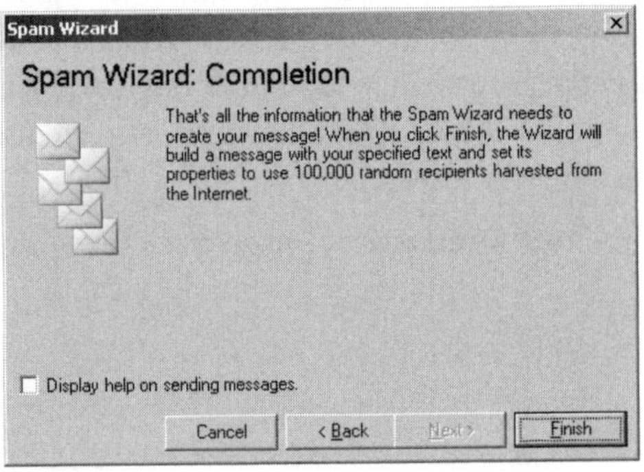

FIGURE 8.28
Confirmation page of a wizard

Summary

In this chapter, you learned about many of the tools and techniques that you can use to make your applications more attractive and usable. Toolbars and menus provide the user with ways to interact with your application. Status bars can give back essential information when the user needs it, whereas splitters allow you to make good use of screen real estate. Wizards are an essential device for helping less-experienced users.

Now we need to look outward from the application to the user for a few chapters. I'll start by examining how users enter data and navigate through an application, and consider what this means to your application's design.

CHAPTER 9

User Input and Navigation

- Five Ways to Work

- Organizing an Application

- Under the Covers

I t's easy to think about the typical user when you're writing software. With some more or less vague idea in mind, you can target your software for this typical user. But, of course, there is no typical user; there are only particular users. In this chapter, I'll discuss some of the things you can do to make your software's user interface work well for all of the particular users who want to use it, regardless of their own preferences.

Five Ways to Work

Suppose that you want to perform a simple operation, such as moving a piece of text from one location to another in a Microsoft Word document. Although one way to do this probably comes to your mind first, there are five distinct methods you can use to perform the actual move operation:

- Keyboard Shortcuts

- Toolbar

- Menus

- Menu Shortcuts

- Direct Action

Although you can't perform every action in every application in all five of these ways, it's worth keeping them in mind. Let's take a closer look at the way these methods might apply to the problem of moving text in Word.

Keyboard Shortcuts

Some users prefer to work without ever lifting their fingers from the keyboard. One of the basic foundations of Windows is to accommodate these users with keyboard shortcuts. That's not just to cater to people's prejudices. Some people (those who can't manipulate a mouse) might have no choice but to use the keyboard or an alternative input device that the system treats as a keyboard.

To move a piece of text using only keyboard shortcuts, you could proceed as follows:

1. Move the cursor to the start of the text to be moved by using the standard cursor-movement keys.

2. Hold down the Shift key and move the cursor to highlight the text to be moved.

3. Click Ctrl+X to cut the selected text.

4. Move the cursor to the new location for the text.

5. Click Ctrl+V to paste the selected text.

Although using only the keyboard in any major application requires learning many arbitrary key sequences, it can be a very fast way for an experienced user to interact with an application. Many of the fastest developers and writers use the keyboard almost exclusively for their work.

Toolbar

The toolbar-oriented user might prefer this approach to moving a piece of text:

1. Highlight the test to be moved by holding down the primary mouse button and dragging across the text.
2. Click the Cut toolbar button on the Standard toolbar.
3. Click the mouse at the new location for the text.
4. Click the Paste toolbar button on the Standard toolbar.

Here I've shown how to combine toolbar actions with mouse selection, but of course you could equally well select text with the keyboard and still use the toolbar for actions. The toolbar buttons don't care how the user selects the text.

Menus

Menus are pervasive in Windows, and are generally the definitive list of what an application can do. That is, the menus usually expose all the commands in an application, whereas keyboard shortcuts and toolbar buttons cover only a subset of the most important functionality. With the menus, text-moving looks like this:

1. Highlight the text to be moved by holding down the primary mouse button and dragging across the text.
2. Select Cut from the Edit menu.
3. Click the mouse at the new location for the text.
4. Select Paste from the Edit menu.

Combining the mouse with the menus allows you to perform many operations without touching the keyboard at all. Although not generally as fast as using the keyboard for everything, this process might work out better for those concerned about the health aspects of excessive keyboard use.

TIP   One case where a mouse makes for fast work is browsing for information on the Internet. If you get a mouse equipped with a wheel, as well as forward and back buttons, you can review large quantities of data without ever touching the keyboard.

Menu Shortcuts

Of course, you can activate the menus by using the keyboard instead of the mouse:

1. Move the cursor to the start of the text to be moved by using the standard cursor-movement keys.

2. Hold down the Shift key and move the cursor to highlight the text to be moved.

3. Click Alt+E,T to cut the selected text.

4. Move the cursor to the new location for the text.

5. Click Alt+E,P to paste the selected text.

As with using keyboard shortcuts, using menu shortcuts lets you operate without having to remove your hands from the keyboard.

Direct Action

There are no real-world objects in your computer. If you open the case, you won't find little customers or calendars inside. But sometimes it's useful to pretend that there are. That's the point of direct actions: They provide an analog to real-world activities but carried out on the digital stage.

Word encourages this view by treating text as something that you can pick up and drag with the mouse. To move a piece of text, you can follow these steps:

1. Highlight the text that you want to move by using either the keyboard or mouse methods discussed earlier.

2. Click the primary mouse button anywhere in the highlighted text. While holding the button down, drag the text to the desired new location.

3. Release the mouse button.

Although direct action provides an easy way to perform some tasks, it's inherently limited in most applications. With dozens of operations and only a limited number of basic ways to use the mouse and keyboard, the developer needs to choose carefully which tasks should map to direct actions.

A Final Way: The Hybrid Approach

It's tempting to suppose that you can use these varied ways of working to come up with a sort of taxonomy of users, and then put in functionality for each kind of user. For example, thinking of some of your users as keyboard-only will encourage you to make every part of the application accessible through the keyboard. Although this is a useful thing to do, it's also far too simplistic a view of users.

The truth is that users vary in their approaches—depending on the application, the task they're performing, or even their mood. Even the most committed keyboard-only user touches the mouse once in a while, and even the user who relies on menus for most of his work sooner or later picks up a shortcut key or two.

As a developer, one of your jobs is to provide the flexibility for users to make their own decisions about how to perform any particular task. It's a mistake, for example, to build in a configuration dialog box that forces the user to choose between keyboard-centric and mouse-centric ways to perform operations in your application. Instead, you should make both modes of operation freely available and let users shift back and forth as they please.

Organizing an Application

The user interface for many applications seems to just grow organically. As developers implement new functionality, they stick on menu items, toolbar buttons, and keyboard shortcuts wherever they can find room. The result is often confusing. The lack of upfront planning can result in keyboard shortcuts being assigned in uncommon ways because the common shortcut was already used, or in toolbar buttons being left off because less-useful buttons are already occupying all the available space.

If you want to develop a good user interface, you should allocate time for planning the user interface when you design the application. In this section, I'll work through a structured approach to organizing the user interface for the (fictitious) SpamOVator application that I used for some other examples.

Start with Functionality

A good starting point for the process is a simple list of the functions that you expect the application to perform. For SpamOVator, such a list might look like this:

Create a new message	Font and size
Import a message from another application	Spell check
Obfuscate a message	Find proxy servers
Set the number of copies	Evaluate subject line for avoiding filters
Suggest a subject line	Report on results of a mailing
Exit the application	About the application
Set the return address	Properties
Send the message	Set up Internet account

Set a time for delay sending	Cut
Convert to HTML	Copy
Convert to plain text	Paste
Save	Delete
Save As	Find
Open saved message	Options
Insert picture in HTML	Next window
Insert tracking GIF in HTML	Previous window
Bold	Arrange all windows
Italic	Help contents
Underline	Help index

This list isn't in any particular order; it's the sort of thing that might arise from a brainstorming meeting, or from going through a set of product specifications to extract functionality.

Finding the Hierarchy

Faced with a heap of functionality, your first job is to put it into some sort of order. I like to start by planning menus. That's because the menu system forms a natural hierarchy, which means that I can focus on one small portion of the problem at a time.

You can create your hierarchy with just about any outlining tool. At this point, I recommend not actually working with a programming language, not even with one as easy to prototype with as Visual Basic. Instead, use a business application so that you can focus on the organization and are not tempted to start writing code.

One possible approach is to use the outlining feature of Microsoft Word. Figure 9.1 shows the list of SpamOVator features converted to a Word outline.

With Word's outlining features, it's easy to move things around, and easy to expand and contract individual menus to focus on. Word also has the advantage of being widely familiar to most computer users.

Note that I identified some of the actions as not actually being on menus. Although making text bold, italic, or underlined is an important action in most text-processing applications, these operations are not normally placed on any menu. Instead, they're accessible only through shortcut keys and toolbar buttons.

Another possibility is Microsoft Excel. Figure 9.2 shows the SpamOVator menu hierarchy rendered as an Excel spreadsheet.

FIGURE 9.1
Working out the menu
hierarchy in Word

- ◇ **File**
  - ▫ *New*
  - ▫ *Open*
  - ▫ *Import*
  - ▫ *Save*
  - ▫ *Save As*
  - ▫ *Exit*
- ◇ **Edit**
  - ▫ *Cut*
  - ▫ *Copy*
  - ▫ *Paste*
  - ▫ *Delete*
  - ▫ *Find*
  - ◇ *Insert*
    - ▫ Picture
    - ▫ Tracking Bug
- ◇ **Format**
  - ▫ *Font*
  - ▫ *Convert to HTML*
  - ▫ *Convert to Plain Text*
- ◇ **Message**
  - ▫ *Properties*
  - ◇ *Subject*
    - ▫ Set
    - ▫ Suggest
    - ▫ Evaluate
  - ▫ *Schedule*
  - ▫ *Send*
- ◇ **Tools**
  - ▫ *Obfuscate*
  - ▫ *Spell Check*
  - ▫ *Find Proxy Servers*
  - ▫ *Set up Accounts*
  - ▫ *Mailing Report*
  - ▫ *Options*
- ◇ **Window**
  - ▫ *Next Window*
  - ▫ *Previous Window*
  - ▫ *Arrange All Windows*
- ◇ **Help**
  - ▫ *Contents*
  - ▫ *Index*
  - ▫ *About*
- ◇ **Not on Menus**
  - ▫ *Bold*
  - ▫ *Italic*
  - ◇ *Underline*

Excel also makes it easy to move around blocks of text by dragging them. There are outlining features available in Excel, but I didn't use them in this example. Excel's outlining is a bit clunky, displaying nesting with lines in the margin rather than traditional indentation. As you'll see a bit later, Excel can be exceptionally handy if you want to record additional information for each menu item.

FIGURE 9.2
Working out the menu
hierarchy in Excel

A final possibility is to use one of the more or less flexible pieces of outlining software on the market. Figure 9.3 shows one alternative that I like: MindManager (http://www.mindjet.com).

The main benefit of outlining software is that it usually contains features to make it easy to rearrange items, which is useful when you're trying to settle on a menu hierarchy. Such software often contains other features designed to encourage brainstorming as well—for example, the ability to add fancy fonts, colors, or pictures to the diagram. Although these features may not benefit you in designing menus, they can have other uses.

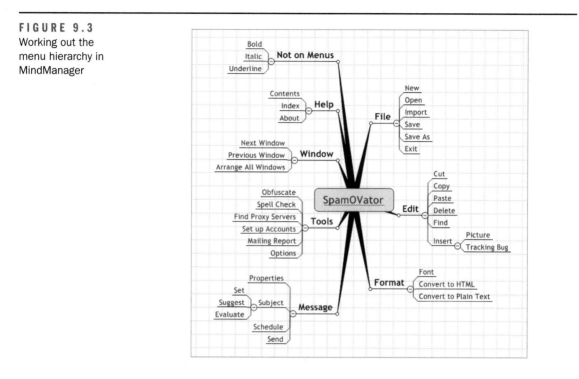

FIGURE 9.3
Working out the
menu hierarchy in
MindManager

Refining the Menus

Having identified which menus and menu items your application will support, your next task is to place these items in a reasonable order. Start by ordering the menus themselves, following these rules:

- The File menu should always come first.

- If there is an Edit menu, it should come directly after the File menu.

- The Help menu should always come last.

- If there is a Window menu, it should come directly before the Help menu.

- If your other menus resemble those of a major application, use the order of that application. For example, Format should follow Insert because both Word and Excel use that ordering.

- Place the most frequently used menus closer to the start of the menu bar.

By using these rules, I was able to settle on an order for the top-level menu items for SpamOVator quickly:

1. File

2. Edit

3. Message

4. Format

5. Tools

6. Window

7. Help

The next step is to order the items within each menu. There are some rules for this as well:

- Group related items together.

- Use separators between groups.

- Place the most frequently used menu items closer to the top of the menu.

- If there's an implied ordering between menu items, keep them in that order. For example, if a menu has separate items to set starting and ending dates for a process, the starting item should come before the ending item.

- If your menu items resemble those of a major application, use the order from that application. For example, Cut, Copy, and Paste always go in that order.

Figure 9.4 shows my Excel spreadsheet of menus after applying these rules to order the items on each menu.

The menu separators are each indicated by a single dash on the worksheet. If you look closely, you'll see that I actually inserted some new menu items in this step of the process. When working through the design of your user interface this way, it's not unusual to need to reconsider previous decisions or to discover that you left something out.

Assigning Menu Shortcut Keys

Remember, every menu item should have a corresponding shortcut key. This is where working in Excel starts to become useful. I like to make a second copy of my menu structure and then remove everything but the shortcut key for each menu and menu item. This makes it easy to scan down each column and make sure that there are no conflicts in shortcut keys.

FIGURE 9.4
The SpamOVator
menu structure refined

	A	B	C
1		Menu Items	
2	File		
3		New	
4		Open	
5		Import	
6		Close	
7		-	
8		Save	
9		Save As	
10		-	
11		Exit	
12	Edit		
13		Cut	
14		Copy	
15		Paste	
16		-	
17		Delete	
18		Insert	
19			Picture
20			Tracking Bug
21		-	
22		Find	
23		Replace	
24	Message		
25		Properties	
26		Subject	
27			Set
28			Suggest
29			Evaluate
30		Schedule	
31		Send	
32	Format		
33		Font	
34		Convert to HTML	
35		Convert to Plain Text	
36	Tools		
37		Set up Accounts	
38		Find Proxy Servers	
39		-	
40		Obfuscate	
41		Spell Check	
42		Mailing Report	
43		-	
44		Options	
45	Window		
46		Arrange All Windows	
47		Next Window	
48		Previous Window	
49	Help		
50		Contents	
51		Index	
52		About	
53	Not on Menus		
54		Bold	
55		Italic	
56		Underline	

Of course, there are some guidelines for selecting good menu shortcut keys. These rules include the following:

- Do not duplicate shortcut keys at any given level. For example, no two menus should have the same shortcut key, and no two menu items on the same menu should have the same shortcut key. It's OK for menu items on two different menus to share a shortcut key.

- Use the first letter of the text of the menu or menu item whenever possible.

- As a second choice, use the first letter of the second word of a longer menu item.

- As a third choice, use a distinctive consonant or vowel in the text.

- As a fourth choice, use wide letters such as w, m, or capital letters.

- Avoid using letters with descenders (g, j, p, q, or y), letters next to letters with descenders, or single-pixel-wide letters (I, i, or l). It's difficult to see the underline for a shortcut key on these letters.

- Use the shortcut keys used by other applications whenever possible. In common cases, this overrides the other rules. For example, the Exit menu item on the File menu should always use x for its menu shortcut key.

Figure 9.5 shows my Excel worksheet for SpamOVator with the addition of menu shortcut keys.

Assigning Direct Shortcut Keys

This is a good time to assign direct shortcut keys (such as Ctrl+X for cut) to the application. If you're using a spreadsheet, you can add one new column to keep track of this information. Here are some guidelines to follow:

- Use common shortcuts, such as Ctrl+X for cut and Ctrl+F for find, whenever possible.

- Use Ctrl+key combinations or the F1 through F12 special function keys for most direct shortcuts.

- If a shortcut reverses the effect of another shortcut, you can add the Shift key to signify the reversal. For example, Ctrl+F6 is the standard shortcut for Next Window, which is why Shift+Ctrl+F6 is the standard for Previous Window.

- Avoid using special characters, such as $ or ^. These characters might not be present on all keyboards.

- Avoid using Alt+letter combinations because these combinations are reserved for menu shortcut keys.

- Avoid using Ctrl+Alt combinations because some language keyboards use these keys as a way to generate alternative characters.

FIGURE 9.5
Coming up with menu
shortcut keys

	A	B	C	D	E	F
1		**Menu Items**			**Menu Shortcut Keys**	
2	**File**			F		
3		New			N	
4		Open			O	
5		Import			I	
6		Close			C	
7		-				
8		Save			S	
9		Save As			A	
10		-				
11		Exit			x	
12	**Edit**			E		
13		Cut			t	
14		Copy			C	
15		Paste			P	
16		-				
17		Delete			D	
18		Insert			I	
19			Picture			P
20			Tracking Bug			T
21		-				
22		Find			F	
23		Replace			R	
24	**Message**			M		
25		Properties			P	
26		Subject			u	
27			Set			S
28			Suggest			u
29			Evaluate			E
30		Schedule			c	
31		Send			S	
32	**Format**			o		
33		Font			F	
34		Convert to HTML			C	
35		Convert to Plain Text			P	
36	**Tools**			T		
37		Set up Accounts			S	
38		Find Proxy Servers			F	
39		-				
40		Obfuscate			b	
41		Spell Check			C	
42		Mailing Report			M	
43		-				
44		Options			O	
45	**Window**			W		
46		Arrange All Windows			A	
47		Next Window			N	
48		Previous Window			P	
49	**Help**			H		
50		Contents			C	
51		Index			I	
52		About			A	
53	**Not on Menus**					
54		Bold				
55		Italic				
56		Underline				

Figure 9.6 shows the plan for SpamOVator with the addition of direct shortcut keys.

RULE   Remember, a direct shortcut saves only a single keystroke over menu shortcuts in most cases. You should define direct shortcuts for only the most common actions.

FIGURE 9.6
Assigning direct short-cut keys

	A	B	C	D	E	F	G
1		Menu Items			Menu Shortcut Keys		Direct Shortcuts
2	File			F			
3		New			N		Ctrl+N
4		Open			O		Ctrl+O
5		Import			I		
6		Close			C		
7		-					
8		Save			S		Ctrl+S
9		Save As			A		
10		-					
11		Exit			x		
12	Edit			E			
13		Cut			t		Ctrl+X
14		Copy			C		Ctrl+C
15		Paste			P		Ctrl+V
16		-					
17		Delete			D		
18		Insert			I		
19			Picture			P	
20			Tracking Bug			T	
21		-					
22		Find			F		Ctrl+F
23		Replace			R		Ctrl+R
24	Message			M			
25		Properties			P		
26		Subject			u		
27			Set			S	
28			Suggest			u	
29			Evaluate			E	
30		Schedule			c		F2
31		Send			S		
32	Format			o			
33		Font			F		
34		Convert to HTML			C		
35		Convert to Plain Text			P		
36	Tools			T			
37		Set up Accounts			S		
38		Find Proxy Servers			F		
39		-					
40		Obfuscate			b		
41		Spell Check			C		F7
42		Mailing Report			M		
43		-					
44		Options			O		
45	Window			W			
46		Arrange All Windows			A		
47		Next Window			N		Ctrl+F6
48		Previous Window			P		Shift+Ctrl+F6
49	Help			H			
50		Contents			C		F1
51		Index			I		
52		About			A		
53	Not on Menus						
54		Bold					Ctrl+B
55		Italic					Ctrl+I
56		Underline					Ctrl+U

Choosing Toolbars

It remains to decide which actions should be presented on the application's default toolbars. In general, every action from the menus should be available when the user is customizing the application's toolbars, but it would be overwhelming to include all these choices by default. So you need to think about which actions to show the new user.

TIP   You'll learn more about toolbar customization in Chapter 11, "User Choice, Customization, and Confusion."

When selecting actions to include on toolbars, consider these factors:

- The most common operations for your application should be readily available through toolbar buttons.

- You should include no more than about 20 items on a toolbar by default, to make sure that it will entirely fit on a low-resolution screen. Remember, if you include controls such as a font selection combo box, the toolbar will hold fewer controls.

- Use different toolbars to hold broad categories of commands. Use separators on a single toolbar to further group commands.

Figure 9.7 shows the tracking spreadsheet for SpamOVator with toolbar information added.

Finishing Touches

The end result of this design process is a document that you can use when implementing a major part of your application's user interface. It doesn't tell you how to hook anything up, but it lets you see at a glance which keystrokes, toolbar buttons, and menu items should be implemented.

But you shouldn't use this document just once and then set it aside. Instead, it can become a continuing adjunct to your iterative design process. To start, you should place the document under some sort of source code control. You can either put the document into your formal source code control system with the other artifacts of your application or simply add a section to note revisions (tracking who made each revision, what the revision was, and the reasoning behind the revision). Either approach lets you trace back the history of design changes if this ever becomes important.

Next, keep the document up to date. Developers should be required to modify the document whenever they add new menu items, toolbar buttons, or shortcut keys. But you also shouldn't depend on every developer to remember to do this. You should review the document at major milestones to make sure that it is still current and correct.

In addition to tracking plans, you can also use this document to track implementation. Make a copy and color-code it to indicate which features have been completed and hooked up to the user interface, which are partially completed, and which haven't been started.

Pass both the full document and the color-coded version to the quality assurance team as well as the development team. They provide a blueprint for testing by indicating both the functionality that will need testing and the functionality that is ready for testing today.

FIGURE 9.7
Planning for toolbars

	A	B	C	D	E	F	G	H	I	J
1		**Menu Items**		**Menu Shortcut Keys**			**Direct Shortcuts**	**Toolbars**		
2	**File**			**F**				**Standard**	**Message**	**Tools**
3		New			N		Ctrl+N	X		
4		Open			O		Ctrl+O	X		
5		Import			I					
6		Close			C			X		
7		-								
8		Save			S		Ctrl+S	X		
9		Save As			A					
10		-								
11		Exit			x					
12	**Edit**			**E**						
13		Cut			t		Ctrl+X	X		
14		Copy			C		Ctrl+C	X		
15		Paste			P		Ctrl+V			
16		-								
17		Delete			D					
18		Insert			I					
19			Picture			P				
20			Tracking Bug			T				
21		-								
22		Find			F		Ctrl+F	X		
23		Replace			R		Ctrl+R	X		
24	**Message**			**M**						
25		Properties			P				X	
26		Subject			u					
27			Set			S			X	
28			Suggest			u			X	
29			Evaluate			E				
30		Schedule			c		F2		X	
31		Send			S				X	
32	**Format**			**o**						
33		Font			F				X	
34		Convert to HTML			C				X	
35		Convert to Plain Text			P				X	
36	**Tools**			**T**						
37		Set up Accounts			S					X
38		Find Proxy Servers			F					X
39		-								
40		Obfuscate			b					X
41		Spell Check			C		F7			X
42		Mailing Report			M					
43		-								
44		Options			O					X
45	**Window**			**W**						
46		Arrange All Windows			A					
47		Next Window			N		Ctrl+F6			
48		Previous Window			P		Shift+Ctrl+F6			
49	**Help**			**H**						
50		Contents			C		F1			
51		Index			I					
52		About			A					
53	**Not on Menus**									
54		Bold					Ctrl+B		X	
55		Italic					Ctrl+I		X	
56		Underline					Ctrl+U		X	

Under the Covers

Although this book is almost free of source code, this is an appropriate place to mention two source code issues that come up when you're writing code to handle user interface interactions.

Shared Code

The first principle should be obvious, but I've seen it overlooked too often when doing code reviews: You should write code only once. Here's a pseudocode view of a bad pattern for user interaction code:

```
Sub Process_Menu_Click (Item)
    If Item = Item1 Then
        Action1a
        Action1b
        Action1c
    ElseIf Item = Item2 Then
        Action2a
        Action2b
        Action2c
    End If
End Sub

Sub Process_Toolbar_Click (Button)
    If Button = Button1 Then
        Action1a
        Action1b
        Action1c
    ElseIf Button = Button2 Then
        Action2a
        Action2b
        Action2c
    End If
End Sub
```

If you're an experienced developer, warning bells should be going off over all the duplicate code in this sample. Yet developers who would consider this pattern unacceptable anywhere else will somehow happily put it into their user interface code. The problem, of course, is that if the implementation of some action changes, you need to update it in two different places. Fortunately, there's an easy fix. You can refactor out the common code, leading to this much superior way to handle the same tasks:

```
Sub Process_Menu_Click (Item)
    If Item = Item1 Then
        Action1
    ElseIf Item = Item2 Then
        Action2
    End If
End Sub

Sub Process_Toolbar_Click (Button)
    If Button = Button1 Then
```

```
        Action1
    ElseIf Button = Button2 Then
        Action2
    End If
End Sub

Sub Action1
    Action1a
    Action1b
    Action1c
End Sub

Sub Action2
    Action2a
    Action2b
    Action2c
End Sub
```

In almost all cases, the event handlers that are called by operations such as keystroke presses or toolbar button clicks should be simple dispatch routines that call common subroutines to do the actual work.

Handling Undo

A related topic is that of handling undo operations. Many applications these days allow the user to recover from an "oops" moment by undoing their most recent operation. Some applications go even further by allowing multilevel undo: keeping track of the last several operations (or in extreme cases, every operation since the application was launched) and letting the user choose to undo some or all of them.

The key issue to remember when coding an undo facility is that tracking menu selections, toolbar button presses, shortcut key invocations, and other forms of direct interaction is not enough. You also need to keep track of the context of the user's actions. Mouse movements or keystrokes such as Tab or End can change the context, and if you don't include this information in your undo tracking, you may severely damage documents when the user invokes your undo facility.

As a simple example, consider the user who decides to type 10 characters. If they move the cursor after the typing and try to undo, you must return to the scene of the insertion before deleting 10 characters. Otherwise, your undo operation won't delete the right characters!

Programming an undo facility can quickly become arduous thanks to this and similar complications. But it's one of those features that can actually make a lot of difference to end users. When considering which features to keep or cut for an application, undo should be on the short list to keep unless development time is exceptionally short.

Summary

In this chapter, I focused on the ways that the user can interact with your application. After looking at the basic styles of user interaction, I concentrated on a process to organize the user interface so that it all makes sense. By using this process, you can help make sure that users are comfortable with the arrangement of the user interface.

In the next chapter, I'll look at some other common interaction patterns between your users and your application, including cut-and-paste operations and drag-and-drop actions.

CHAPTER 10

Common Interaction Patterns

- More Ways to Work with Windows

- Handling Data Transfer

The whole point of a user interface is to let the user interact with the application, and vice versa. Well, not the *whole* point; in many cases, there are aspects of the user interface that are purely decorative. But most developers will leave the decorative aspects to graphic designers and concentrate on the functional aspects of their application's user interface. In this chapter, I'll look at a few interaction patterns that don't fit anywhere else, including various uses of windows and ways to move data around from one place to another.

More Ways to Work with Windows

In a windowing operating system, windows are of prime importance. That's why I've spent much of this book already discussing things that you can do with windows. But I'm not out of topics in that area yet. In addition to the features that I covered in previous chapters, you should know about several other topics when planning your windows strategy:

- Always-on-top windows
- Autohide windows
- Efficient use of dialog boxes

Always-on-Top Windows

The computer screen is two-dimensional, but that doesn't stop it from being used in a three-dimensional fashion. Applications that implement multiple windows generally keep an internal record of the *z-order* of those windows. The z-order determines which windows will be drawn "in front" of other windows on the screen. A window is said to have a lower z-order value if it will be drawn on top of another window. Figure 10.1 gives you a schematic look at this idea.

Most applications with multiple windows manage the z-order of their windows according to a simple rule: Any time you click on a window, it comes to the top of the stack, pushing other windows down beneath it. This is the way that Windows itself works, so it feels natural to most users. Figure 10.2 provides a sketch of the way this algorithm works.

However, it's possible for applications to define other rules when it comes to rearranging windows in the z-order. In particular, an individual window can be marked as an *always-on-top* window, so that it persists at the top of the z-order—no matter what order the other windows are in. Figure 10.3 shows how having an always-on-top window can change the behavior of clicking on windows in an application.

Always-on-top behavior can be applied to windows both within an application and between applications. In the first case, a window stays on top of all the other windows within an application. In the second case, an application itself stays on top of all other windows on the screen.

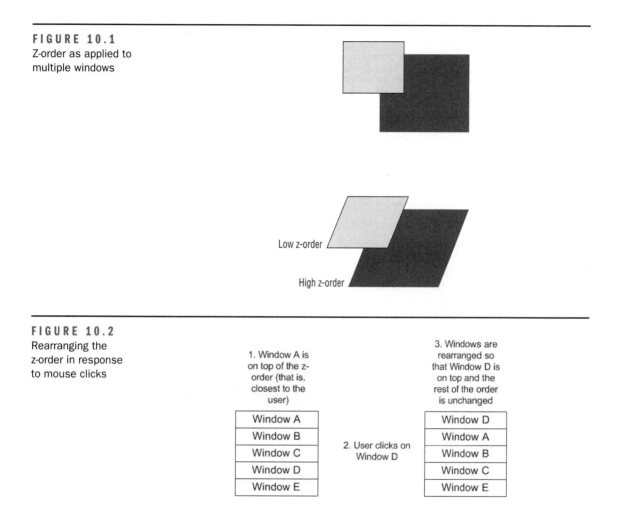

FIGURE 10.1
Z-order as applied to
multiple windows

Low z-order

High z-order

FIGURE 10.2
Rearranging the
z-order in response
to mouse clicks

1. Window A is
on top of the z-
order (that is,
closest to the
user)

Window A
Window B
Window C
Window D
Window E

2. User clicks on
Window D

3. Windows are
rearranged so
that Window D is
on top and the
rest of the order
is unchanged

Window D
Window A
Window B
Window C
Window E

As an example of always-on-top behavior within an application, consider the Find and Replace dialog box from Microsoft Word, shown in Figure 10.4.

When you enter some search text and click Find Next, Word highlights and displays the next instance of the text. It also keeps the Find and Replace dialog box visible on top of the Word document, even if you click on the document and reformat or edit the text. This lets you switch back and forth from working on the document to finding more instances of the specified text. This technique works because the Find and Replace dialog box is both modeless and always-on-top.

FIGURE 10.3

Rearranging the z-order with an always-on-top window

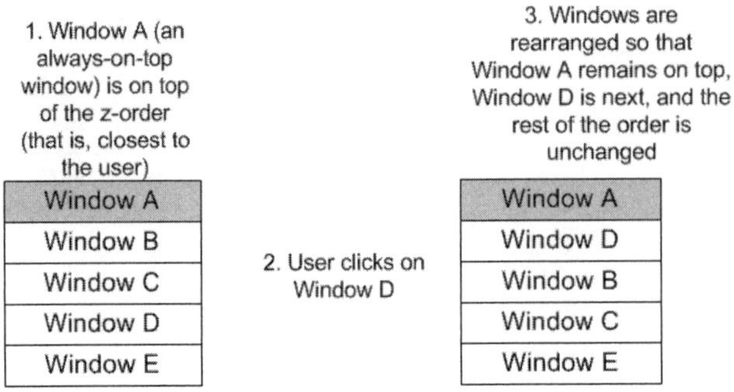

1. Window A (an always-on-top window) is on top of the z-order (that is, closest to the user)

3. Windows are rearranged so that Window A remains on top, Window D is next, and the rest of the order is unchanged

Window A
Window B
Window C
Window D
Window E

2. User clicks on Window D

Window A
Window D
Window B
Window C
Window E

FIGURE 10.4

Using Find in Microsoft Word

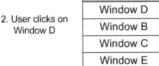

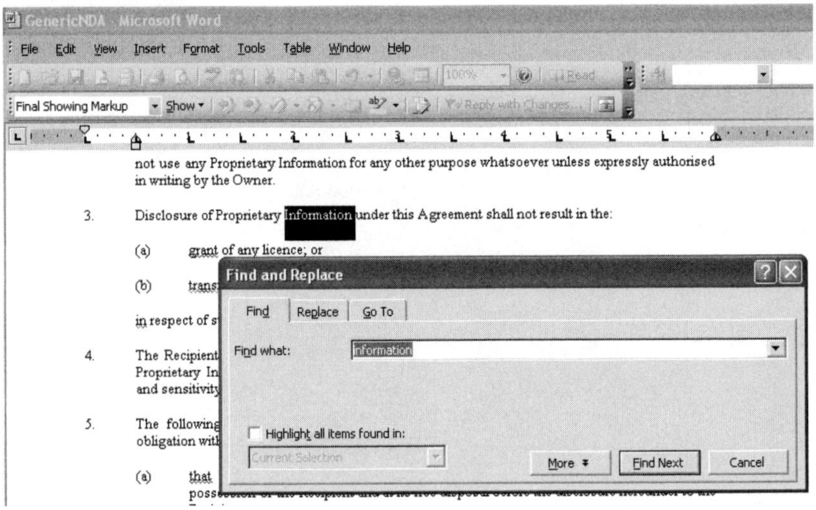

NOTE Modal dialog boxes are automatically always-on-top with respect to other windows in their own application because you can't even activate the other windows.

Figure 10.5 shows another example of an always-on-top window within an application. The various tool windows in Visual Studio .NET all float on top of editing windows.

The tool windows in VS .NET (such as the Solution Explorer shown here) contain information that might be of interest to the user, but which normally won't be the focus of their actions. When editing code, it's sometimes useful to see a list of the other source code files that are available. If the Solution Explorer were not set to be always-on-top, it would vanish while the user was editing code.

FIGURE 10.5
An always-on-top
window in Visual
Studio .NET

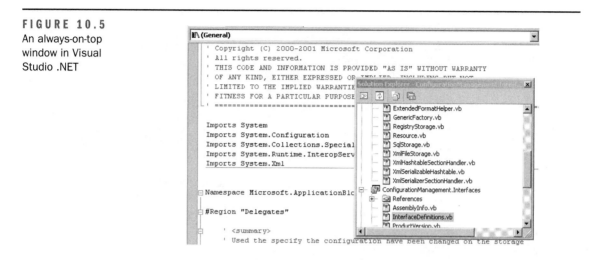

Here is a checklist of things to think about when considering whether to make a particular window within your application always-on-top:

- You need to worry about the decision only for non-modal windows. That is, modal windows will automatically be always-on-top, and you can't change this.

- An always-on-top window should offer information or controls that the user will need frequently in conjunction with other application windows.

- An always-on-top window should be small enough not to block the view of other application windows.

- You should offer an easy way for the user to disable the always-on-top property or to hide the window in case it becomes too obtrusive for them.

- Consider alternative ways to convey essential information that leaves the user interface free of always-on-top windows. For example, ToolTips or status bars do not interfere with the user's other work as much as extra windows.

A second form of always-on-top window is the always-on-top application. Such an application covers up other applications on the user's screen, whether it has the focus or not. In Windows, for example, the Task Manager application is always-on-top, as Figure 10.6 shows.

In Figure 10.6, the Task Manager application is on top, even if the Explorer window has the focus. This behavior is extremely rare among Windows applications, and rightfully so. When you force an application to the top, you're saying that the application is so important that no other application should be allowed to be in its way, no matter what the user thinks.

FIGURE 10.6
An always-on-top
application

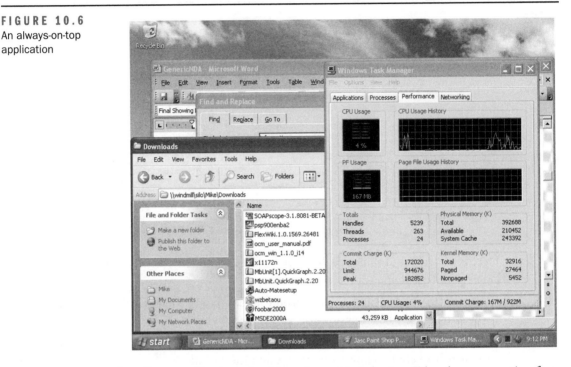

In general, ordinary applications should not have this behavior. I'd make an exception for debugging applications that you expect advanced users to work with under exceptional circumstances. Even then, you should offer a way to revert to normal window behavior.

Autohide Windows

Another unusual option that some applications can take good advantage of is *autohide*. You may be familiar with autohide from the Windows Taskbar, which offers it as an option, as shown in Figure 10.7.

In the upper part of Figure 10.7, the Taskbar is reduced to a single row of dark pixels at the bottom of the screen. Moving the mouse pointer to this row causes the Taskbar window to unhide itself, resulting in the appearance shown in the lower part of Figure 10.7. The Taskbar window slides out to position itself normally, allowing the user to work with the controls that it contains. When the user moves the cursor outside of the Taskbar area, it slides back off the screen. There's a built-in delay to keep it from vanishing too quickly if you move the cursor by mistake.

Autohide windows are almost always set to be always-on-top windows as well. It's possible to have an autohide window that is not always-on-top, but it often isn't useful. The problem is that the autohide window slides out behind other windows on the screen, making it difficult or impossible to find.

FIGURE 10.7
Displaying an autohide window

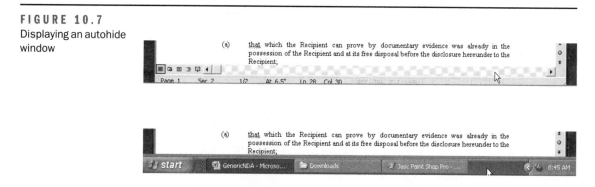

Windows supports up to four autohide windows at the same time, one for each edge of the screen. The user can choose the edge of the screen for such a window by dragging the window and dropping it to that edge.

Autohide windows are useful for functionality that the user may require at any time, but that doesn't need to be permanently displayed on screen. But you need to balance this usefulness against the fact that many users aren't familiar with this behavior (the Windows Taskbar is not set to autohide by default), that hitting a one-pixel-wide target may be difficult for some users, and that there are only four available screen edges for such windows. Follow these guidelines when deciding whether to make a window autohide:

- An autohide window should offer information or controls that the user will need on an unpredictable schedule. It should be important enough that the user won't want to wait for an application to load.

- An autohide window should be small enough not to block the view of other application windows.

- You should offer an easy way for the user to disable the autohide feature, in case it becomes too obtrusive or when there are no free screen edges.

- Consider alternative ways to convey essential information that leaves the user interface free of autohide windows. For example, you may be able to place an icon in the tray area of the Taskbar and attach information to it with a ToolTip or shortcut menu.

Avoiding Modal Dialog Boxes

After so much information in previous chapters on how to design dialog boxes, it might seem a bit strange to devote a section to avoiding their use. But as convenient as they are for the application designer, dialog boxes can offer serious problems for the user.

To be precise, modal dialog boxes can trouble users for a number of reasons:

- They prevent working with other parts of the application's user interface while they're displayed.

- They vanish after the user clicks an action button, making it difficult for the user to remember what they just did.

- They interrupt a smooth flow of work.

- Functionality hidden in dialog boxes can be hard to discover.

Although modal dialog boxes are undeniably useful, it's worth taking a few moments to think about alternatives as you design and build your applications. Otherwise, you might end up with a morass of dialog boxes and no easy way for the user to find the features that they're looking for.

Fortunately, you have lots of other choices for handling bits of user interaction functionality. The long-term trend in Windows applications has been to make more functionality available in modeless form. This doesn't mean just moving from modal to modeless dialog boxes. In addition to using modeless dialog boxes, you should consider whether you can provide tools for the user in one of these ways:

- Through a simple menu item

- Through controls on a toolbar

- Through a palette window

- Through direct functionality, such as mouse selection and dragging

Even in cases where you can't move the entire complexity of a particular function to one of these simpler interfaces, you can use a modeless interface as the jumping-off point for a modal one. Consider configuration management within Visual Studio .NET. A configuration controls various factors about the program that the user is running within the application, such as whether it should run in release or debug mode. At any given time, a user might want to select a particular configuration to test with. Less frequently, the user may want to create an entirely new configuration.

To handle these requirements, the Visual Studio .NET designers came up with a two-step user interface. The first step is shown in Figure 10.8.

The Solution Configurations combo box on the Standard toolbar includes one entry for each existing configuration. It also includes a final entry for the Configuration Manager. Most of the time, the user can just select an existing configuration and proceed with their work. To define a new configuration or modify an existing one, they select the Configuration Manager entry to open the modal dialog box shown in Figure 10.9.

FIGURE 10.8
Selecting an existing
configuration

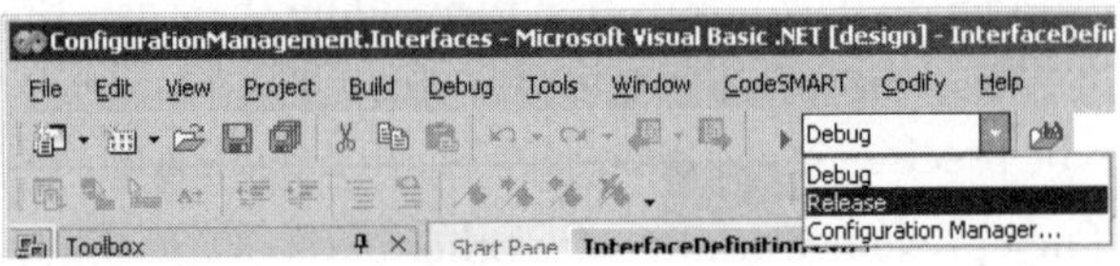

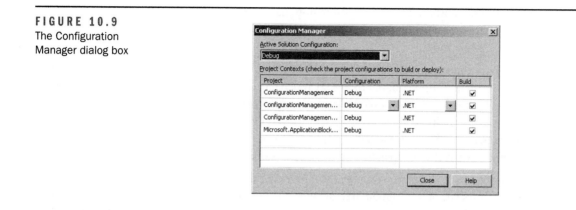

FIGURE 10.9
The Configuration
Manager dialog box

Handling Data Transfer

It's a rare application that doesn't exchange data with other applications. In the pre-Windows days, this was usually accomplished with some indirect mechanism. For example, a DOS application might save a data file to disk, and a second application could open that same data file later.

Windows, however, lets you short-circuit this process by providing several different mechanisms for direct data transfer. You should support these mechanisms in your own applications wherever the user might expect them to work:

- Cut, copy, and paste
- Drag and drop

Cut, Copy, and Paste

Windows maintains an invisible holding pen for data known as the Clipboard. Users can interact with the Clipboard by using the Cut, Copy, and Paste commands (as well as some special variants that I'll discuss later). The basic function of these commands is as follows:

Cut   Cut removes the currently selected information from an application and places it on the Clipboard.

Copy   Copy makes a copy of the currently selected information from the application and places it on the Clipboard.

Paste   Paste takes the contents of the Clipboard and replaces the current selection in the application with it.

A cut operation followed by a paste operation effectively moves information from one application to another; a copy operation followed by a paste operation copies information from one application to another. The Clipboard maintains its contents until another cut or copy operation is performed. Pasting does not empty the Clipboard, so that you can paste the same information multiple times.

You might think that what gets pasted from the Clipboard is exactly what the original application placed on the Clipboard, but things are much more complicated than that—for two reasons. First, the originating application can decide which format to place on the Clipboard. It can even choose to place multiple formats of the same data on the Clipboard as the result of a single cut or copy operation. Second, the target application can decide which format to use and how to transform it when the user performs a paste operation.

Consider one of the more complex cases, copying data from Microsoft Excel to Microsoft Word. If you select a rectangular area of cells in Excel, press Ctrl+C to copy it, activate Word, and press Ctrl+V to paste the contents of the Clipboard, the result is a Word table that is formatted to look like the original Excel region. But that's far from the only way that you can choose to paste the data into Word. If you select Paste Special from the Edit menu, Word will open the Paste Special dialog box, shown in Figure 10.10.

As you can see, there are many choices in this Paste Special dialog box. You can choose from numerous different formats to paste the information. You can also choose to paste a link to the original information, so that it gets updated when the original Excel document is updated. Finally, you can choose to display an icon instead of the full information from Excel.

Although your application is unlikely to offer as many paste choices as this, you should still consider whether you need to offer choices to the user. In addition to the options shown in Figure 10.10, you might also want to offer a Paste as Hyperlink or Paste Shortcut option, for times when you can help the user navigate to the original source document instead of displaying its information.

FIGURE 10.10
Paste Special
dialog box

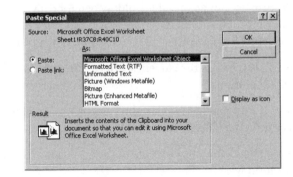

There have been many attempts to extend the Windows copying system to support more than one piece of information on the Clipboard at one time. It's common for programmer's editors, for example, to support more than one paste buffer. As another example, Microsoft Office now implements its own Clipboard to collect items that are copied among the various Office applications. You can also download utilities such as Yankee Clipper (http://www.yankee-clipper.net/) to help you manage information placed on the Clipboard. Rather than attempting to build non-standard Clipboard functionality into your own applications, you should let the user decide whether they want to install such a utility.

Drag and Drop

Although cut, copy, and paste operations work well (for one thing, they're familiar to nearly every Windows user), there's a second alternative that is often more natural: drag and drop. With drag and drop, you simply select something in one application, then use the mouse to drag the selection to another application (or to another location). When you release the mouse button, the dragged information is "dropped" at its new location.

RULE   Don't rely on drag and drop as the sole means to move information around. Some users might lack the motor skills to reliably carry out drag-and-drop operations.

There are two different forms of drag-and-drop operations available in most applications: default and non-default. To launch a default drag-and-drop operation, the user holds down the primary mouse button and drags the selection. When the user releases the selection, the destination application performs whatever it considers the default operation. This may be a copy, a move, or even some other operation such as printing the dragged object. In a default drag-and-drop operation, there's no user interaction beyond deciding where to release the mouse button.

To launch a non-default drag-and-drop operation, the user holds down the secondary mouse button and drags the selection. When the user releases the selection, the destination application displays a shortcut menu, as shown in Figure 10.11.

FIGURE 10.11
Performing a non-default drag and drop

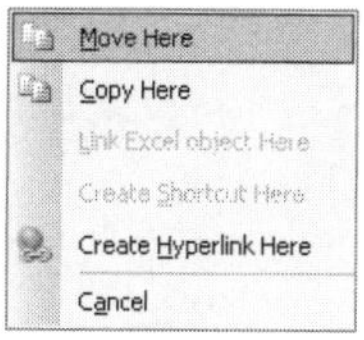

Figure 10.11 shows the shortcut menu produced by performing a non-default drag-and-drop operation from Excel to Word. The first option on the shortcut menu should be the default drag-and-drop operation. The application can also decide to add as many other options as it likes to the menu. Note that in this case, the menu for the non-default drag-and-drop operation doesn't include all the choices that you saw for cut and paste between the same two applications. In cases where paste functionality is exceptionally rich, you should choose the most common options for the non-default drag-and-drop shortcut menu.

If the user presses the Esc key while performing a drag-and-drop operation, you should cancel the operation.

Summary

In this chapter, you learned about some additional techniques to help users tap the power of your applications. You saw how always-on-top and autohide windows can help in specific situations. I also introduced the basics of data-transfer operations, including cut and paste and drag and drop.

In the chapters to this point I've been assuming that you set up your application and the user makes use of it, just as you set it up. But that's not always the case. In the next chapter, I'll look at the sometimes-thorny questions of user customization.

User Choice, Customization, and Confusion

- Menu and Toolbar Customization

- Docking and Anchoring

- Color Choices and Skinning

- Application-Specific Customization

- The Computer Is Not a Puppy Dog

Almost every Windows application offers the user some choice in the way that it works. Whether it's a matter of adding buttons to toolbars, selecting options from a menu, or picking an entire "skin" to change the look of the application, users have grown to expect customization. In this chapter, I'll discuss some of the ways that you might offer customization, as well as some of the pitfalls to avoid.

Menu and Toolbar Customization

Menus and toolbars in Windows applications didn't start out being customizable. But over time, applications have introduced ways to customize almost every aspect of these tools. You need to consider carefully which level of customization is appropriate for your own application. In general, there are three levels of customization used in Windows applications for toolbars and menus:

- No customization
- Simple customization
- Complex customization

No Customization

If your application is relatively simple, with only a few menu items and toolbar buttons, you should consider simply not allowing customization at all. This is the approach taken by Microsoft Paint, Microsoft Notepad, and many utilities from both Microsoft and other vendors. For example, Paint does not allow the user any control over the contents of its menus, and it doesn't display a toolbar. By not allowing menu customization, Paint can keep its interface standardized, no matter what the user does.

There's one big advantage to not allowing customization: This approach lowers support costs. If you allow the user to customize the user interface, you must check during any support communication to see whether they're using the stock user interface or not. This leads to additional time spent doing support, and additional confusion on both sides of the conversation.

On the other hand, if you don't allow any customization, users may feel that you've left something out. Even if you don't believe the customization will add anything to the application's functionality, users may feel cheated if they can't customize toolbars in your application just like they can in other applications.

Simple Customization

Applications that support a single toolbar often use a simple customization dialog box like the one shown in Figure 11.1.

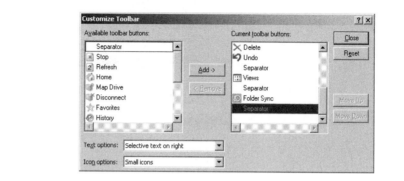

FIGURE 11.1
Simple toolbar
customization

Figure 11.1 shows the Customize Toolbar dialog box from the Windows Server 2003 version of Windows Explorer. To display this dialog box, right-click the toolbar and select Customize. The Customize Toolbar dialog box provides the following functionality:

- Add new buttons to the toolbar
- Remove existing buttons from the toolbar
- Rearrange buttons on the toolbar
- Toggle between large and small icons
- Decide whether to show text with icons
- Reset the toolbar to its original state

The list of potential toolbar buttons is a subset of the menu items for the application. Most applications with simple customization work this way: The menus are comprehensive, and the toolbars offer at most a subset of the menu functionality.

Simple customization is appropriate when your application has a single toolbar, and you want to allow users to exercise some control without doing an overwhelming amount of support. It does not offer users the chance to precisely choose every detail of the user interface, but it also steers clear of the dangers of allowing them to customize everything.

Complex Customization

Complex customization has been brought to a high art by Microsoft Office. In recent versions of Office, practically every aspect of the menus and the toolbars can be customized. In fact, the menu is treated as just another toolbar that happens to display its options as text rather than as icons. Right-clicking on any menu or toolbar within an Office 2003 application and selecting Customize will display the dialog box shown in Figures 11.2, 11.3, and 11.4.

FIGURE 11.2
Complex toolbar
customization
Toolbars tab

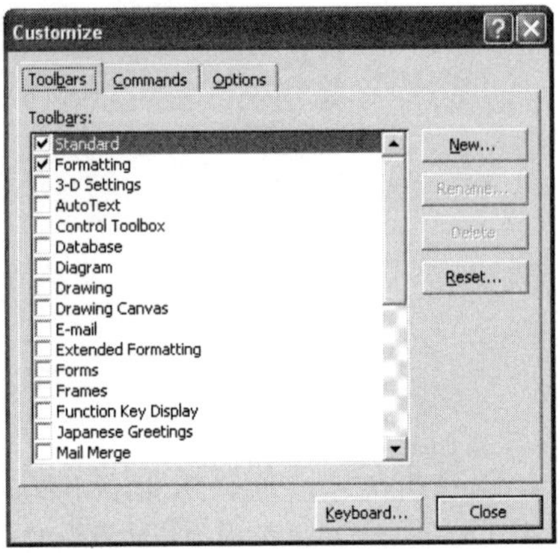

NOTE   Older versions of Office also allow complex customization, though the dialog boxes and particular choices may be different than those I've shown here.

The Toolbars tab of the Customize dialog box exists primarily so that you can decide which toolbars should be displayed by default. It lists all the toolbars; checking a toolbar puts it on screen. If you scroll down the list, you'll find the menu bar listed as an available toolbar. Other functionality available from this tab include the following:

- Create a new toolbar
- Rename a toolbar
- Delete a toolbar
- Reset toolbars to their original state
- Customize keyboard shortcuts

The Options tab of the Customize dialog box offers some miscellaneous options that don't fit anywhere else. Depending on your own application, you may or may not need such a tab. In the Office applications, it includes these capabilities (among others that apply to individual applications):

- Display important toolbars spread across two rows of buttons
- Disable or reset adaptive menus
- Use large icons
- Use screen tips
- Animate menus

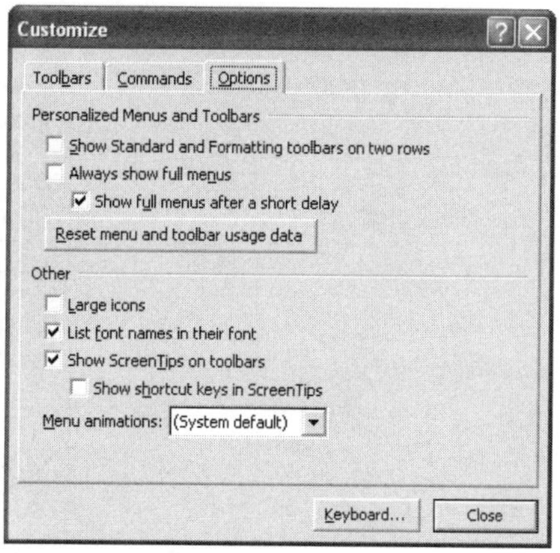

FIGURE 11.3
Complex toolbar
customization
Options tab

Finally, Figure 11.4 shows the Commands tab of the Customize dialog box, which offers the user almost unlimited options for customizing menus and toolbars. The two list boxes of categories and commands between them offer every option that's on the menus of the application by default, and some that aren't. You can add any of these commands to an existing menu or toolbar by dragging it from the Customize dialog box and dropping it on the toolbar. You can also remove an existing command while this dialog box is visible by dragging it from a menu or toolbar and dropping it anywhere else. The Customize dialog box also lets you rearrange the commands on an existing menu or toolbar.

While the Customize dialog box is open, you can also right-click on any existing toolbar button or menu item to pop up a customization menu that applies to that item, as shown in Figure 11.5.

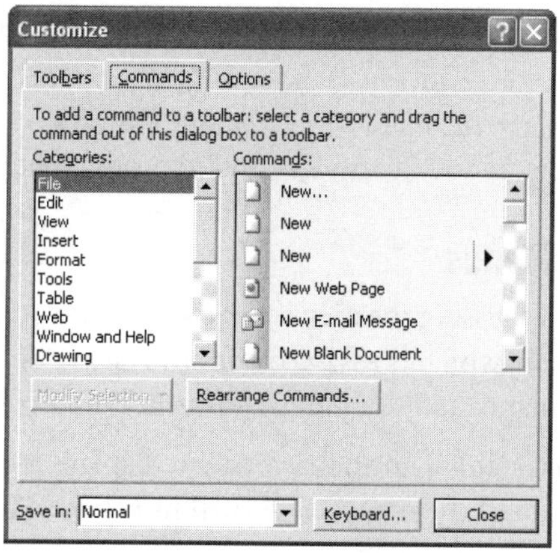

FIGURE 11.4
Complex toolbar
customization
Commands tab

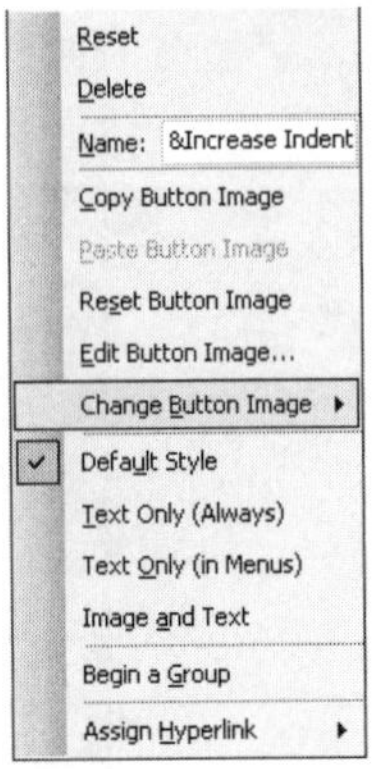

FIGURE 11.5
Customizing a toolbar
button

Reset
Delete
Name: &Increase Indent
Copy Button Image
Paste Button Image
Reset Button Image
Edit Button Image...
Change Button Image ▶
✓ Default Style
Text Only (Always)
Text Only (in Menus)
Image and Text
Begin a Group
Assign Hyperlink ▶

The options on the customization menu include renaming the button; changing the image it displays; and changing whether it displays text (as on a menu), an image (as on a toolbar), or both. With enough time and patience, you can use this menu to change a toolbar into a menu or vice versa.

Should you implement this level of customization for your own applications? Unless your application has the complexity and depth of Office, you probably don't need to offer quite as much customization as Microsoft does. With millions of users, Office needs to do everything that it can to cater to individual tastes. Your user base will almost certainly be smaller, meaning that you need to balance that sort of catering off against increased programming and support costs.

> **TIP**   If you do allow complex customization, consider providing a means for resetting everything to its default setting. That provides a safety net for users who get lost in the choices and end up with a less-functional application as a result. Microsoft does this with a Reset button in the Customize dialog box.

Still, users expect customization.

> **RULE**   At a minimum, you should implement the sort of simple customization interface that will allow users to add, rearrange, and remove toolbar buttons from a predetermined list.

Adaptive Menus

While I'm discussing the menu and toolbar customization system in Office, I must mention the *adaptive menu*, which is a Microsoft innovation designed to make it easier for users to find the menu commands that they need without being overwhelmed by complexity.

The initial state of an adaptive menu displays a few commands, along with a chevron button at the bottom of the menu, as shown in Figure 11.6.

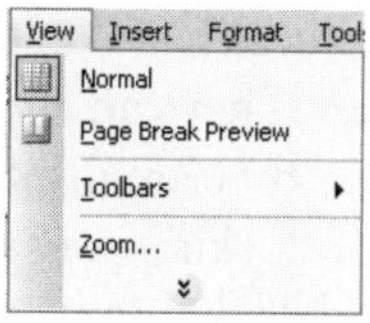

FIGURE 11.6
An adaptive menu
before expansion

If you move the cursor to the chevron and click, the menu expands to display all its commands, as shown in Figure 11.7. The menu also expands if you just hover the cursor over it for a few seconds.

But there's more to adaptive menus than just hiding and showing commands. The Office application keeps track of which commands you actually use. Commands that you haven't used are gradually demoted until they do not show on the short form of the menu. Commands that you use frequently are promoted so that they are always displayed, even before the menu is expanded.

Some users find this useful, but so many found it maddening that Microsoft has been forced to include an option to completely disable both the promotion and demotion behavior and the menu expansion itself. Other software manufacturers (and even other groups within Microsoft) have not followed the lead of the Office team here. My own view is that adaptive menus cause more confusion than they are worth.

FIGURE 11.7
An adaptive menu
after expansion

Docking and Anchoring

Another area in which many applications offer user choices is window arrangement. Specifically, it's possible to dock windows to each other or to the parent window, or to anchor them in various places. Another Microsoft application, Visual Studio .NET, offers the most overwhelming array of choices, so I'll use it for my examples.

To begin with, every toolbar in VS .NET has a handle at its left end. You can drag the toolbar by this handle to a new location. Toolbars can be docked (that is, attached) to any edge of the main VS .NET window. They can also be dragged free entirely to float in the middle of the work area, in which case they are displayed with a half-height caption bar. A floating toolbar can be dragged back to a docking position, or you can double-click the caption bar of a floating toolbar to automatically dock it in its most recently docked position.

Visual Studio also contains more than a dozen tool windows of various sorts. You can change the appearance of these windows in many ways. In Figure 11.8, I simplified things by closing all but two of these windows: the Solution Explorer and Properties windows. They're both docked at the right side of the workspace.

FIGURE 11.8
VS .NET with two docked windows

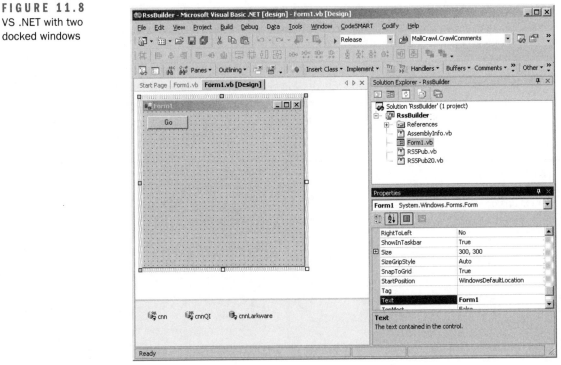

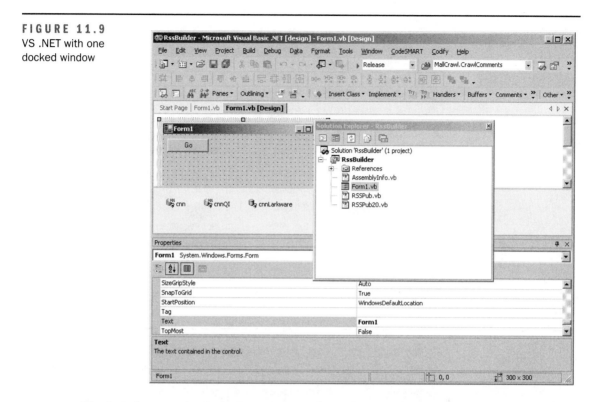

Tool windows can be docked on any side of the workspace or dragged to float free, just like toolbars. In Figure 11.9, I redocked the Properties window to the bottom border of the main window, and left the Solution Explorer window to float.

If you have multiple floating windows, you can stick them together. Figure 11.10 shows the Solution Explorer and Properties windows docked to one another, with both floating free.

Windows can be docked together side by side (as in Figure 11.10) or top-and-bottom. There's also a third style, which you can see in Figure 11.11. In this style, the different tool windows are presented as tabs in a single larger window. The tabs at the bottom of the tool window switch between the Solution Explorer and the Properties windows.

You can also dock tabbed windows, as shown in Figure 11.12.

FIGURE 11.10
VS .NET with two float-
ing windows

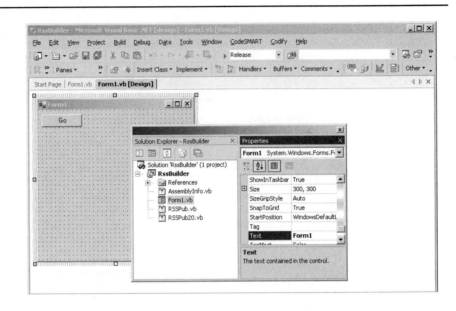

FIGURE 11.11
VS .NET with floating
tabbed windows

FIGURE 11.12
VS .NET with docked
tabbed windows

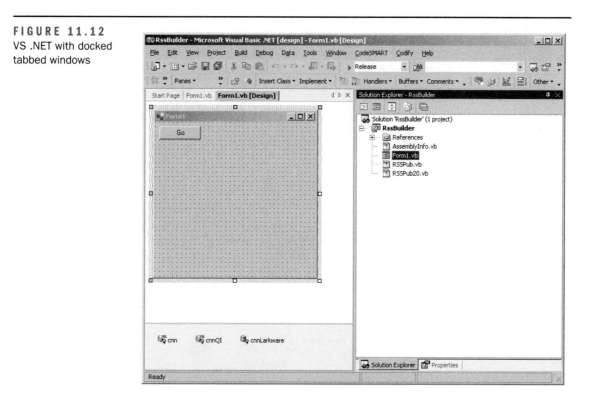

When a tool window is docked, it gains a pushpin icon in its caption bar. Clicking this pushpin turns the tool window into an autohide window. Like autohide applications (which I discussed in Chapter 10, "Common Interaction Patterns"), these tool windows are tucked away at the side of the application. However, the appearance is a bit different, as you can see in Figure 11.13. Here, the Properties window has been set as an autohide window and displays as a single tab.

As with menu and toolbar customization, it's easy to go overboard with window customization. But if your application does depend heavily on tool windows, you should probably implement most or all of these features. Because they're controlled with the mouse, with immediate visual feedback, window customization features are not too confusing to the user. The good news is that you can buy an off-the-shelf windowing package that allows you to add these features to any application with little or no additional development work on your part.

FIGURE 11.13
VS .NET with an
autohide window

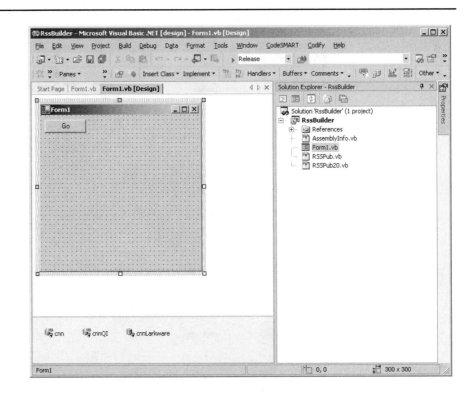

Color Choices and Skinning

Every application should allow the user to customize the colors for its display—even though they should not provide a dialog box to perform this customization. How is this apparent paradox resolved? The answer is that Windows offers its own facility for color customization, as shown in Figure 11.14.

The Display Properties dialog box lets the user specify system-wide colors. They can do this either by selecting a predefined set of colors collected into a color scheme, or by customizing the color of individual elements such as ToolTips or command buttons. As long as your application uses system colors in its construction, it automatically picks up color changes made by the user in this dialog box.

In fact, this dialog box goes beyond color customization to allow the user to select standard fonts and other user interface features such as the spacing of icons. A well-designed application will respond to changes in these factors by customizing its own interface. That way, your application will automatically fit in with the way that the user likes their desktop to look. This is especially important for users with visual disabilities, who may need particular color combinations or large fonts to make applications usable at all.

There are a few cases for which you'll still want to use custom colors instead of system colors within an application:

- For branding, as on a corporate logo
- To display photos or other realistic images
- When the color conveys particular information

WARNING Be sure that you don't use color as the only means to convey some piece of information. Remember that a relatively large proportion of the population has some form of color-blindness. Always supply alternative interfaces, such as ToolTips or reports, to duplicate information that you convey with color. You also need to be sure that at least one of your alternatives is accessible to screen readers for users with severe vision problems.

At the far end of the customization spectrum from using system colors is the increasingly common use of "skinning" to customize applications. Some applications, such as the popular Winamp music player, let you change every aspect of their interface. This applies not just to the colors used, but also to the location of controls, shape used for the main window, size and position of the Windows controls such as the minimize button, and so on. Skinning lets artistic designers rearrange an application to look like anything from a block of wood to a futuristic toaster.

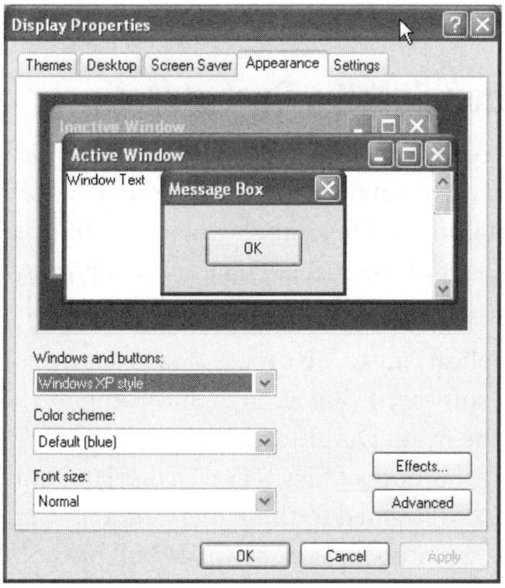

FIGURE 11.14
The Appearance tab of
the Display Properties
applet

Figure 11.15 shows a typical Winamp skin. If you didn't know in advance, you'd be hard-pressed to identify this as a Windows application.

Although you can buy frameworks that enable skinning for your application with little or no work on your part, I believe that you should think long and hard before doing so. On the plus side, a skinned application undoubtedly gives the user the feeling of being in complete control, and lets them make their system look "cool." But on the minus side, such applications fly in the face of all the conventions that make using Windows easier. Your application may look more futuristic when skinned, but it will be harder for most users to use. In almost every case, that's a bad trade-off to make.

FIGURE 11.15
A skinned application

Application-Specific Customization

All the customizations that I discussed so far in this chapter have been very generic—they apply equally well to a great many applications. Beyond that, of course, your application may require its own customizations. For example, there may be a default directory where you look for templates, or perhaps a set of colors that you use when portraying new objects on a drawing canvas. Such choices are typically wrapped up in an Options dialog box such as the one shown in Figure 11.16.

Many applications today expose dozens or even hundreds of customization options in this way. With software being as large and complex as it is, it's easy to understand where these choices come from. Developers look at their work and realize that they're about to hard-code something: a number of files, a path, a display status. Rather than placing a constant in the code (which we're all trained to think of as somehow inelegant), they decide that this is something that could be put under user control. And presto! Another user customization option is born.

FIGURE 11.16
Options from Microsoft
PowerPoint

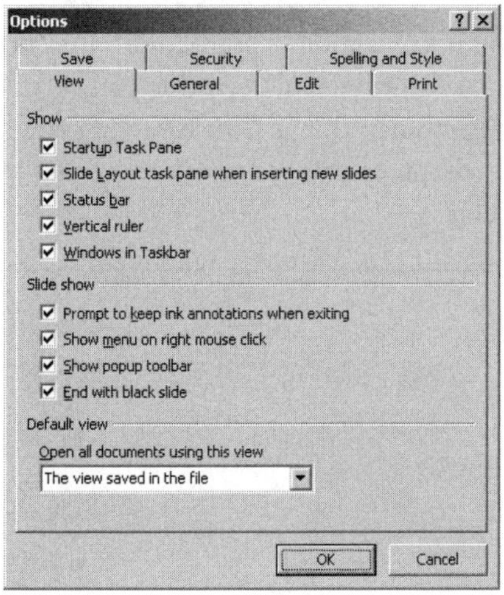

The fallacy here lies in the assumption that just because something *can* be placed under the user's control it *should* be placed under the user's control. When faced with the opportunity to add another customization option to your application, you should consider several questions:

- *Is there a single best setting for this option that will be optimal for every user of the application?* If so, you should code that setting and eliminate the option.

- *Is the option setting something that will need to be updated only occasionally by power users, perhaps with the aid of technical support?* If so, you should consider exposing it via a Registry setting rather than in the user interface. Alternatively, you can ship a separate utility application that performs the customizations, but which won't be obvious to the casual user.

- *Is the option setting something that the user will choose only once?* If so, prompt for it during installation rather than exposing it in the user interface.

As with many other choices in user interface design, there are trade-offs here. The more users you have, the more likely it is that someone will appreciate the ability to change some setting that you thought should be fixed. But the more settings you expose, the higher your support costs will be, and the more confusing your application will be. Most users seem to feel that dialog boxes like the one shown in Figure 11.16, which spread dozens of option settings over several rows of tabs, go too far.

It's all too easy to say "Oh, add an option" when you're developing an application. But keep the end user in mind before you do so, and try to decide whether there's another approach that makes better sense. That will help both you and your users in the long run.

The Computer Is Not a Puppy Dog

The anthropomorphization of applications may not quite be a matter of customization, but it fits in as well here as anywhere else. Anthropomorphizing is the process of ascribing human characteristics to non-human things. In a more informal sense, I'd also include ascribing animal characteristics to computer programs. Microsoft has been one of the pioneers here, as Figure 11.17 will remind you.

FIGURE 11.17
Search window in
Windows XP

Perhaps I'm simply unable to see the wonder of this user interface, but if so, I'm in good company; it's descended from the almost universally detested "Clippy" character who offers not-so-helpful help in Office. Presumably the motivation behind slapping an organic interface on a computer program is to make the program seem less threatening and more friendly. The main problem is that (to stretch the dog metaphor just a bit) it can turn around and bite the user.

What is the user to think when they ask the cute little puppy to fetch a file, and the puppy comes back empty-mouthed? Has the puppy not been properly fed? Is it distracted by needing to go out to the lawn? Is it, perhaps, just being mean to the user on purpose because it's tired of being shut up in the little box? Maybe its feelings are hurt.

Although humanized computers might be cute and friendly in Disney movies, in real life this theory doesn't seem to work out so well. If the illusion is not well done, it just ends up annoying users, who don't know why this stupid program looks like a dog when it won't act like one. If the illusion is well done, the user starts to think of the application as having feelings, and starts to interact with their perception of a real dog instead of the reality of the application underneath.

Either way, there's a mismatch between what the application is doing and what the user is trying to make it do, which makes the user less efficient at getting any actual work done.

Like skins, I think that animated characters should be left off any user interface that's actually intended to let people get some work done.

Summary

This chapter drew together some thoughts on customization in a wide variety of contexts. I looked at how menu and toolbar customization works, and at the various options that current applications offer for window management. I also talked about color choices, skinning, application customization, and animated characters.

Now it's time to turn our attention outside the individual computer and on to the World Wide Web. In the rest of the book, I'll look at web applications, which in some areas play by a different set of rules than Windows applications. To begin with, I'll develop a framework for thinking about web applications in general.

CHAPTER 12

The Web Is Not Windows

- Expanding Your Skills to the Web

- Pages, Sites, and Applications

- New Rules and New Challenges

In the old days (say, before 1995), most developers could just ignore the entire Internet and all that it entailed. Now most developers need to pay attention to web design as much as to designing applications for their own individual platforms. Even if you're not involved in building a public Internet site, most companies have at least experimented with delivering applications over an *intranet*. In the remainder of the book, I'll talk about design techniques for web applications and the skills that you need to cultivate to produce such applications.

Expanding Your Skills to the Web

If you're a long-time Windows developer, you might be wondering why you should even consider writing web applications. Aren't there enough opportunities for work in the environment you already know? Well, right now there probably are enough opportunities. But there are good reasons why you should learn about web design even if you feel secure in your present niche.

First, although Windows has had a good long run, it won't last forever. Already a new version of Windows, code-named Longhorn, is on the horizon. Although it's still similar in many respects to current versions of Windows, Longhorn will have rather different user interface conventions. When it starts to dominate the market (probably around the end of the decade), your existing Windows design skills will start to become obsolete.

Meanwhile, the technologies behind the World Wide Web have spread to the inside of many corporations. By now, most companies have their own intranets: private networks that use the same communication protocols as the larger Internet. A web page or a web application can be designed for use solely on an intranet; anything from a Customer Relations Management (CRM) system to an accounting entry system might be implemented using these technologies.

Finally, it's worth noting that the worlds of the Web and the Windows desktop application are converging. Longhorn (the next version of Windows) uses markup languages, similar to HTML or XML, to define its user interface. Learning these technologies now will position you for the future of the Windows platform if you choose to remain a Windows developer, as well as for the continuing use of the Internet or intranets as a way to deliver applications to users.

> **NOTE**   A second type of convergence is provided by *smart client* technologies, which allow you to deliver a Windows application through a web browser. I won't cover these technologies specifically because the user interface of a smart client application is the same as the user interface of any other Windows application.

Fortunately, although the Web offers different ways to do things (and different limitations) than Windows does, the basic principles of user interface design remain the same. It's still your job to create applications that let users do their job with a minimum of confusion and chaos. You need to make allowances for the way the Web works, but if you keep the user in mind you won't go far wrong.

Pages, Sites, and Applications

I like to think about web design for application developers on three different levels:

- The web page
- The website
- The web application

Each of these is a distinct realm of design. You need to understand which realm you're working in before you can do any effective design work.

Web Pages

The basic unit of work on the Web (whether the World Wide Web or a smaller, private intranet), is the *web page*. A web page is the response returned by a web server when it receives a single request from a browser. Figure 12.1 shows this interaction schematically.

As a developer, you generally control only the web server side of the equation. People viewing the pages that you design might do so in a variety of web browsers. As you'll see later in this chapter, this fact leads to some serious challenges in application design. When requests come in, you send responses back, but you can never be quite positive what's happening at the other end of the pipeline.

A single web page might be *static* or *dynamic*. These terms refer to the way in which the page is constructed at the server side of the conversation. A static page is one that contains only content determined in advance. A dynamic page contains content that is generated at the time that the page is delivered to the client.

For example, consider a web page that contains a customer contact list on your corporate intranet. If the customer list does not change frequently, you might choose to create a static page and to edit it by hand when a customer is added, removed, or updated. But normally you create such a page as a dynamic page so that it will be up-to-date whenever it's requested. In such a case, you can use a technology such as Microsoft's ASP.NET to let the web server get the current customer list from a database and build the corresponding web page when it's needed.

FIGURE 12.1
Lifecycle of a web page

When you're designing a single static web page, the design is mostly limited to esthetics. Such pages are usually designed by people whose entire job is web page design, rather than by developers. Of course, there are plenty of cases in which a developer might put together a single static web page for one reason or another. In such a case, you'll need to grasp the relevant web standards and potential problems that I'll discuss later in this chapter.

With a single dynamic web page, things get a bit more interesting (more interesting from a developer's point of view, at least). In most cases, dynamic pages will require some user input. This requires you to design the user input controls as well as the display of the requested information.

Websites

A *website* is an interconnected collection of web pages delivered (usually) by a single web server. Websites range from simple sites containing half a dozen pages to huge sprawling monsters such as the Microsoft or IBM websites, which might contain hundreds of thousands of web pages.

Designing a website offers the challenge of designing all the individual web pages, but it also adds the new dimension of coordinating them. Site designers need to worry about issues that apply to multiple web pages:

- Providing consistent navigation from page to page
- Providing a consistent look and feel for all pages in the site
- Tracking user actions and identity as they move through the site

Visual design for a website is normally the job of a professional designer. But as a developer, you're more likely to get involved with a website than with a web page. Things like navigation, identity, and data entry all require developer participation in the site design. Even if you're not responsible for the user interface design, your decisions affect the user interface. For example, if you're prompting the user to enter a date, it's up to you to figure out how (or whether) to limit the data entry to legitimate dates.

Web Applications

At the top of the web food chain (at least for now) is the *web application*, which is an interconnected collection of dynamic web pages designed to perform some function for the user. As an example, Figure 12.2 shows Microsoft Outlook Web Access.

Outlook Web Access is a particularly complex example of a web application. The developers at Microsoft went to great lengths to duplicate much of the user interface of the stand-alone version of Outlook, but hosted in a web browser. Most web applications are less elaborate than this, but they still allow the user to interact with the web server by working with controls, just as if they were dealing with a Windows user interface.

Web applications are often written with an application platform such as Microsoft's ASP.NET, which is designed to help work around the limitations that otherwise apply to websites. Such platforms make it easier for the developer to manage problems like authentication or identity tracking within an application. They also provide standard controls that a developer can use to put together a user interface. Figure 12.3 shows a page from a fictional ASP.NET application open in a web browser.

With a web application, the application developer's design skills come to the fore. It's still helpful to have input and help from a professional web designer (if you can afford one), but often the development platform limits what can be done. For small web applications, or those with a limited budget, the reality of the situation is often that the developer has to do all the user interface design as well.

FIGURE 12.2
Outlook Web Access

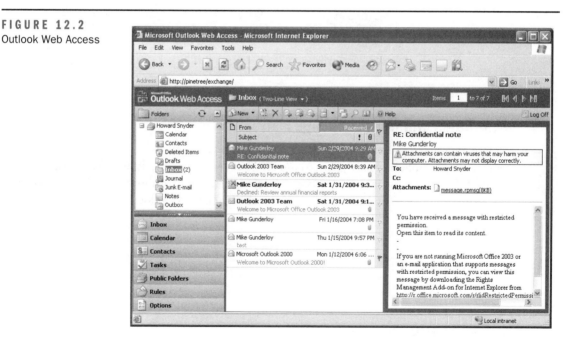

FIGURE 12.3
A web application in
action

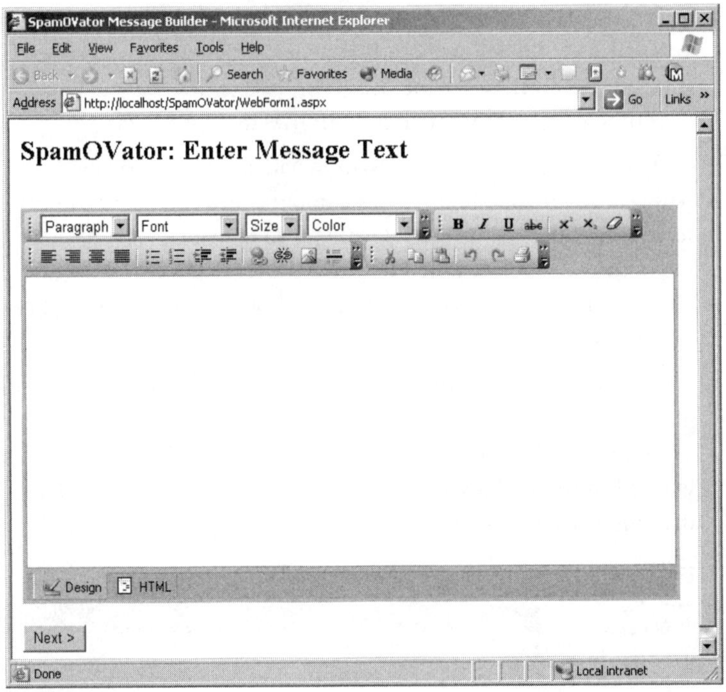

New Rules and New Challenges

You're undoubtedly already aware that there are many differences between Windows applications and web applications. It's hard to use the Web (as we practically all do) and not be aware of the differences. Still, it's good to know in detail what you're dealing with. Here are some of the things that make designing for the Web a challenge for Windows developers trying to make the transition:

- Limited control selection
- Statelessness
- Varying browsers
- Varying standards
- Unpredictable infrastructure

I'll consider each of these issues in turn.

Limited Control Selection

In Chapters 4, 5, and 6 you learned about the rich variety of controls that are available for building Windows application user interfaces. Sadly, web applications are much more limited on this front. Figure 12.4 shows the standard user interface controls that are part of the HTML 4.0 specification.

However, the picture isn't as bleak as Figure 12.4 perhaps makes it out to be. With clever use of images, fonts, and colors, you can use simple HTML to build a reasonably attractive user interface, even without introducing additional controls. Figure 12.5, for example, shows Microsoft's Hotmail user interface. Even though it's built from the same basic pieces as any other HTML page, Hotmail manages to look attractive and be reasonably functional.

WARNING   Unfortunately, you're not guaranteed that your beautiful and innovative use of HTML will display properly on an arbitrary user's computer. See the section "Varying Browsers" later in this chapter for more details.

The distributed nature of the Internet makes it unlikely that we'll see new standard controls any time soon. HTML works largely because a wide variety of browsers and servers agree on how it is structured and what it means. Forcing the adoption of changes or extensions to HTML is a long and arduous process, overseen by the World Wide Web Consortium (`http://w3c.org`). Although there is continuing progress on defining new web standards, the overall state of HTML (the core technology for designing web pages) has been mostly unchanged for years now.

FIGURE 12.4
HTML controls

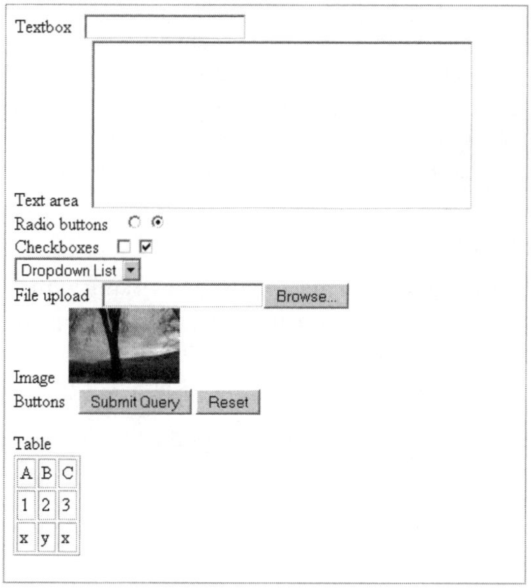

FIGURE 12.5
Microsoft HotMail

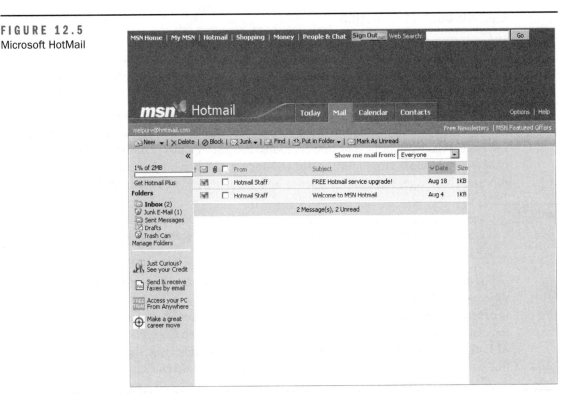

WARNING There are several vendor-specific technologies that let you use a greater variety of controls in a web application than HTML supplies. For example, Microsoft Internet Explorer supports embedding ActiveX controls on a web page. The problem with such technologies is that they limit you to customers using a particular web browser. In general, such extensions are not feasible unless you control the browser choice, as might be possible on an intranet.

Statelessness

One of the biggest differences between working with a Windows application and working with web pages is that web pages are *stateless* (by default, the server does not remember anything about the user between interactions). To see what this means, consider designing a very simple program to handle loan applications, following these requirements:

1. Prompt the user for their name and address, and the amount of the loan.

2. Display the terms of the loan and require the user to click OK.

3. Determine whether to grant the loan.

A Windows application could handle these requirements by creating a wizard interface, as shown in Figure 12.6. The user would first fill in their information and click next on this form.

With a web application, it's easy to start out creating the user interface the same way, as shown in Figure 12.7.

But after this first page, there's a problem. When the user clicks Submit, the web page sends its data to the web server and receives a new page in return. Then the web server forgets all about the interaction. There's no continuing connection between the browser and the server. So at the end of the process, when it's time to determine whether the user qualifies for a loan, the server no longer knows who applied or how much money they wanted.

FIGURE 12.6
Designing a Windows
loan application

FIGURE 12.7
Designing a web
loan application

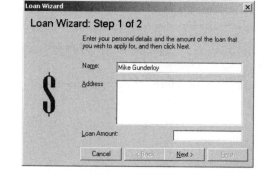

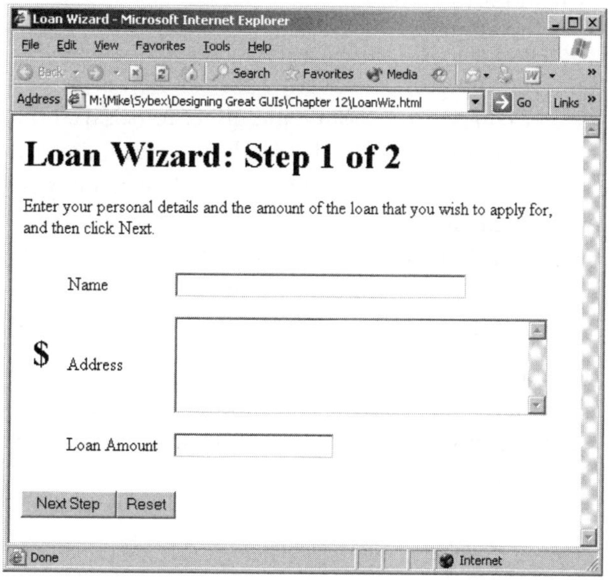

The difference here is between an application that runs as a single process on a single machine (the Windows application) and a conversation between two separate processes: the web browser and the web server. In the original design of the Internet, the web server was a provider of static information. Sitting somewhere on the Internet, a server is bombarded by hundreds or thousands of requests for pages. Each time it gets a request, it satisfies the request by returning the appropriate HTML page, and then forgets about the whole transaction. There's nothing in this design that ties two different page requests together into an application.

The fundamental problem is that there's no easy, foolproof way for the server to tell that two requests belong to the same session. You might think that the server could track the Internet Protocol (IP) address of the requesting computer to know whether two requests belong together, but that doesn't work. Network Address Translation (NAT), a common technology for using one computer to forward requests from many computers to the Internet, means that two requests might appear to the server to come from the same computer, even though they don't.

Of course, faced with this situation, developers have come up with a number of workarounds. All are based on a simple notion: If the server can't tell when it's already heard from a particular client, the client must remind the server. Starting with this premise, information can be stored on either the client or on the server between page requests.

There are three general approaches to creating *stateful* (the opposite of stateless) web applications in wide use:

- Cookies
- Hidden fields
- Data in URLs

A *cookie* is a collection of data stored on the client computer, either temporarily for the time that the browser is open or permanently as a disk file. A cookie can contain any information that the web server chooses to transmit and direct to be saved there. Each time the browser makes a new request to the server, it also sends the cookie along. In the hypothetical loan application, you might use cookies in one of two ways. The first way is to save the name, address, and other information in the cookie; then this information is passed back and forth between browser and server with each request. The second way is to save the information on the server, perhaps in a database, and to put a unique key in the cookie. With this approach, the cookie is smaller, but the web server has to do more to look up the information when the cookie arrives.

Although the use of cookies is reasonably elegant, it suffers in practice from sometimes justifiable fear and suspicion on the part of computer users. Cookies have been used in some dubious and unethical ways. For example, some providers of banner advertisements have used cookies to build up dossiers on particular customers, tracking their interests for more targeted ads in the future. Because some people object to this as an invasion of privacy, most web browsers now include facilities for blocking cookies. If the user blocks the cookies that your web application depends on, the application will break.

A second approach to creating stateful applications is to use *hidden fields* on the web page itself. A hidden field is similar to a text box, but it isn't displayed by the web browser. When the user sends the next request to the server, the hidden field is packaged up and sent along. Hidden fields are a good alternative to cookies in many circumstances because they're difficult to block (although not impossible, if the user cares to handcraft a copycat page without the hidden field to pass back).

A final alternative is to store data directly in the URL sent to the server for a request. For example, suppose that the second page of the loan application were located at

```
http://example.com/LoanWiz2.html
```

In this case, the browser could place extra information in the URL to represent the user's choices on the page:

```
http://example.com/LoanWiz2.html?Name=Mike&Address=PO%20Box%2057&Amount=35000
```

Storing data in the URL is fast and easy, but it's subject to limits on the maximum length of a URL, which can be as small as 256 characters for some web servers.

Even if these approaches help turn a stateless application into a stateful one, none of them is perfect. Users can click the Back button or close the web browser entirely, for example, and confuse or completely disconnect their web application session. Overall, the best approach is probably to choose an approach to maintaining state but also to accept (and allow for) user sessions that simply vanish without ever being completed.

Varying Browsers

Another big challenge in writing web applications is that you generally don't know for sure what's on the other end of the communications link. As the web developer and designer, you're working with the web server—but the web browser isn't under your control. This means that it's very hard to be sure how your carefully crafted site design will look when it ends up in front of the user. For example, Figure 12.8 shows a website in Mozilla Firefox, an up-to-date graphical web browser.

TIP An excellent reference when you're trying to figure out what will work in various browsers is the Webmonkey browser chart at `http://webmonkey.wired.com/webmonkey/reference/browser_chart/index.html`.

FIGURE 12.8
A website in Firefox

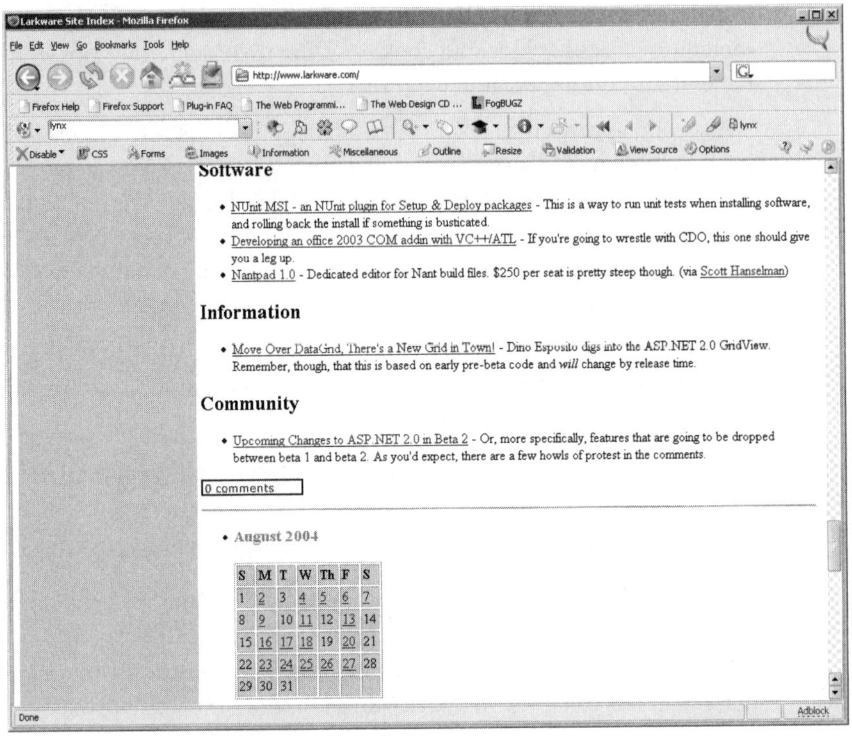

But Firefox isn't the only browser out there. The most common browser in use these days is Microsoft Internet Explorer, but even with IE any given user might be browsing with one of a dozen or more different versions. There are also other choices in the graphical browser market, notably Opera and Netscape. With all these choices, you can expect subtle display differences between computers.

NOTE   For a few years it looked as if Internet Explorer would become so dominant in the browser market that there was little or no point in designing pages that worked well in other browsers. Recently, though, other browsers—such as Opera, Mozilla, and Firefox—have started making inroads into Internet Explorer's market share, thanks to the perceived feature stagnation and security risks of continuing to use Internet Explorer. It's impossible to know just how much market share the various browsers have, but on some sites non-IE browsers are accounting for as much as 30 percent or more of visitors in late 2004.

NOTE   In addition to varying browsers, users can affect the appearance of your site by changing the settings in their browser. For example, some users choose to browse with graphics turned off, so pages will download more quickly. These users will never see your website's pretty graphics. Other users disable scripting or cookies, which might affect any programming you've done.

Sometimes, though, the differences are less subtle. What if someone gets to your website with a wireless connection from a PDA? Figure 12.9 shows what the result might be.

FIGURE 12.9
A website on the
PocketPC

Different sizes are not the only changes your site might hit with different browsers, though. Lynx is a browser that's still popular in some circles, where people are used to command-line tools and speed takes precedence over flashiness. As Figure 12.10 shows, any site is reduced to text when viewed in Lynx.

FIGURE 12.10
A website in Lynx

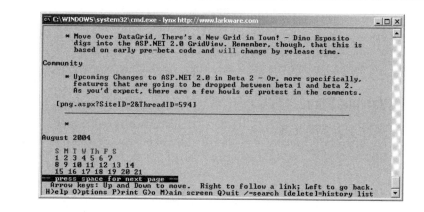

There's more to these display differences than you might think at first sight. Although you might design a dialog box with a particular size in mind, the user is always free to resize their browser window. In some cases, this will cause the controls you've designed on the web page to rearrange themselves. For example, Figure 12.11 shows the same web page that you saw in Figure 12.7.

As you can see, the heading of the page and the instructional text have been rewrapped to fit the new window. On the other hand, the data entry controls, being located in an HTML table, are cut off by the window's borders. Comparing Figure 12.11 with Figure 12.8 will give you some notion of the control that you do and don't have when building user interfaces in HTML.

Varying Standards

Another problem that you'll run into with browsers is that they all support standards just a little bit differently. The Web is governed by standards, of which HTML is only one. You'll learn more about these standards in Chapter 13, "Building a Web Page." You should be aware, though, of the major standards that play a part in web design:

HTML (Hypertext Markup Language) continues to be the most common language for authoring Web pages.

DHTML (Dynamic HTML) is a specification for making things change dynamically after a page has been rendered. For example, DHTML can change the fonts or colors of part of a page in response to a mouse action.

ECMAScript is a standardized version of the JavaScript language, which can also be used for programming on the web browser.

CSS (Cascading Style Sheets) is a specification for adding styles (such as fonts and colors) to web pages.

XML (Extensible Markup Language) is a general-purpose language to adding metadata to data through markup tags.

XHTML (Extensible Hypertext Markup Language) is the next-generation successor to HTML.

XForms is the next-generation successor to the part of HTML that deals with forms and controls.

There are many other Web specifications, most of which are managed by the Worldwide Web Consortium (`http://w3c.org`), but these are the chief ones that you'll need to know to design web pages. Of these, HTML and CSS are the most important for visual design today, with XML playing the part of a general-purpose data transport mechanism. ECMAScript probably has an edge over DHTML for client-side programming because it's supported more consistently by a wider variety of browsers. XHTML and XForms are not widely supported by the current generation of browsers.

Even when a browser supports a particular standard, it's important to ask what "supports" means. These web standards are complex, and browsers often don't render the same page the same way for a variety of reasons:

- The browser vendor might choose to leave out support for parts of the standard that it considers unimportant or too hard to implement.

- The browser's implementation of a particular part of the standard might be incomplete or buggy.

- The standard might have been revised after the browser was developed. For example, some browsers have shipped with preliminary implementations of standards such as XML that were rendered partially incorrect when the final standard was released.

- The browser vendor might choose to ship its own proprietary technology rather than an equivalent standard. Thankfully, this sort of "extension" of web standards is becoming less and less common.

As an example of the sort of difficulty that you can run into when dealing with browsers and standards, consider Figures 12.12 and 12.13, which show the same page rendered in two different browsers.

FIGURE 12.12
Experimental list in Firefox

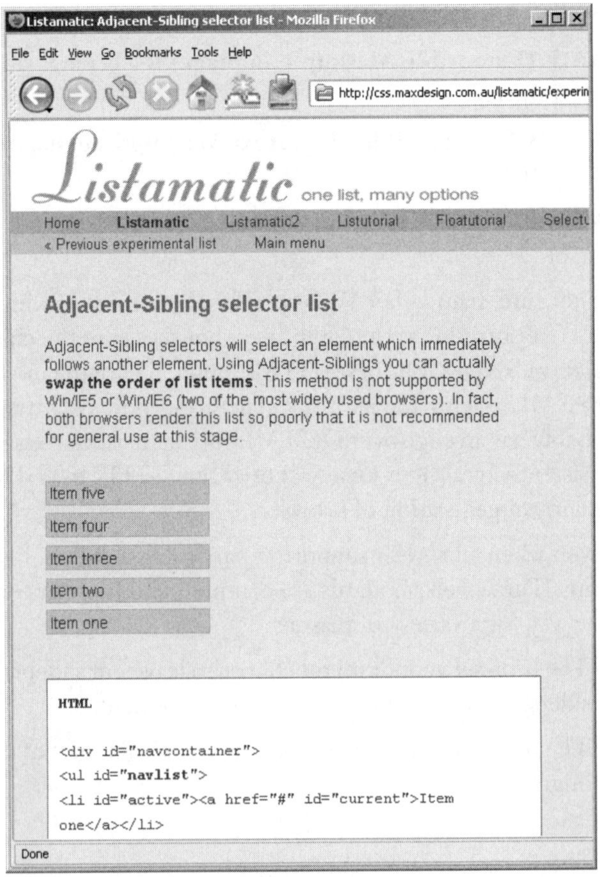

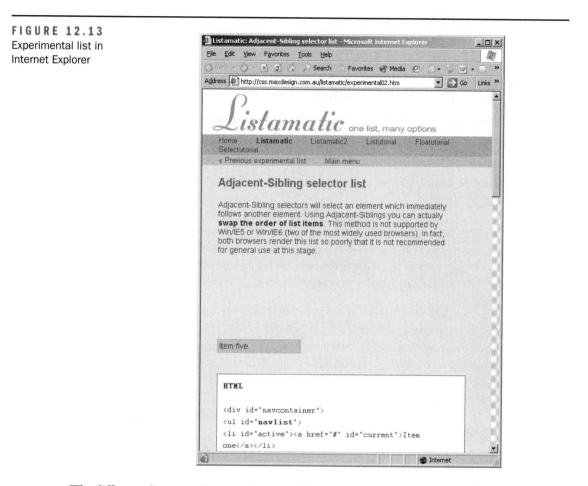

The difference between these two figures is that Firefox supports a relatively unusual part of the CSS standard, whereas Internet Explorer does not. As a result, Firefox renders the page correctly; Internet Explorer does not render it correctly. From a developer's point of view, it's tempting to say that you're writing CSS to the standard, and that some browsers render it correctly, so this is Internet Explorer's problem. Unfortunately, that statement ignores the reality that 90 percent or so of all users are browsing with Internet Explorer.

Although you're not likely to hit such discrepancies in the most common core parts of the standards, they're inevitable as you venture into the more advanced (and obscure) corners of those same standards. In some cases, you can work around this issue by detecting the browser that the user is accessing your web server with and delivering different HTML to a different browser. But there are several problems with this approach:

- Detecting the exact browser isn't always possible. Browser detection depends on an identifying string that the browser sends to the server, and some people suppress or alter this string for reasons of their own.

- Maintaining multiple versions of HTML is more work than maintaining a single version.

- When you customize your site to different browsers, you take on the added work of checking each new feature to see how (or whether) it works in each browser that you want to support.

All in all, I think you're better off just avoiding problematic parts of the standards.

TIP	Some tools do part of the work for you. For instance, Microsoft's ASP.NET uses the browser string to automatically adjust the HTML that it delivers on the fly. Although its browser detection is far from perfect (for example, by default ASP.NET thinks that Firefox does not understand CSS at all), having this support as part of the tool frees the developer from some of the work of supporting different browsers.

From the developer's point of view, the ideal solution is to be able to control the browser that is used to access your web server. Although this is not possible on the public Internet, it might be a possibility on a corporate intranet, depending on company politics. If your corporation standardizes on Mozilla as a browser, for example, you can design and test your web applications in that browser and not worry about any other—as long as you're sure that the applications will remain confined to the intranet.

Unpredictable Infrastructure

A final factor that can make designing web applications difficult is that the Internet itself is unpredictable. Factors utterly out of your control can have a major impact on your website and applications:

- Users connect to the Internet through a variety of hardware, ranging from dial-up modems to fast cable modems and even faster dedicated lines. You can't be sure how long any particular web page will take to load, or what delay there will be between the user sending a request to your server and getting back a response.

- The infrastructure of the Internet itself is subject to attack. Major network worms or denial-of-service attacks can have a major effect on website performance.

- Keeping websites secure is an increasingly difficult task. One missed patch can leave your server vulnerable to spoiled children who will break in and deface your web pages for no reason except to say that they did it.

- Websites come and go. If you depend on links to or resources from another site, you might wake up some morning to discover that the other site is no longer available.

Of course, there are some strategies that you can use to mitigate these problems. Keeping your individual web pages small means that they will load reasonably quickly—even on slow connections (and nearly instantaneously on fast ones). Paying attention to your network and server security, and applying patches from vendors in a timely fashion, will help protect you from attackers. You should also test all the links on your website on a regular basis and include some way (normally on your feedback form) for users to report broken links.

TIP   There are many applications that you can use to check all the links on a website to see whether any are broken. One free application to do this is Xenu's Link Sleuth: `http://home.snafu.de/tilman/xenulink.html`.

Design Strategies

Given the potential difficulties and pitfalls of moving from Windows user interface design to web interface design, how should you proceed? There's no hard-and-fast answer to that question. Rather, you can select from a variety of different design strategies based on your needs and preferences:

- KISS design
- Bleeding-edge design
- Extra frosting design
- Single-browser design
- Multiple-browser design
- Tool-driven design

In the rest of this chapter, I'll discuss these various different approaches.

KISS Design

KISS, of course, is the time-honored acronym for "Keep It Simple, Stupid." One easy way to get started in the Web world is to limit yourself to the simplest technologies that can possibly work. That generally means using the tags from HTML 3.2 (some older browsers still in use don't support some of the tags that were introduced in HTML 4.0) and nothing else: no CSS, no XML, and certainly nothing like Flash or DHTML.

This approach has at least three substantial benefits:

- A lower learning curve makes it easier to get started.
- Using lowest–common-denominator standards means that your pages should render in any browser.
- Simple pages tend to be smaller and load more quickly.

The major drawback to KISS design is that by limiting yourself to a small number of tools you also limit yourself to relatively simple page designs. In an age where people have learned to expect "flashy" websites, this might put you at a disadvantage. Even so, if you're new to web design, this is an excellent place to start. You can always expand your toolset and repertoire of design techniques later.

Bleeding-Edge Design

Other developers argue that there is little or no point to learning outmoded technologies. From this point of view, you should immerse yourself in web technologies, read the latest articles, and see if you can create a site that is attractive, flashy, and functional.

This strategy tends not to be a great idea for the novice web designer because there's simply too much to learn all at once. But experienced designers can use all the tools of the trade to do some pretty amazing things. Often, you can incrementally arrive at this design strategy by starting with simpler designs and then gradually learning new tools and techniques.

There's a danger here, though. As you use more and more complex designs, you're more and more likely to cut yourself off from users who are equipped with older web browsers. Come up with a stunning way to use DHTML to implement dynamic menus, for example, and users browsing from version 3.0 browsers will simply be out of luck. Although it's easy to say that those users should upgrade, in some cases users can't upgrade. For example, there might be a corporate IT department that doesn't allow unauthorized browsers on the network. Even worse, users might have devices (such as PDAs or cell phones) that make upgrading browsers difficult or impossible.

Extra Frosting Design

Rather than use the cutting-edge tools to come up with sites that demand users with the latest browser, you can spread those technologies on top of an otherwise-functional site as "extra frosting." As a simple example, consider the case of constructing a page that contains an image. You can do this with very simple HTML:

```
<html>
<head>
<title>Image demo 1</title>
</head>
<body>
<img src="winter_small.jpg">
</body>
</html>
```

Figure 12.14 shows this web page in Internet Explorer. As you expect, it displays the specified image.

FIGURE 12.14
A web page with an image

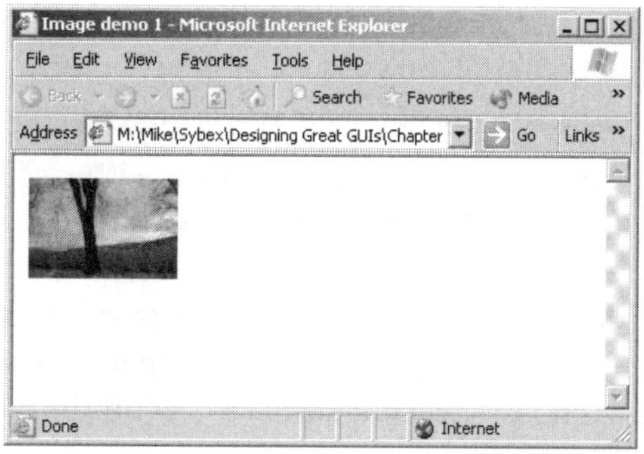

Figure 12.15 shows the same page in Lynx. Being a text-mode browser, Lynx doesn't have any way to display the picture, so all it can do is put up the filename. This isn't very user-friendly.

A simple change to the HTML can make the page friendlier to Lynx:

```
<html>
<head>
   <title>Image demo 2</title>
</head>
<body>
<img src="winter_small.jpg" alt="Photo of leafless tree in
front of backlit clouds on a winter morning">
</body>
</html>
```

FIGURE 12.15
A web page with an image in Lynx

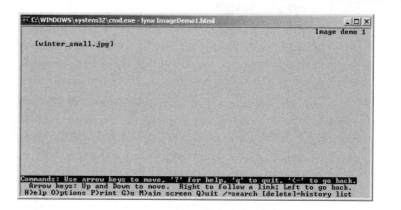

The alt attribute of the image tag supplies alternative text to be used by browsers that can't display the actual image. This inability to display images doesn't apply just to text browsers; people with graphical browsers sometimes choose to turn image display off to speed page loading. Figure 12.16 shows how the revised page looks in Lynx.

Similar tricks can be used to make other advanced technologies friendlier to older browsers. Whether it's CSS, DHTML, or ECMAScript, it's possible to design pages so that the more complex technologies are simply invisible to less-capable browsers. There's a subtle trap lurking here, though: You need to make sure that the essential parts of your site don't depend on the spiffy new technologies. It doesn't help to hide the scripting from old browsers if users of those browsers are suddenly unable to get off the home page of your site.

FIGURE 12.16
A web page with
alternative text
in Lynx

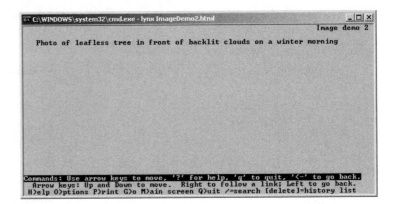

Single-Browser Design

If you're fortunate enough to have control over which browser people use with your web application (which is normally only the case for intranet applications), then you're in luck. You can design pages specifically to take advantage of the features and foibles of that browser, without worrying about how they'll look in any other browser.

If you're in this situation, you can use the browser vendor's documentation as your primary technology guide, rather than relying on the standards and testing to see what actually works. But you need to be aware of two potential downsides to this tightly constrained design strategy. First, you might be in for rough sailing if the approved browser is ever changed and you took advantage of quirks that no longer exist in the new version. Second, you need to be careful of linking your own skills too tightly to a particular browser. If you ever want to change jobs, you'll want to be able to present yourself as a web designer rather than just an Internet Explorer 5.01 designer.

Multiple-Browser Design

At the far end of the spectrum from designing for a single browser is a technique that I mentioned earlier: designing multiple versions of a website for multiple browsers. You might, for example, have different versions for each of these potential clients:

- Text-only browsers
- Older graphical browsers
- Current graphical browsers
- Small-screen browsers

You can also add user choice into the mix. For example, some people like the animated graphics that can be produced with Macromedia's Flash, whereas others detest them. That's why you'll sometimes see sites offering a Flash version and a non-Flash version that let users choose which version of the site to view. You can also try to detect which browser is being used to view the site and serve the appropriate version of the pages (although there are potential problems with this approach, as I discussed earlier in the chapter).

On the plus side, a multiple-browser approach can leave all or most of your visitors very satisfied with the site by making good use of the features that their browsers support. On the minus side, maintaining more than one version of a site introduces a lot of extra work into the equation. Not only do you need to keep each version working, you need to make sure that changes are made consistently across all the versions.

Tool-Driven Design

Finally, you can choose to abdicate all responsibility for underlying technology choices and instead rely on a tool to help you write web pages. Although this approach seems like a cop-out, it's actually consistent with the way in which almost everyone develops Windows applications. It's a very rare developer who writes Windows applications using assembly language, or even C++ and the Windows API. Instead, most of us rely on tools such as Visual Studio .NET to abstract away the routine details. We write code using high-level objects, design the user interface with forms and controls, and let the compiler worry about translating everything to compiled code.

Similarly, rather than building web pages and sites in HTML, you can use a visual design tool such as Macromedia Dreamweaver, Microsoft FrontPage, or Visual Studio .NET to design pages graphically. Your designs are then converted into HTML and other web standards behind the scenes. When the process is complete, the server is still sending HTML, but you never have to look at it if you don't want to.

Tool-driven design can be the fastest way to move from Windows interface design to web interface design. These modern integrated environments make it very easy to create and customize web pages while hiding complexity from the user. But it helps to have some understanding of what you're creating. For example, with Visual Studio .NET, you can choose which of several browsers to target with your HTML. The choices you make affect both the capabilities of the tool and the ultimate generated HTML. If you treat the system as a completely black box, you might be powerless to understand or fix any problems that users report.

Summary

In this chapter, you learned a little bit about moving user interface design skills from Windows applications to web applications. You saw why you might want to make the transition. I then discussed some of the problems that await you in trying to be a web designer with a Windows outlook, and offered some potential design strategies to help you deal with this new world.

Now it's time to look at some of the web technologies in more detail. The next chapter looks at the pieces of a web page in more depth, and I discuss the capabilities of the standard HTML controls and tags that you can use to build a user interface for a web application.

CHAPTER 13

Building a Web Page

- The Elements of Page Design

- A Brief Look at Cascading Style Sheets

- General Principles of Web Page Design

o design a user interface for a web application, you need to be familiar with the basic tools at your disposal. This means understanding the basic elements of HTML, even if you will use a graphical design tool that does the heavy lifting for you. Even the best of tools occasionally needs a bit of help in the form of hand-editing of the generated HTML, and if you don't know what you're looking at, you'll be out of luck. In this chapter, I'll show you what HTML provides as building blocks for your web user interfaces and go over some general principles of good web page design. If you already know the basics of HTML and web page design, you might like to just skim this chapter for suggestions on how to most effectively use the standard tags and controls.

The Elements of Page Design

Web pages are built of HTML tags. These tags specify the content and layout of the page (within limits) to the web browser. In this section of the chapter, I'll go over the most common and useful HTML tags, and show how they fit together to build a user interface. It's convenient to divide these tags into two groups: basic tags that support the non-interactive features of a web page, and forms that supply an interface somewhat similar to dialog boxes with controls in a Windows application.

> **NOTE**   The picture gets more complex when you add in other web standards such as CSS. CSS is a non-HTML language that modifies the presentation of HTML pages. Even in this case the page itself will still be HTML.

> **TIP**   For more details on any of the web standards discussed in this chapter visit the World Wide Web Consortium site at www.w3c.org.

Basic Elements

In this section, you'll learn how to put together a web page, including the most common non-interactive elements:

- Text
- Lists
- Hyperlinks
- Images
- Tables

> **TIP**   There's a lot more to HTML than I'm going to show you in this chapter. If you'd like an exhaustive reference, try *HTML Complete* (Sybex, 2003).

The Structure of an HTML Page

I'll start with an extremely simple web page that will show you the general structure that all HTML pages should follow:

```
<html>
<head>
<title>First Web Page</title>
</head>
<body>
<!-- A sample web page -->
Some text
</body>
</html>
```

The first thing to note here is the selection of *tags* sprinkled through the file. A tag is delimited by angle brackets (< and >), and it's not meant to be displayed to the user. Rather, a tag is an instruction to tell the web browser what's going on. Tags come in pairs; each opening tag has a closing tag that is the same as the opening tag with a slash character; for example, </body> is the closing tag for the opening tag <body>. Opening tags can contain *attributes* that further specify their purpose (although none of them do in this particular example).

TIP   Strictly speaking, HTML does not require every opening tag to have a corresponding closing tag. But some of the other web standards, such as XML, do impose this requirement, and HTML doesn't object to closing tags. It's good practice to always include explicit closing tags.

Tags can be nested. That is, there can be tags within the opening and closing pair for other tags. Looking at just the structure of the first example with some indentation makes this clear:

```
<html>
    <head>
        <title>
        </title>
    </head>
    <body>
    </body>
</html>
```

The <head> and <body> tags in this example are nested inside of the <html> tag; the <title> tag is further nested inside of the <head> tag. You can't overlap tags; the inner tag must be closed before the outer tag is closed. Thus, HTML with this structure would be illegal:

```
<html>
    <head>
        <title>
    </head>
        </title>
    <body>
    </body>
</html>
```

WARNING   Some web browsers make an attempt to interpret illegal HTML, but it's best not to depend on any such behavior.

Every HTML document should contain these three tags:

- `<html>` identifies the document as being HTML.
- `<head>` contains information about the document.
- `<body>` contains information to be displayed in the browser.

In the `<head>` section, you'll almost always want to include a `<title>` tag. As you can guess from the name, this tag specifies the caption text to be shown at the top of the web browser.

The sample document includes two things inside of the `<body>` tag. The first line is an HTML comment:

```
<!-- A sample web page -->
```

HTML comments are introduced by the special characters `<!--` and terminated by the special characters `-->`. As in any other programming language, you can use comments to make the intent of your HTML clear, to keep notes for future implementation, and so on. Finally, anything that's not a tag or a comment is text to be displayed:

```
Some text
```

Figure 13.1 shows this document in a browser.

Text

Anything outside of tags is treated as text to be displayed in the browser. One thing to note is that white space in the HTML source is generally *not* significant to web browsers. Consider this source file:

```
<html>
<head>
<title>Unbroken text</title>
</head>
<body>
    Text with leading spaces.
And another paragraph with some more text.
Even more text on this line, with a big     gap in it.

Text after a blank line.
</body>
</html>
```

You might expect this file to display in the browser much as it looks here. If so, you'd be surprised, as Figure 13.2 shows.

FIGURE 13.1
A very simple HTML
document

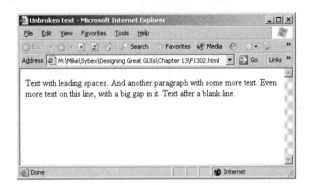

FIGURE 13.2
HTML without white
space markup

Most browsers just don't consider spaces and carriage returns to be significant. They ignore these things and pour the text into the browser window as one long chunk. This can get pretty hard to read, which is why HTML provides some ways to lay out the display of the text:

** ** is a non-breaking space character that displays an explicit space in the browser.

<p> indicates a paragraph of text that most browsers render with surrounding blank lines.

<div> indicates a division of text that can be aligned within the browser.

**
** indicates a line break.

Here's an HTML document that uses these tags:

```
<html>
<head>
<title>Layout tags</title>
</head>
<body>
<p>    
This text will be indented four spaces</p>
```

```
<div align="left">The text in this section of the document
will be left-aligned.</div>
<div align="right">And the text in this section of the
document will be right-aligned</div>
<p>Here's a short paragraph of text.</p>
<p>And here's another, slightly longer, paragraph of
text to round out the document. This particular paragraph
includes<br /> a line break embedded in it.</p>
</body>
</html>
```

There are a couple of things to note about this document. First, because the layout and line breaks are controlled by the markup and browser, you're free to wrap text however you like in the HTML source. You can also insert tabs and blank lines for readability if you like. Second, the `<div>` tag here shows how to use HTML attributes. The `<div>` tag supports a number of attributes, including the `align` attribute to specify the alignment of text in the section. To use an attribute, you include the attribute name, an equal sign, and a quoted value inside the opening tag. In addition to the left and right values shown in this sample, you can also use the align tag to center text with `align="center"`. Figure 13.3 shows this file in the web browser.

TIP   The `<p>` tag also supports the `align` attribute.

NOTE   CSS provides alternative ways to align text and other parts of a web page. Many developers prefer to use CSS for this purpose, and to limit HTML to holding content. Splitting design from content often makes it easier to fine-tune each.

The bulk of your web page work is likely to be text. Web pages would be pretty dull if all the text on the page looked the same—although there are some pretty severe limitations to what you can specify about the appearance of the text. For example, you can't specify a font or an absolute text size in HTML (although CSS eases this restriction a bit; see the section "A Look at Web Page Standards" later in this chapter). But HTML does supply a variety of tags that you can use to alter the appearance of text. Here are just a few of them:

- `<h1>` through `<h6>` tags for headings.
- `<b>` or `<strong>` for bold text.
- `<i>` or `<em>` for italic text.
- `<u>` for underlined text.
- `<code>` for source code.
- `<pre>` for preformatted text.

FIGURE 13.3
Laying out HTML
with tags

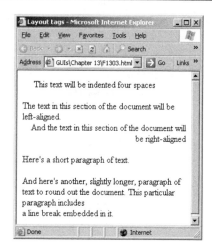

Here's a sample document that uses these tags:

```
<html>
<head>
<title>Formatting text</title>
</head>
<body>
<h1>Heading 1</h1>
<h2>Heading 2</h2>
<h3>Heading 3</h3>
<h4>Heading 4</h4>
<h5>Heading 5</h5>
<h6>Heading 6</h6>
<p>A paragraph with <b>bold</b> and <strong>strong</strong> text.</p>
<p>A paragraph with <i>italic</i> and <em>emphasized</em> text.</p>
<p>A paragraph with <u>underlined</u> text.</p>
<p>This paragraph includes some embedded source code:
<code>For i = 1 to 10</code>.</p>
<pre><code>
' Preformatted source code
For i = 1 to 10
    Debug.Print i
Next i
</code></pre>
</body>
</html>
```

Figure 13.4 shows this page in the browser.

FIGURE 13.4
Formatting text
with HTML

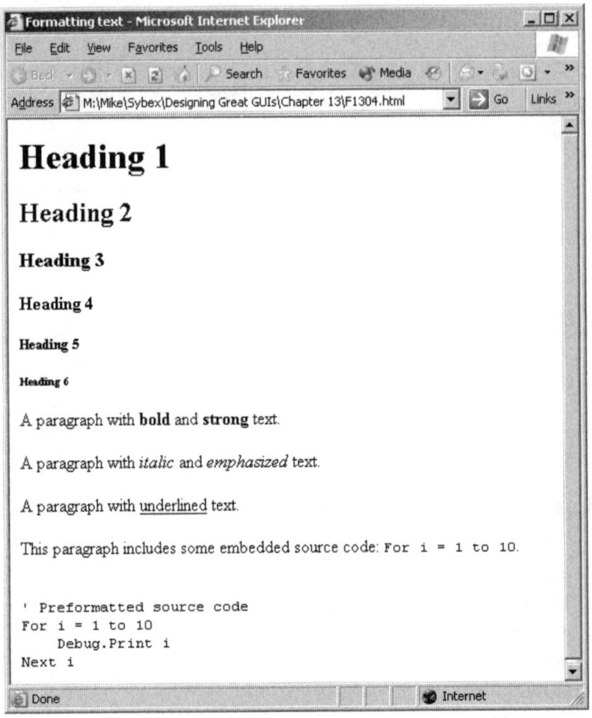

The heading tags <h1> through <h6> provide six different styles that can be used for outline-style heads within a document, from largest to smallest. There's no particular requirement as to how the browser renders these headings, although usually <h4> is the same font size as normal paragraph text.

Why two sets of tags for bold and italic text? The answer is that <b> and <i> are *physical style tags*, which dictate to the browser exactly what it should do: display text as bold or italic. The other two tags, <strong> and <em>, are *content-based tags*. These tags tell the browser to emphasize the text, but don't specify how the emphasis should be done. In practice, though, every modern browser uses bold and italic text for these tags.

The <code> tag tells the browser to use a monospaced font; it's usually used for computer programming source code. Often, you'll see this tag nested in the <pre> tag, as shown in the final part of this sample. The <pre> tag indicates that text is preformatted; that is, the browser should not change the spacing or word wrap within this text. Although this is really a layout tag, it's most often used with the <code> tag, which is why I saved it for this example.

The formatting tags, such as <b> and <i>, date back to very early versions of the HTML standard. In fact, these tags are currently deprecated. That is, the applicable standards bodies recommend you use CSS instead of these HTML tags. While avoiding the HTML formatting tags will keep you on the cutting edge, the plain fact is that there will never be a browser that doesn't understand these tags; they're just used on far too many web pages already. My advice is to use the tags that you're comfortable with and that suit your needs, and not to worry too much about whether a standards body says you're doing it right.

NOTE   If you'd like to check your work to see whether it conforms to the standards, you can use one of the online validation services: Bobby (http://bobby.watchfire.com/bobby/html/en/index.jsp), Vischeck (www.vischeck.com/vischeck/vischeckImage.php), or the W3C validator (http://validator.w3.org/). But use your judgment when deciding which recommendations to accept.

Lists

Another variation of plain text in HTML is the list. HTML supports two types of lists: ordered lists and unordered lists. This sample shows both types in action:

```
<html>
<head>
<title>Lists</title>
</head>
<body>
<p>Ordered list:</p>
<ol>
<li>First item</li>
<li>Second item</li>
<li>Third item</li>
</ol>
<p>Unordered list:</p>
<ul>
<li>First item</li>
<li>Second item</li>
<li>Third item</li>
</ul>
</body>
</html>
```

Lists such as these always involve nested tags. The outer tag specifies the type of list: <ol> for an ordered list and <ul> for an unordered list. The inner tag is always <li> (for *list item*); there are as many of these tags as there are items on the list. As you can see in Figure 13.5, ordered lists are numbered, and unordered lists are bulleted.

FIGURE 13.5
Ordered and
unordered lists

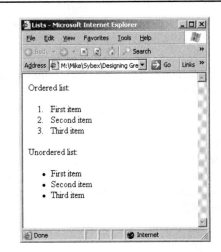

Lists can also be nested. This is most useful with unordered lists, which create additional levels of indentation and distinctive bulleting. For example, here's a page with a nested unordered list:

```
<html>
<head>
<title>Nested List</title>
</head>
<body>
<ul>
<li>First item</li>
    <ul>
    <li>First nested item</li>
    <li>Second nested item</li>
    <li>Third nested item</li>
    </ul>
<li>Second item</li>
    <ul>
    <li>First nested item</li>
    <li>Second nested item</li>
    <li>Third nested item</li>
    </ul>
<li>Third item</li>
    <ul>
    <li>First nested item</li>
    <li>Second nested item</li>
    <li>Third nested item</li>
    </ul>
</ul>
</body>
</html>
```

FIGURE 13.6
Nested list

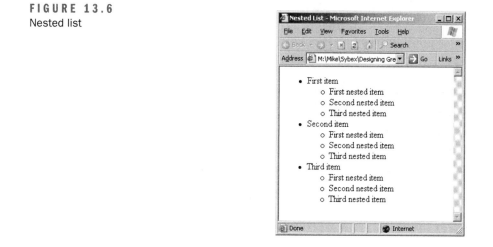

Figure 13.6 shows this file in Internet Explorer.

Images

Any modern web browser can display images in three common formats: GIF, JPG, and PNG. To insert an image in your document, use the <img> tag, which supports many attributes including the following:

src for the source (image file) location.

alt for text to be displayed when the browser can't display the image or when the user has images disabled.

align to specify the alignment of the image with the surrounding text.

height to specify the image height in pixels.

width to specify the image width in pixels.

Here's a document that includes two images:

```
<html>
<head>
<title>Images</title>
</head>
<body>
<img src="happy.png" alt="Happy face" align="left"
height=100 width=100>
<p>The happy face graphic is aligned to the
left side of the browser window,
and the text flows around it on the right.</p>
<img src="sad.png" alt="Sad face" align="right"
```

```
height=100 width=100>
<p>The sad face graphic is aligned to the
right side of the browser window,
and the text flows around it on the left.</p>
</body>
</html>
```

Figure 13.7 shows this document in the browser.

The src attribute of the <img> tag specifies a file relative to the HTML page on the server. In this case, with no folder listed, the web server looks for the images in the same folder as the HTML file itself.

FIGURE 13.7
Images in HTML

Hyperlinks

You're aware, of course, that web pages are connected to other web pages by hyperlinks. In HTML, hyperlinks are indicated by the <a> tag. The general form of the <a> tag, when used for hyperlinks, is:

```
<a href="link URL">Link text</a>
```

For example, here's a page that links to several well-known locations on the Web:

```
<html>
<head>
<title>Hyperlinks</title>
</head>
<body>
```

```
<ul>
<li><a href="http://www.microsoft.com"
     title="Microsoft home page">Microsoft</a></li>
<li><a href="http://www.yahoo.com"
     title="Yahoo home page">Yahoo</a></li>
<li><a href="http://www.google.com"
     title="Google home page">Google</a></li>
</ul>
</body>
</html>
```

Figure 13.8 shows the page generated by this HTML, which wraps three hyperlinks in a list.

To be useful, hyperlinks need to include the `href` attribute, which specifies the target page that the jump will take the user to. You should also include the title attribute, which specifies a title for the target page. This is usually the same as the page's title, though it can be different. This attribute is used by screen readers to give users a hint as to where the hyperlink will take them. Another common attribute is `target`, which dictates which window a hyperlink will open in. You can use `target="_blank"` to cause a hyperlink to open in a new window.

There are quite a few different possibilities for the link URL, but you're most likely to see five of these:

http://www.example.com/test.htm   HTTP URL pointing to a page on another site.

https://www.example.com/test.htm   Secure HTTP URL pointing to a page on another site.

Page2.html   Relative URL pointing to the same site. In this case, the link would be to `Page2.html` stored by the web server in the same directory as the current page.

ftp://example.com/test.zip   FTP URL for downloading a file from an external site.

mailto:MikeG1@example.com   E-mail URL for sending mail to the specified user.

You can enclose just about any other tag inside of the <a> tag. For example, it's quite common to hyperlink images. Here's a page that uses a graphical button instead of a text link:

```
<html>
<head>
<title>Linked graphic</title>
</head>
<body>
<p>Click the arrow to go to the Microsoft Website.</p>
<a href="http://www.microsoft.com">
<img src="MS.png" alt="Microsoft arrow" height=50 width=200>
</a>
</body>
</html>
```

Figure 13.9 shows the result. Note the hand cursor over the graphic, which shows that it's a hyperlink. This figure also shows how Internet Explorer handles the alt attribute of the <img> tag, by displaying a ToolTip with the text of the attribute. The alt attribute is also used by screen readers to describe an image that they can't see, so you should strive to make the description stand by itself.

WARNING   Beware of hyperlinking images without making it very clear to the user that that's what you are doing. It's okay to create a menu in graphics, for example, as long as there is text that cues the user to click. But creating a menu purely out of graphics with no text leads to what is sometimes called "mystery meat" navigation, where it's impossible to find the hyperlinks without madly waving your cursor around the web page. This is a bad idea that only annoys users.

Tables

The last of the major basic tools is the table. *Tables* are the most complex part of basic HTML, and I'm going to show you only the most common of the table tags here. In almost every case, you'll be using a graphical tool to define tables, rather than writing raw HTML.

FIGURE 13.9
A hyperlinked image

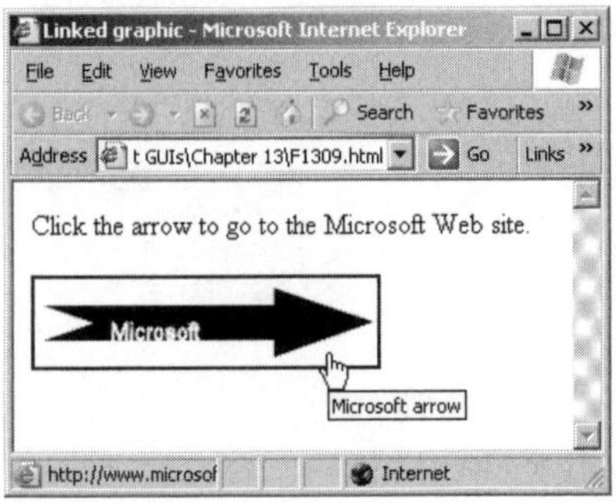

In HTML, tables are created as cells within rows within the table itself. Here's a first simple example of defining a table:

```html
<html>
<head>
<title>Table #1</title>
</head>
<body>
<table>
    <tr>
        <th>State</th>
        <th>Capital</th>
    </tr>
    <tr>
        <td>Alabama</td>
        <td>Montgomery</td>
    </tr>
    <tr>
        <td>Alaska</td>
        <td>Juneau</td>
    </tr>
    <tr>
        <td>Arizona</td>
        <td>Phoenix</td>
    </tr>
</table>
</body>
</html>
```

Figure 13.10 shows the table defined by this structure. The <table> tag marks the overall table. Each row is defined by the <tr> tag. Individual cells are within <th> or <td> tags—the difference being that the browser renders the former with more emphasis so that they can be used as headers.

FIGURE 13.10
Simple HTML table

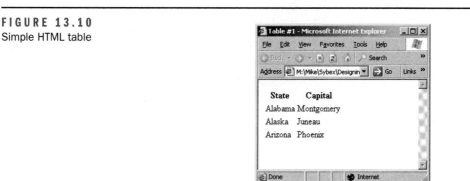

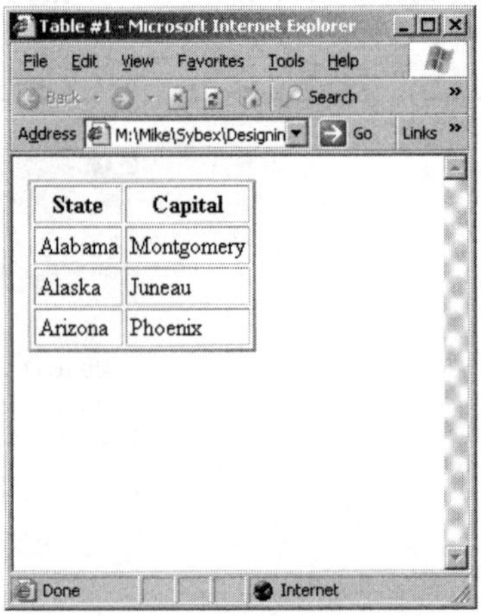

The `<table>` tag has a set of attributes that let you draw borders around the cells, as in this example:

```
<html>
<head>
<title>Table #1</title>
</head>
<body>
<table border=2 cellspacing=2 cellpadding=2>
    <tr>
        <th>State</th>
        <th>Capital</th>
    </tr>
    <tr>
        <td>Alabama</td>
        <td>Montgomery</td>
    </tr>
    <tr>
        <td>Alaska</td>
        <td>Juneau</td>
    </tr>
    <tr>
        <td>Arizona</td>
        <td>Phoenix</td>
    </tr>
</table>
</body>
</html>
```

Figure 13.11 shows the result. Now each cell in the table is surrounded by a chiseled border.

FIGURE 13.11
HTML table with borders

The three attributes that control the borders are as follows:

border   The width of the border around the table, in pixels. By default, this is zero.

cellspacing   The amount of space placed between adjacent cells in a table and along the outer edges of cells along the edges of a table, in pixels.

cellpadding   The amount of space between the edge of a cell and the text or image that it contains.

Two other attributes that are worth knowing about are colspan and rowspan. These attributes allow you to create irregular tables. Here's an example:

```
<html>
<head>
<title>Table #1</title>
</head>
<body>
<table border=2 cellspacing=2 cellpadding=2>
    <tr>
        <td></td>
        <td colspan=2 align="center">Details</td>
    </tr>
    <tr>
        <td></td>
        <th>State</th>
        <th>Capital</th>
    </tr>
    <tr>
        <td rowspan=3>States</td>
        <td>Alabama</td>
        <td>Montgomery</td>
    </tr>
    <tr>
        <td>Alaska</td>
        <td>Juneau</td>
    </tr>
    <tr>
        <td>Arizona</td>
        <td>Phoenix</td>
    </tr>
</table>
</body>
</html>
```

In this case, the colspan attribute indicates a cell that spans two columns; the rowspan attribute later on dictates that a cell is spread across three rows. Figure 13.12 shows the result.

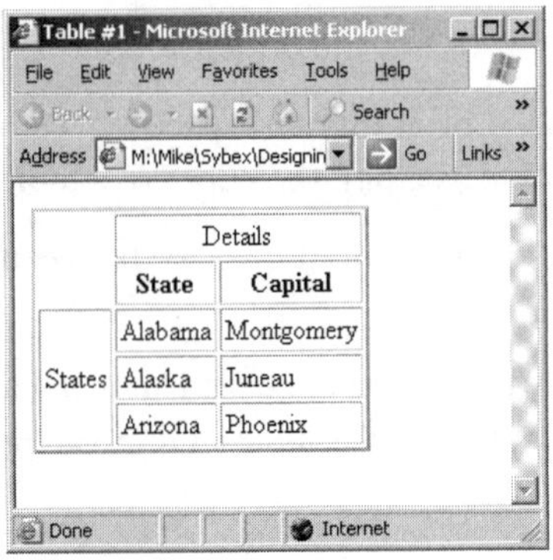

FIGURE 13.12
An irregular HTML
table

FIGURE 13.12
An irregular HTML
table

Forms

So far, all the HTML elements that you've seen in this chapter are static. They can be used to display data (perhaps quite complex data) to the user, but they don't allow the user to interact with the server beyond clicking a hyperlink to load another page. As such, they don't allow the richness that's needed for an interactive application.

The <form> tag, and the tags that it contains, fills this gap in classic HTML. An HTML form, like a Windows dialog box, is a collection of controls that the user can interact with. When the user has entered or selected values, they can click a button to send the information they chose back to the server for further processing. It's important to understand that this model is independent of the particular web server or the software on the server side. HTML forms provide a mechanism for packaging up data into standardized messages; these messages can be handled by a variety of server applications.

For starters, here's a very simple HTML form:

```
<html>
<head>
<title>Simple form</title>
</head>
<body>
<form action="http://www.example.com/testform" method="post">
What's your name? 
<input type="text" name="UserName" size="40"><br />
<input type="submit" value="Log In">
</form>
</body>
</html>
```

Figure 13.13 shows this form in the browser.

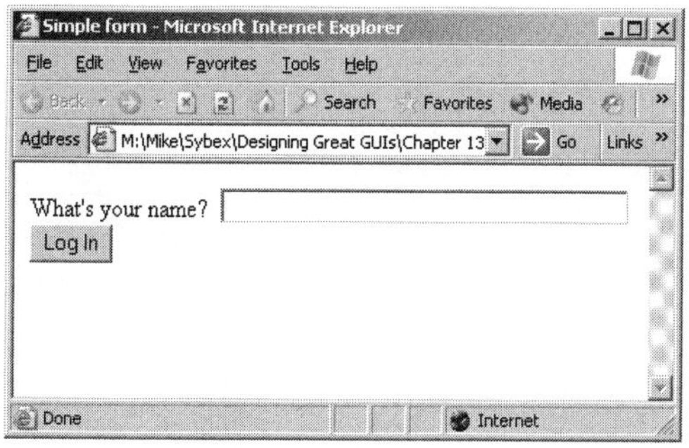

FIGURE 13.13
A very simple
HTML form

When the user types in their name and clicks the Submit button, the browser sends the information on the form to the server. This information is sent in the HTTP headers for the request, where it's available for any server software that cares to make use of it. Data from the form is sent as name-value pairs. For example, if you type **Horace Horsley** into the form in Figure 13.13 and click Submit, the data sent to the server includes

```
UserName=Horace+Horsley
```

Note that the space in the user input is automatically replaced by a plus sign.

The <form> tag requires both the action and method attributes. The action attribute specifies the target URL for the data sent by the form. Depending on your server software, this could be the same HTML page that contains the form, a different HTML page, or something else entirely. The method attribute can be either post or get. Which one you use depends on the server software that's dealing with the form; they refer to two slightly different standards for uploading the data.

Figure 13.14 shows the standard controls that you can use on HTML forms:

- Text box
- Text area
- Radio button
- Check box
- Drop-down List
- Listbox
- File Upload
- Buttons

FIGURE 13.14
HTML form controls

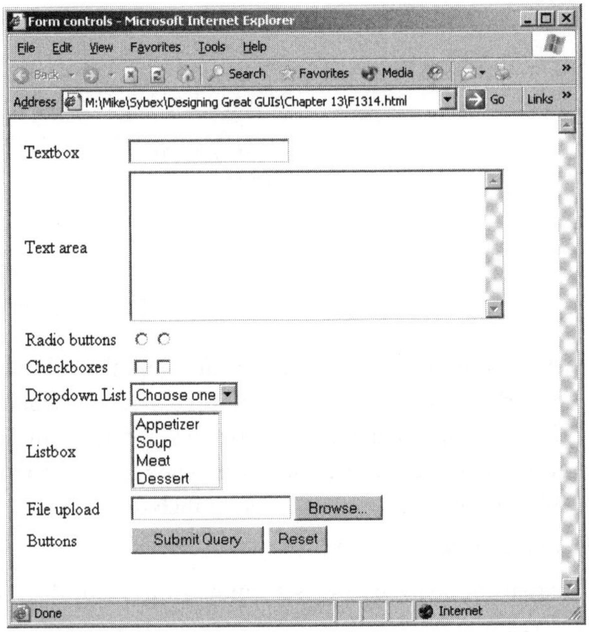

Text Box

The text box control provides a single-line input area where the user can type whatever they like. The text box in Figure 13.14 was produced by this code:

```
<input type="text" name="txt1">
```

As you can see, a text box is actually part of the more generic <input> tag. In fact, most of the controls in Figure 13.14 are created by the <input> tag. The type attribute specifies the type of control to create, and the name attribute (which is also required) is sent back to the server with the form's data to identify the particular control. Other useful attributes for text boxes include:

size   The size of the text box, taken as the number of characters to display.

maxlength   The maximum number of characters that the text box will accept.

As on Windows dialog boxes, text boxes are useful when you need to allow completely free-form input. For cases where the user should select from a small number of alternatives, other controls offer a better user interface.

Text Area

The text area control allows you to define a multiple-line input area on an HTML form:

```
<textarea cols="40" rows="8" name="area1">
```

The cols attribute specifies the number of columns to display, and the rows attribute specifies the number of rows to display. Normally, the control displays text exactly as the user types it and sends exactly that text to the server; to go to a new line, the user must press Enter. You can adjust this behavior with the wrap attribute. If you set wrap=virtual, the text will be wrapped on screen, but not when transmitted to the server. If you set wrap=physical, the text will be wrapped on screen and sent to the server with line breaks as well.

Radio Button

Radio buttons are also created by the <input> tag:

```
<input type="radio" name="r1" value="1">
<input type="radio" name="r1" value="2">
```

Note that the name attribute is the same for both of these radio buttons. That's what tells the browser to use the standard radio button behavior of allowing only one to be marked at any given time. Each radio button has an associated value, and when the user submits the form to the browser, the value of the checked radio button is sent back as the value of the entire group. If you want to display the form with one of the buttons preselected, include the checked attribute in its tag:

```
<input type="radio" checked name="r1" value="1">
```

Check Box

Check boxes, too, are created by the <input> tag:

```
<input type="checkbox" name="c1" value="1">
<input type="checkbox" name="c1" value="2">
```

The only major difference between radio buttons and check boxes is that even if two check boxes have the same name attribute, the browser allows the user to check both of them. The values of all checked check boxes are sent back to the server when the user submits the form.

Drop-Down List

To create a drop-down list of choices on an HTML form, you use the <select> and <option> tags:

```
<select name="ddl1">
<option>Choose one</option>
<option>News</option>
<option>Sports</option>
<option>Talk</option>
</select>
```

The `<select>` tag itself specifies that there will be a list of items here. By default, this tag creates a drop-down list. Each option within the list is represented by an instance of the `<option>` tag. The browser displays the first option in the list as the default value of the drop-down list when the user first loads the page.

The value of the drop-down list is the text of the selected option. If you prefer to somehow encode values, you can use the `value` attribute of the `<option>` tag:

```
<select name="ddl1">
<option value=0>Choose one</option>
<option value=1>News</option>
<option value=2>Sports</option>
<option value=3>Talk</option>
</select>
```

In this case, the browser will send the server 0, 1, 2, or 3 as the value of `ddl1`.

List Box

You can also create a list box by using the `<select>` tag:

```
<select name="s1" size="4" multiple="multiple">
    <option>Appetizer</option>
    <option>Soup</option>
    <option>Meat</option>
    <option>Dessert</option>
</select>
```

The `size` attribute of the `<select>` tag controls how many rows will be displayed in the list box at one time. To allow multiple selection, include the `multiple` attribute.

File Upload

HTML includes a variation of the `<input>` tag to make it easy for the user to select and upload a file:

```
<input type="file" name="f1">
```

This tag is actually rendered as two different controls: a text box and a button labeled Browse. Clicking the Browse button opens a File Open dialog box provided by the operating system to allow the user to choose a file.

For the file upload control to work properly, you must use the `post` method for the form and set the `enctype` attribute of the `<form>` tag:

```
<form enctype="multipart/form-data"
method=post action="process_file.html">
```

Buttons

Finally, HTML forms contain buttons. There are two standard button types—submit and reset:

```
<input type="submit">
<input type="reset">
```

The submit button sends the current contents of the form to the server; the reset button clears the form so that the user can start over. You can also create as many custom buttons on the form as you want by supplying values for the `name` and `value` attributes:

```
<input type=submit name=action value="Add">
<input type=submit name=action value="Update">
<input type=submit name=action value="Delete">
```

In this case, the form will have three different submit buttons, labeled Add, Update, and Delete. When the user clicks one of these buttons, the form's data is sent back to the server along with a parameter named `action` that contains the value of the button that the user clicked.

A Brief Look at Cascading Style Sheets

There are attributes to set display preferences such as fonts and colors in HTML, but I haven't shown you any of them. That's because most web designers these days agree that Cascading Style Sheets (CSS) are a better choice for dictating these visual aspects of your web page. CSS is more flexible than HTML formatting attributes, and it also encourages a separation of content and design that makes it easier to focus on each piece of the process individually.

In addition to the benefits they offer to developers, Cascading Style Sheets can also be a boon for users. That's because the major web browsers allow the user to substitute their own CSS for the one supplied by the website. If you're using Internet Explorer, for example, select Tools ➤ Internet Options. On the General tab of the Internet Options dialog box click Accessibility. In the Accessibility dialog box, check the Format Documents Using My Style Sheet option and fill in the name of a CSS file on your own computer. Using your own style sheet lets you alter fonts, colors, alignment, and just about anything else about a web page. For example, you can make the default font of a site larger if you have trouble reading it, or get rid of a background image that you find difficult to live with.

CSS styles can be included as part of an HTML page or collected into an external file called a style sheet. Usually, the external style sheet is a better choice. By collecting styles in an external style sheet, you can reuse them across many web pages. This gives you benefits analogous to those derived from reusing library code across many applications.

To demonstrate styles in action, I'll start with a very simple HTML document:

```
<html>
<head>
<title>CSS demo</title>
<link rel=stylesheet type="text/css"
      href="Sheet1.css">
</head>
<body>
<h1>Heading</h1>
<p>Some text in the document.</p>
</body>
</html>
```

Note that there's a new tag in the <head> section of this file. The <link> tag in question specifies an external style sheet, and gives the name of the style sheet in the href attribute. In this case, the style sheet is in the same folder as the web page. Here are the contents of the style sheet Sheet1.css:

```
h1 {font-size: 120pt}
p {font-style: italic}
```

Figure 13.15 shows the result of displaying the indicated web page with this style sheet. Note that the <h1> and <p> text looks very different than it would with the default style for these sections.

A *style sheet* is a collection of styles. Each style consists of a selector, plus one or more property-value pairs, enclosed in curly braces. The selector matches the HTML tag to which the style will be applied. The property is separated from its value by a colon. So, you might read the Sheet1.css file as "make the font in all <h1> tags 120 point, and make the style in all <p> tags italic."

FIGURE 13.15
Using a Style Sheet

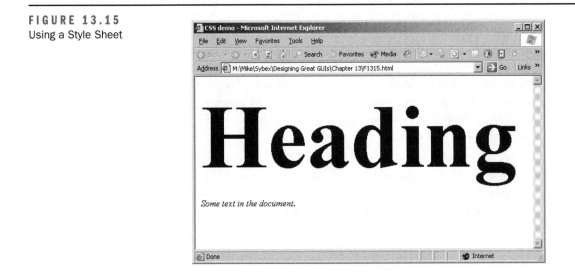

You can also apply a style to just part of a tag. The trick is to use the <span> tag to delimit the text whose style you want to change. The <span> tag is an HTML tag that has no effect by itself, but it can be used in conjunction with CSS to apply formatting wherever you'd like it. Consider this HTML file:

```
<html>
<head>
<title>CSS demo</title>
<link rel=stylesheet type="text/css"
      href="Sheet2.css">
</head>
<body>
<h1>Heading</h1>
<p>Some <span class=bigtext>text</span> in the document.</p>
</body>
</html>
```

And here are the contents of the Sheet2.css file that goes with the HTML:

```
span.bigtext {font-size: large}
```

Figure 13.16 shows the results. As you can see, the span.bigtext style is applied only to the text within the <span> and </span> tags. You can define as many classes of <span> tag as you like, and apply individual styles to each of them.

FIGURE 13.16
Using CSS for part of a paragraph

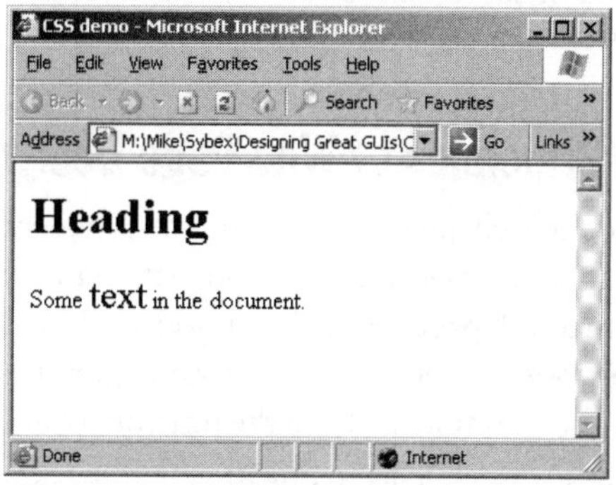

TIP You can also use the class attribute for other tags. For example, if you start a paragraph with <p class=bold>, it is formatted according to a p.bold style in the associated style sheet.

Table 13.1 lists some of the properties that you can set with CSS. There are many more than this available; for a full listing, see the CSS pages at the Worldwide Web Consortium site (http://www.w3c.org/Style/CSS/).

TABLE 13.1 Selected CSS Properties

Property	Description
background-color	Background color of an element
background-image	Image file to use as the background of an element
border-color	Border color of an element
border-style	Style of the border of an element
border-width	Width of the border of an element
color	Foreground color of an element
font-family	List of font names to use for an element
font-size	Font size for an element
font-style	Control normal versus italic for text
font-weight	Control amount of boldness for text
margin	Margin of an element
text-align	Text alignment for an element
vertical-align	Vertical alignment for an element

TIP   For some stunning examples of CSS design, visit the CSS Zen Garden (`http://www.csszen-garden.com/`). This site uses a single HTML file with dozens of different CSS files to show you what a wide variety of effects CSS can achieve. Even better, you can download all of the files to use as learning aids.

General Principles of Web Page Design

To conclude this chapter, I'll give you some general guidance on designing web pages that will be a part of a web application. Of course if you've spent time on the Internet (and who hasn't?), you know that web pages come in an overwhelming variety of designs. Unlike Windows, which has some history of standards that constrain graphic design, the Web has been wide open to innovation. It's also traditionally been the territory of graphic artists rather than application designers.

However, you don't have to put all of your time and energy into artistic work to design usable web applications. Paying attention to page design, the use of links, and the way that you set up forms can help your application's usability, even if it doesn't end up being flashy.

Web Page Design for Applications

Many of the general principles that you learned in Chapter 7, "Dialog Boxes," apply equally well to web page design:

• Use borders and boxes to clarify which controls work with each other.

- Keep controls arranged in neat rows and columns. On a web page, the easiest way to do this is with a table whose border width is set to zero.

- Place command buttons after other controls, where the user will naturally find them after working through the rest of the form.

- Arrange controls left to right and top to bottom, to take advantage of the user's natural reading order.

- Use tabs to break up large pages into smaller subpages.

The last point deserves some further explanation. Although HTML doesn't include a native tab control, it's easy enough to fake it with a proper use of images and hyperlinks. For instance, consider the well-known tabbed interface used by Amazon.com, as shown in Figure 13.17.

FIGURE 13.17
Tabbed user interface
in HTML

Here's the HTML that produces the portion of the page shown in Figure 13.17, somewhat simplified (I removed long paths and shortened filenames):

```
<a href="home.html">
    <img src="welcome-on-whole.gif">
</a>
<a href="your-store.html">
    <img src="yourstore-unrec-off-sliced.gif">
</a>
<a href="books.html">
    <img src="books-off-sliced.gif">
</a>
<a href="apparel.html">
    <img src="apparel-off-sliced.gif">
</a>
<a href="electronics.html">
    <img src="electronics-off-sliced.gif">
</a>
<a href="toys.html">
    <img src="toys-off-sliced.gif">
</a>
<a href="kitchen.html">
    <img src="kitchen-off-sliced.gif">
</a>
<a href="homegarden.html">
    <img src="homegarden-off-sliced.gif">
</a>
```

You get the idea. On other pages in the tab set, the HTML is almost identical, except that a different graphic is darker than the rest to indicate the active tab.

There are some other principles that are more applicable to web pages than to Windows dialog boxes. Chief among these principles is the notion that important content should be "above the fold," a term borrowed from newspaper publishing. This is an extension of the notion that reading order starts at the top left of the page, coupled with the fact that web pages render progressively: In most browsers, you'll see the content at the top of the page before the content at the bottom of the page is written to the screen. To keep the user's interest, the most important content should be in this area. Thus, on web pages you should always keep menus at the top, where they'll quickly be available for users to choose from.

You should also make sure that the web page looks good on more than just your computer with your preferred browser. At the very least, I suggest checking any page with the current versions of Internet Explorer, Mozilla/Netscape/Firefox (all of which use the same core rendering engine), and Opera. Depending on your target audience, you might wish to include less-common browsers on the list as well. If you're designing many web pages, you'll find it useful to set up test machines or virtual machines with a variety of browsers installed.

Tips for Using Hyperlinks

There's an art to finding the right level of hyperlinking for a web document. If you're designing a web application where you expect the user to stay within a set of pages that link to each other, it's relatively easy. In this case, you'll use links to move the user through a data entry process or to different areas of the application, and links will be relatively rare.

But you may also be designing other web pages, such as portal pages or training pages, which work in conjunction with your application. In this case, things get a bit trickier. One of the nice things about hyperlinking is that it provides a way for users to get more information on demand. Sometimes developers go a bit overboard with this, as shown in Figure 13.18.

In this style, developers seem to mistake their web page for an encyclopedia, adding a hyperlink to every noun on the grounds that the user might want to go look up more information. This is generally pretty overwhelming for users. It's better to limit yourself to links that are relevant to the user's current needs. These links usually include the following:

- Links to terms that are specific to your application
- Links to other pages in the application
- Links to generic pages such as help or the company home page

FIGURE 13.18
Overlinked page

FIGURE 13.18
Overlinked page

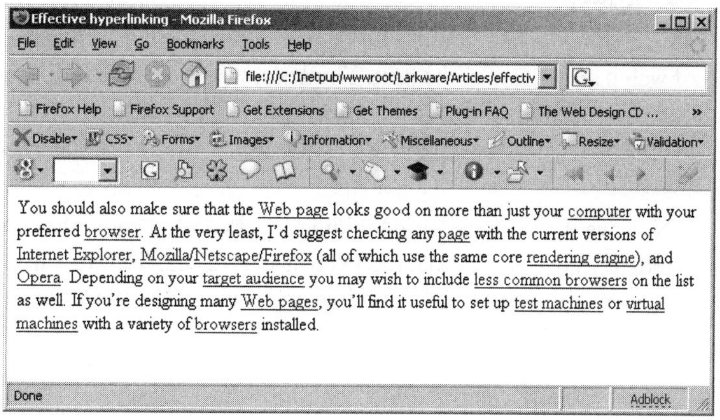

Remember, the user can always open another browser window and search if they feel in need of the definition for a generic term.

Try not to place two links next to one another. Most browsers make it impossible for the user to tell where one link stops and the other begins, and they may not even realize that there are two links there. Put a non-breaking space between the links, put them in a list, or find some other wording to separate the adjacent links.

Avoid using graphics for links unless it's crystal-clear that the graphic will be a link. Don't fall prey to the mystery-meat navigation problem where the user has to get lucky with the mouse to find out where the hyperlinks on a page are located.

Tips for Using Forms

Good HTML form design takes practice. But you can keep some basics in mind as you get started:

- Help the user with input whenever possible. Use drop-down lists, list boxes, radio buttons, or check boxes for constrained input. If the user must type free-form input into a text box, try to size the text box to indicate the amount of input that you're expecting.

- Use tables to lay out the form so that controls line up neatly.

- Make use of CSS to indicate important information on the form.

- Always indicate which fields on the form are required. Remember, when the user clicks the submit button, they have to wait for the server to respond. Don't make them do this only to find out that they left out some required information.

Summary

This chapter covered quite a bit of ground, especially if you've never looked at the nuts and bolts of web page design in the past. You learned about basic HTML, and how HTML tags are put together to form a page. I also introduced CSS, which provides the most widespread standard for adding display formatting to web content. Finally, I offered a few hints for effective web page design.

Now we'll take these basic building blocks and see how they can be used to create a variety of standard web pages. Even if the Web displays a near-infinite variety, there are common metaphors that users are accustomed to seeing, and they're the subject of the next chapter.

CHAPTER 14

Common Web Design Patterns

- Common Web Pages

- Handling Site Navigation

- Creating Web Applications

N ow that you know about the basic pieces of a web page, it's time to start putting them together into larger groups. Although the Web is much less constrained than Windows in its user interface or application flow, users are still accustomed to some common sorts of pages. In this chapter, I'll offer advice on those common pages, discuss website navigation, and close with some thoughts about creating web applications.

Common Web Pages

As you learned in the first part of this book, Windows applications share a more-or-less uniform look and feel. Web pages (and by extension, web applications) are much less constrained. But although the look of web pages varies widely, there are still similarities that you'll run into as you navigate between websites. For example, just about every website has a home page—the page where most visitors will start their browsing experience on that site. By using standard pages, you can help the first-time visitor find their way around your site. Common web pages include these:

- Home
- Site Map
- Search
- About
- Contact
- Frequently Asked Questions
- Privacy Policy
- Trademarks
- Terms and Conditions

Home Page

If you're only going to spend time designing one web page for your site, make it the home page. The *home page* is the page—usually with a name such as default, index, or welcome—where you expect most users to start their interaction with your website.

Because outside sites can link to anywhere, or users can send links in e-mail, there's no way to guarantee that everyone starts at the home page. You can do a couple of things to make it easier for people to find the home page, though:

- Provide a prominent link to the home page on every other page of the site. You might simply use the text "Home" for this, although many websites use the site name, company name, or site logo as a link to their home page. For example, on the Microsoft home page shown in

Figure 14.1, the Microsoft logo in the upper-left corner is a link to the home page, and this design element is repeated on every page in the site.

- Set your website's properties to specify the site's home page as the default page for the site. How you do this depends on which web server you're using. What this procedure does is direct people who type just the site URL to a particular page on the site. If you're running example.com, setting the default page to index.html would have the effect of directing people who type www.example.com to http://www.example.com/index.html. If you're using IIS 6.0 to serve your website, for example, you can do this by launching Internet Information Services Manager and opening the Properties dialog box for your site. Click the Documents tab and check the Enable Default Content Page check box. You can supply a list of possible names for the default page in the list box, as shown in Figure 14.2. IIS will return the first of these pages that actually exists in the site's folder on the hard drive.

FIGURE 14.1
Microsoft home page
in fall 2004

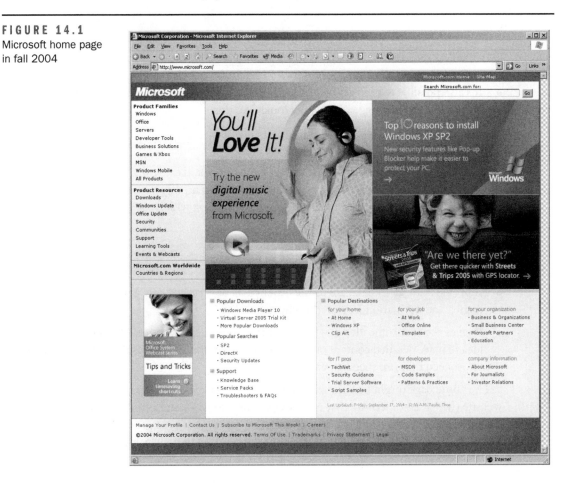

- It's also possible to redirect from one page to another by including a meta refresh tag in the HTML of the first page. Such a tag looks like this:

```
<META http-equiv="REFRESH" content="0;
    url=http://www.example.com/welcome.htm">
```

Including such a tag in the HTML for default.htm would cause the user to get welcome.htm in its place. The problem with this scheme is that there's no way to use the meta refresh tag to provide a default page for the entire site; you have to guess which pages the user might try and then redirect all of them.

The home page normally serves several purposes:

- It introduces your company, organization, or website to the new visitor.

- It provides a way to navigate to the other parts of your website. You'll learn more about menus and navigation later in this chapter.

- It gives the user some idea of what else they'll find on the website. Although it's not a good idea to place detailed content on the home page, an overview helps the user decide whether to proceed to more specific pages.

The home page might be your only chance to convince a user to spend more time with your website (which is something that most website developers want to do). It's important to consider what you want to emphasize. Typically, the goal of the home page is to tell users what sort of information they can find on your website as well as what they can do there. Take another look at the Microsoft home page in Figure 14.1. There's a lot going on here (not surprising because the Microsoft website itself is huge, with more than a hundred thousand pages); but size, graphics, and placement are used to make some parts of the page stand out:

- The upper-left part of the page (where most people automatically start reading) contains jumps to Microsoft's product families. This is appropriate because Microsoft is a software product company.

- The main area of the page contains three large graphics that advertise the content Microsoft was trying to promote the week that I took this screenshot.

- Other links are grouped by their purpose or intended audience to make them easier to find.

You probably won't have as much content on your website as Microsoft does on its site, but you should still carefully construct your home page to act as a showcase and a launching pad for the rest of the site.

TIP   One thing that Microsoft does not have on its home page or elsewhere is a cute little animated "under construction" icon. The Web is always under construction, and most users are just annoyed by those icons. Users expect web pages to be dynamic and to evolve. If you're using one of those icons, I urge you to get rid of it.

Site Map Page

Most websites are not as large as Microsoft's or IBM's, but they can still be confusing. As the site designer, you know exactly which pages exist on the site and how they're arranged, but visitors don't have that luxury. To deal with this problem, a convention called the *site map* has evolved. A site map lists pages or groups of pages on a site, and usually consists almost entirely of hyperlinks. Figure 14.3 shows a partial site map for a fictional software company.

The key to an effective site map is to keep it simple and well-organized. Usually a hierarchical organization will work. That is, identify groups of similar pages (in Figure 14.2, they include "Products" and "Services") and then list individual pages underneath them, with each individual page name hyperlinked to the actual page. In some cases, you may also want to provide links for the groups themselves, if the groups have their own home pages on your site. You should generally avoid graphics and flashy content on the site map page. Users typically visit this page only if they're trying to find something quickly, so it's paramount that the page load quickly and be easy to scan.

If you're maintaining a huge site, you can't list every single page on the site map. In this case, the main site map page should list the major sections of your website. For example, Figure 14.4 shows the site map for the Microsoft website. Each of the links on this page takes the user to an area of the site with its own navigation aids for drilling in to more detailed content.

FIGURE 14.3
A typical site map

Site Map

Products

SpamOVator

Bulk Mailing Wizard

Phone Essentials

Services

Custom Programming

Outsourced E-mail Services

Downloads

Trial Software

Registered User Section

Support

Feedback

About IGS

Corporate Information

Contact Us

Press Releases

FIGURE 14.4
Site map for a
large site

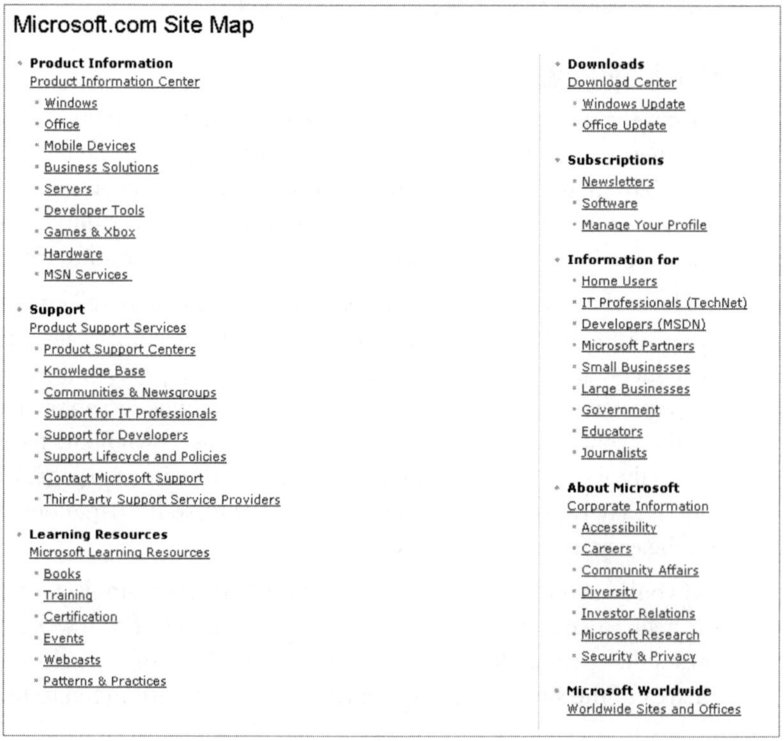

Microsoft.com Site Map

• **Product Information**
  Product Information Center
  ○ Windows
  ○ Office
  ○ Mobile Devices
  ○ Business Solutions
  ○ Servers
  ○ Developer Tools
  ○ Games & Xbox
  ○ Hardware
  ○ MSN Services

• **Support**
  Product Support Services
  ○ Product Support Centers
  ○ Knowledge Base
  ○ Communities & Newsgroups
  ○ Support for IT Professionals
  ○ Support for Developers
  ○ Support Lifecycle and Policies
  ○ Contact Microsoft Support
  ○ Third-Party Support Service Providers

• **Learning Resources**
  Microsoft Learning Resources
  ○ Books
  ○ Training
  ○ Certification
  ○ Events
  ○ Webcasts
  ○ Patterns & Practices

• **Downloads**
  Download Center
  ○ Windows Update
  ○ Office Update

• **Subscriptions**
  ○ Newsletters
  ○ Software
  ○ Manage Your Profile

• **Information for**
  ○ Home Users
  ○ IT Professionals (TechNet)
  ○ Developers (MSDN)
  ○ Microsoft Partners
  ○ Small Businesses
  ○ Large Businesses
  ○ Government
  ○ Educators
  ○ Journalists

• **About Microsoft**
  Corporate Information
  ○ Accessibility
  ○ Careers
  ○ Community Affairs
  ○ Diversity
  ○ Investor Relations
  ○ Microsoft Research
  ○ Security & Privacy

• **Microsoft Worldwide**
  Worldwide Sites and Offices

Search Page

Some people prefer to search for the content they desire, rather than browsing through a list of links. For those people, it's important to have a *search page* on your website. Figure 14.5 shows a search page from the Microsoft website.

This particular search page caters to people with differing levels of search skills, which is a good idea. To just search the entire site for a word, you can type the word into the text box at the top of the page and click Go. Otherwise, you can use the advanced search section to set additional options. Note that there's also a link to Search Help, in case the user needs further guidance.

You might think that the search page is superfluous because users can use a search engine such as Google to locate pages on your site. Although that's at least partially true, it doesn't take into account users who might not know the syntax for making Google do a site-specific search (include `site:example.com` in the search terms to return only results from the `example.com` site).

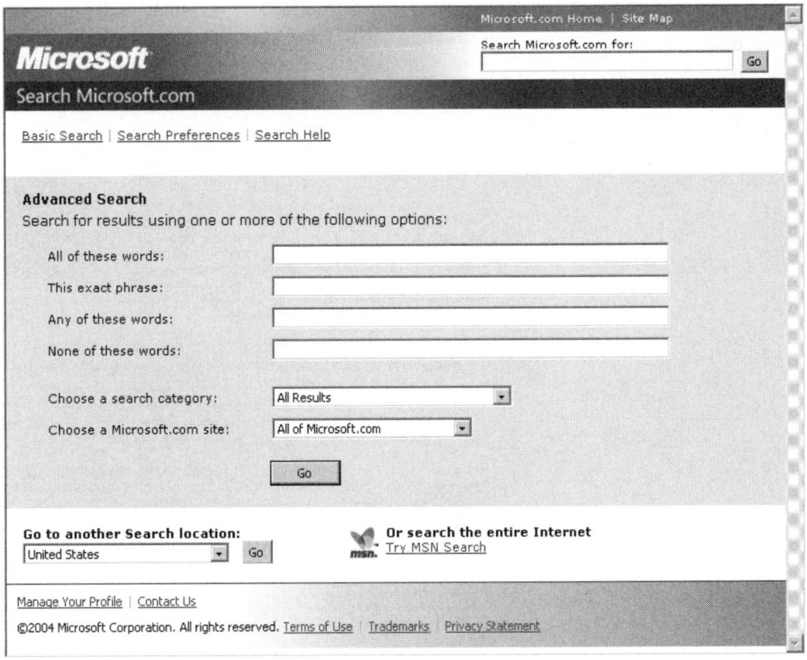

FIGURE 14.5
A search page

About and Contact Pages

Most sites also contain an *about page* and a *contact page*. Both of these pages pertain to the company or organization behind the website, instead of to the site itself, but they have slightly different purposes. The about page is designed to give the user basic information about the company at greater length than the home page can accommodate, whereas the contact page tells the user how to get in touch for more information.

Figure 14.6 shows a portion of the about page from the John Deere website, cropped to show only the content area. John Deere is a major manufacturer of agricultural equipment, and the about page explains this quite clearly.

Note that the about page presents the company in a positive light, explains what it does, and provides hyperlinks for more information. The about page is usually very information-oriented; it explains things without offering any action items to the user.

By contrast, the contact page is very task-oriented. Figure 14.7 shows a portion of the contact page from Borland's website.

About Us

In 1837, John Deere founded the company that would come to bear his name. Incorporated as Deere & Company in 1868, it has grown from a one-man blacksmith shop into a worldwide corporation that today does business in more than 160 countries and employs approximately 46,000 people worldwide. It is one of the oldest industrial companies in the United States.

Our company is guided today, as it has been since its beginning, by John Deere's original values of quality, innovation, integrity and commitment. We strive to create shareholder value through the pursuit of continuous improvement and profitable growth.

How We're Organized
We have four manufacturing divisions:

- Agricultural Equipment - creating fine products for the farmsite;
- Commercial and Consumer Equipment - creating lawn and grounds care equipment for residential needs, golf and turf, and commercial operations;
- Construction and Forestry Equipment -building products that help build your world; and
- John Deere Power Systems - creating the engines and components that power our equipment and other products around the globe.

We also provide world-class financial solutions and tools through John Deere Credit. John Deere Health offers quality health care benefits at a reasonable cost. John Deere Parts provides quality parts and service to John Deere equipment owners, as well as owners of competitive brands of equipment.

Our History
In 1837, John Deere, an enterprising country blacksmith forged a special plow in his shop in Grand Detour, Illinois. Made from a discarded saw blade, the plow allowed settlers to cultivate the sticky soil and transform the prairie into fertile farmland. Read more about our company's history or visit our Deere & Company Archives site.

Integrity
Quality
Innovation
Commitment

When someone visits the contact page, you can assume that they want to contact the company somehow. Your goal here should be to provide as many alternatives as possible for making that contact. Note that the Borland page offers addresses, phone numbers, fax numbers, and e-mail links for a variety of units within the company.

TIP   In some cases, you might not want to publish phone numbers or e-mail addresses on the Web. In that case, your contact page should contain a web form that allows users to submit questions or suggestions to the company. Make sure that someone reads and responds to these messages on a regular basis!

Frequently Asked Questions

Many sites include a frequently asked questions, or FAQ, page. Figure 14.8 shows the FAQ page from the popular technical discussion site SlashDot.

FIGURE 14.8
An FAQ page

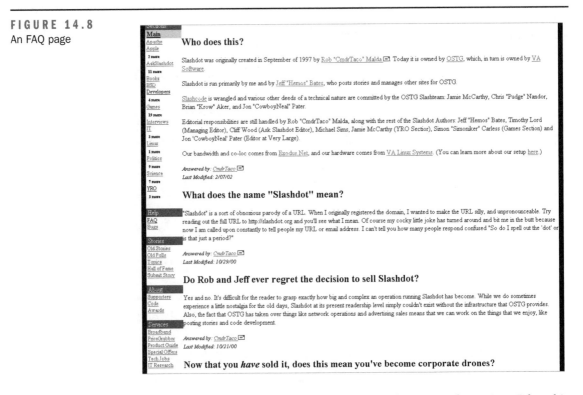

Like an About page, an FAQ page gives visitors a place to go for more information. Often this information is categorized, with sections devoted to the company, its products, the site itself, and so on. For a small FAQ, you might choose to present the questions and answers as one long page. For larger FAQ pages, it's generally useful to create a single page listing all of the questions with hyperlinks to the individual answers so that the page will load more quickly.

A properly designed FAQ page can also have a benefit for your organization by providing a first line of support for visitors. When visitors can answer questions in this self-serve fashion, they don't have to phone or e-mail you for answers. That cuts down on your support and customer service expenses.

WARNING The key to making an FAQ page useful to visitors is to make sure it really does answer the most frequently asked questions. Sometimes FAQ pages are just disguised marketing material designed to explain how great your company is, regardless of what people ask. Such pages might make the marketing department feel good, but in the long run they're of little use to visitors.

Legal Pages

Finally, when you're designing a website, don't neglect the legal aspects. That's good advice when it comes to almost any activity in our modern world, of course. But there are three areas in particular that most sites spell out, which makes many users expect them:

- Privacy policy
- Trademark claims
- Terms and Conditions

Privacy Pages

Rightly or wrongly, web surfers are extremely concerned about their privacy online. Some users of the Web have this feeling that their every action is being watched, recorded, and correlated for later nefarious use. Although this is almost entirely a paranoid fantasy, some practices on the Web go beyond what some users are comfortable with. For example, sites that deliver advertising banners can set cookies on the user's computer and later use those cookies to correlate visits to different sites with the same banner.

Some sites also collect personal information on users. For example, if you're sending an e-mail newsletter out, you'll need e-mail addresses. Beyond that, though, many sites collect demographic information such as name and address, or even income and interests. Users are sometimes confused about what this information will be used for and who will have access to it.

To allay these fears, your site should have an explicit privacy policy that's easy for users to find (linking it from the home page is a good idea). Figure 14.9 shows a small portion of the privacy page for Microsoft's website.

There are four essential parts to a privacy policy:

- A list of the information collected by the website
- A list of the purposes that the information will be used for
- Information on who can access the information
- A warning that use of the site implies acceptance of the policy

There have been several efforts to formalize standards for privacy on websites. The most important of these are TRUSTe and P3P.

TRUSTe (http://www.truste.org) is an independent nonprofit organization that exists as a central review authority for privacy policies. It works with your site to make sure that your privacy policy is acceptable under its standards, which are designed to strike a balance between the needs of businesses and the rights of consumers. TRUSTe certification is not free; charges are on a sliding scale based on your annual revenue (they start at about $600 per year).

Microsoft.com Privacy Statement

Updated: July 30, 2004

Microsoft is committed to protecting your privacy. This privacy statement explains data collection and use practices of the Microsoft.com site (the "Site"); it does not apply to other online or offline Microsoft sites, products or services. By accessing the Site, you are consenting to the information collection and use practices described in this privacy statement.

Other Microsoft services with links from this Web site, including MSN, Windows Update, Office Online, have their own privacy statements which can be viewed by clicking on their links.

On This Page

⇩ Collection of your Personal Information

⇩ Use of your Personal Information

⇩ Control of your Personal Information

⇩ Access to your Personal Information

⇩ Security of your Personal Information

⇩ Protection of Children's Personal Information

⇩ Use of Cookies

⇩ Use of Microsoft Passport

⇩ Enforcement of this Privacy Statement

⇩ Changes to this Statement

⇩ Contact Information

TRUSTe Privacy Program

TRUSTe is an independent, non-profit initiative whose mission is to build users' trust and confidence in the Internet by promoting the principles of disclosure and informed consent.

Related Links

• Manage Your Profile

• Safe Internet

Collection of your Personal Information

We will ask you when we need information that personally identifies you (personal information) or allows us to contact you to provide a service or carry out a transaction that you have requested such as receiving information about Microsoft products and services, entering a contest, ordering e-mail newsletters, joining a limited-access premium site or service, signing up for an event or training, or when purchasing, downloading and/or registering Microsoft products. The personal information we collect may include your name, title, company or organization name, work e-mail, work phone, work or home address, information about your job function, information about your company, and credit card information.

The Site may collect certain information about your visit, such as the name of the Internet service provider and the Internet Protocol (IP) address through which you access the Internet; the date and time you access the Site; the pages that you access while at the Site and the Internet address of the Web site from which you linked directly to our site. This information is used to help improve the Site, analyze trends, and administer the Site.

P3P stands for Platform for Privacy Preferences, a project sponsored by the Worldwide Web Consortium. P3P provides a standard file format for privacy policies, with the goal of enabling automatic privacy policy management by various tools. For example, a user of a P3P-enabled web browser can specify their own privacy requirements as part of setting up the browser, and the browser will warn them whenever they visit a site without a proper P3P file. You can find more information about P3P at http://www.w3c.org/P3P/.

You probably won't need TRUSTe certification unless you're running a large commercial site, but you should consider P3P for any website that collects personal information or uses cookies.

The actual format of a P3P file is fairly complex. It's worth investigating tools such as the free IBM P3P Policy Editor (http://www.alphaworks.ibm.com/tech/p3peditor) or the commercial P3Pwriter (http://www.p3pwriter.com/) when you're ready to create a P3P file for your own website. Figure 14.10 shows the IBM P3P Policy Editor in action.

To use the P3P Policy Editor, you select pieces of information and associate them with groups of possible uses. The tool automatically generates a list of the privacy implications, as well as policy files in both human-readable (HTML) and machine-readable (XML) formats.

Trademark Pages

If you own a trademark, it's your duty to protect that trademark. Part of this duty involves notifying people that something *is* a trademark. If you're selling a single software product, it might make sense to simply include the appropriate trademark symbol after every reference to that product on your website. But once you're dealing with more than a couple of products, that approach can be cumbersome. That's why most large sites include a trademark page similar to the one shown in Figure 14.11, which is taken from Microsoft's website.

Of course, if your site doesn't involve any trademarks or other intellectual property that you're required to protect, you can safely skip creating a trademark page.

Terms and Conditions Pages

To be honest, most users pay no attention at all to the Terms and Conditions of use (sometimes called Terms of Use, Terms of Service, or some other similar name) for a website. However, if you have lawyers, they will pay attention. Most such pages have language to the effect that using the website indicates agreement to the listed conditions. Although there's some controversy as to whether this is in fact a legally binding contract, it's certain that not listing any terms is even less binding.

FIGURE 14.10
Editing a P3P policy

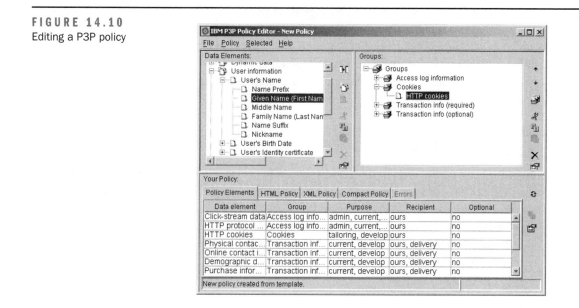

Microsoft Trademarks

Published: June 9, 2003 | Updated: August 18, 2004

This page contains the most current information on Microsoft trademarks. For guidance on how to refer properly to Microsoft product names and trademarks, review the General Trademark Guidelines.

- General Microsoft Trademark Guidelines

On This Page

↓ Microsoft Corporation Trademarks
↓ Xbox Video Games-Japan
↓ Great Plains Software, Inc., Trademarks
↓ Microsoft Business Solutions ApS Trademarks
↓ FRx Software Corporation Trademarks

Microsoft Corporation Trademarks

The absence of a name or logo in this list does not constitute a waiver of any and all intellectual property rights that Microsoft Corporation has established in any of its product, feature, or service names or logos.

Trademark	Status	Descriptor
ActiMates	®	Interactive toy
Active Accessibility	®	Programming interfaces tools
Active Desktop	®	Interface item
Active Directory	®	Directory service
ActiveMovie	®	Application programming interface
ActiveStore	®	Retail technology architecture
ActiveSync	®	Technology

Figure 14.12 shows the start of Microsoft's Terms of Use page.

Because the Terms and Conditions are intended to be a legal contract between the website operator and the user, it's impossible to give any general guidance as to their content. You should consult your own lawyer about whether you need such a page, and what its contents should be. I'll limit my advice to noting that it's not worth spending too much effort on a pretty design for this page because the number of users visiting it will probably be quite low. Concentrate on a readable presentation of information and move on.

Handling Site Navigation

You can spend all the time in the world creating interesting and useful content for a website, and then not have visitors go anywhere besides the home page. If you don't provide clear, consistent, and easy-to-use navigation around the site, that's what will happen. Remember, you know what pages are on the site and how they're related to one another. Your visitors do not, at least not when they first come to the site. If you want repeat traffic and happy users, it's up to you to provide a workable navigation system.

FIGURE 14.12
Terms of Use page

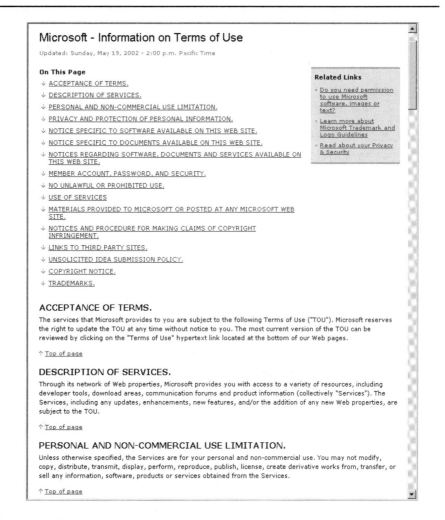

Fortunately, a number of navigation conventions have grown up over the lifetime of the Web. If you use these conventions, users are likely to think "Ah, I know how to get around this site." I already mentioned three of these conventions:

- The home page provides a fixed reference point for the site, reachable by a single click from anywhere within the site. If the user feels completely lost and wants to start over, a click on your site logo should take her back to the beginning (unless, of course, she's so frustrated that she just gives up and goes somewhere else).

- The site map provides a quick way to locate major chunks of the site by browsing through a list of links.

- The search page provides a way to locate information of interest by searching the entire site or some subset of the site.

But there are many other navigation conventions to consider using, including the following:

- Persistent navigation

- Hierarchical navigation

- Breadcrumb navigation

- What's New pages

- Adaptive websites

I'll discuss these techniques in the following sections.

Persistent Navigation

The idea of *persistent navigation* is simple: Keep the navigation controls visible and obvious at all times. The easiest way to do this is to make sure that the main navigation controls are the same—and in the same location—on every page. This might be at the top of the page or in a column to the left of the page, depending on your design preference. Figure 14.13 shows how persistent navigation works on the SlashDot website.

As you move through the SlashDot site, the content of the pages change (of course). But whether you're looking at the home page, at a particular story, or at your user preferences page, the navigation links down the left side of the page remain constant. After only a short while of using the site, the user will develop a sense of "Oh, to go to user preferences I always click *here*." This makes the site easier to use.

Almost every large website uses some form of persistent navigation, from drop-down menus created with DHTML to the tabs at the top of Amazon's shopping pages. The persistent navigation controls don't take to you every page of a large site, but they do provide a consistent and reliable way for users to jump to major areas. As a side benefit, they also indicate what those major areas are, letting users know what's on the site that they might like to explore.

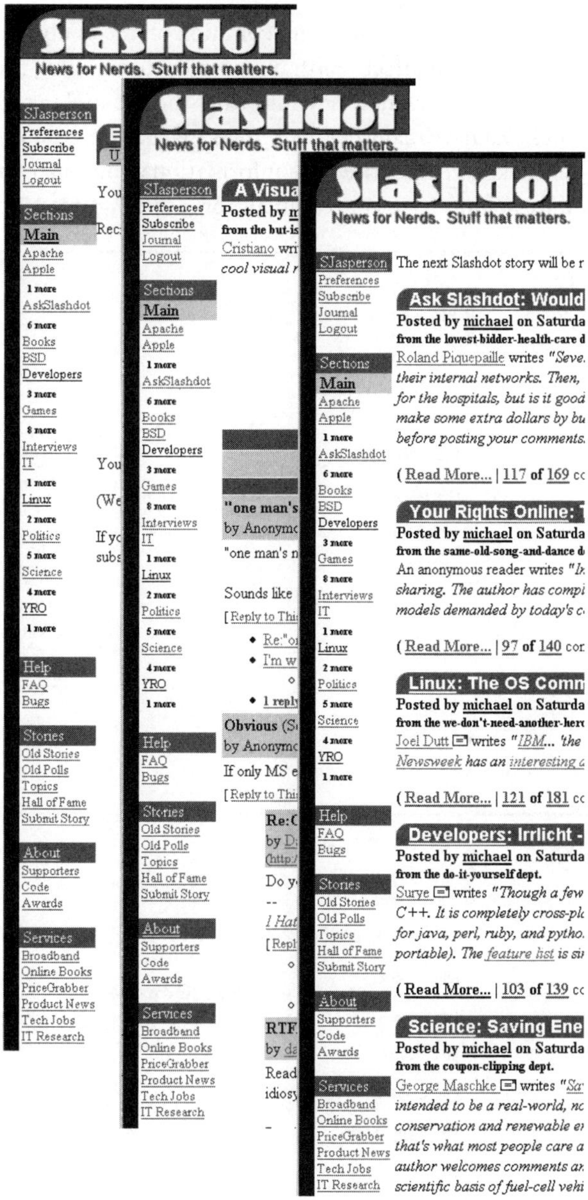

FIGURE 14.13
Persistent navigation
in action

Hierarchical Navigation

Hierarchical navigation is also very common on the Web, and it's often combined with persistent navigation to good effect. With hierarchical navigation, the user follows links down a logically organized hierarchy until they find what they're looking for. This approach often works well with sites that have many detailed pages that can be grouped into sections and subsections. This might be a knowledge base with information about many products, a zoology site that lets you view information on various animals, or (as in Figures 14.14 through 14.17) a shopping site.

FIGURE 14.14
Hierarchical navigation: top level

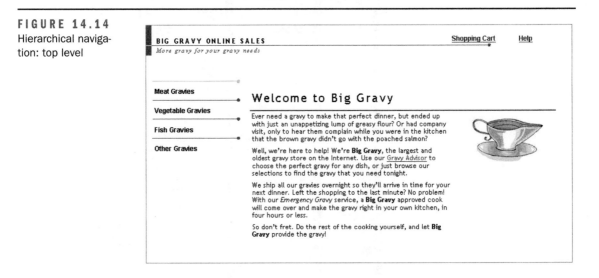

FIGURE 14.15
Hierarchical navigation: second level

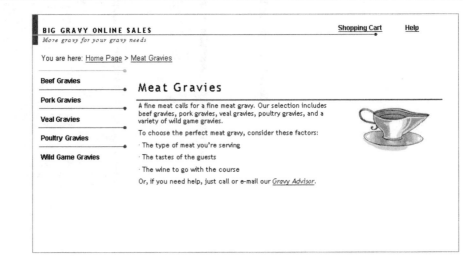

FIGURE 14.16
Hierarchical naviga-
tion: third level

BIG GRAVY ONLINE SALES   Shopping Cart   Help
More gravy for your gravy needs

You are here: Home Page > Meat Gravies > Wild Game Gravies

Venison Gravies

Moose Gravies

Wild Boar Gravies

Yak Gravies

Alligator Gravies

Wild Game Gravies

When you need to impress your guests with your lavish,
spare-no-expense lifestyle, consider one of our fine wild game
gravies. We spare nothing to bring you great taste in these
gravies, but just as importantly, we spare nothing to make the
price tag impressive. Each shipment comes with a handy
duplicate invoice that you can leave casually on your desk to
impress the snoopy guest.

For an even more exotic experience, contact our Special
Gravies department and ask about a **Gravy Safari**. Imagine being
the first one on your block to come home with rhinoceros
gravy!

FIGURE 14.17
Hierarchical naviga-
tion: products

BIG GRAVY ONLINE SALES   Shopping Cart   Help
More gravy for your gravy needs

You are here: Home Page > Meat Gravies > Wild Game Gravies > Yak Gravies

Yak Gravies   TO CONTACT US CALL:
                                 1-888-555-GRAVY

List the products that your company offers. To add more products, copy and paste additional
text boxes.

Best Yak Gravy
Our "five star" yak gravy, made exclusively from the marrow of contented yaks
raised on the sunny southern slopes of the mountains and fed pure imported
Alaskan summer hay.

SKU/Item Number: Y0101   Add to Cart   **Price: $199.95**

Everyday Yak Gravy
You can use this reasonably-priced yak gravy for every occasion. The yaks may not
be the best, but they're still flavorful!

SKU/Item Number: Y0102   Add to Cart   **Price: $29.95**

Yak Gravy for Kids
Problems getting your kids to eat meals with healthy, nutritious gravy? Try this
alternative! Each pint of yak gravy is mixed with one pint of pure clover honey.
They'll think they're getting a sticky treat while you load them with vitamins.

SKU/Item Number: Y0103   Add to Cart   **Price: $59.95**

You can see in this series of figures how this hypothetical store handles navigation for its website, which contains thousands of products. Across the top of each page there's a persistent navigation section with tabs for the major departments, the company logo to jump back to the home page, and utility links (such as help and shopping cart links). Down the left side of the page you'll find the hierarchical navigation links. As you click each link, you're presented with further choices to narrow down your selection until ultimately you arrive at a page containing products. Note that each page also has clear text telling you exactly where you are; if you click on a Meat Gravies link, the next page is clearly marked as being Meat Gravies. Thus at any time the user can see where they are, how to get back to the top level of the site, or what their choices are for drilling down further.

Breadcrumb Navigation

Another navigation aid found on many web pages goes by the rather informal name of "breadcrumbs." Figure 14.18 shows some breadcrumbs (in fact, these breadcrumbs are also visible in Figure 14.17).

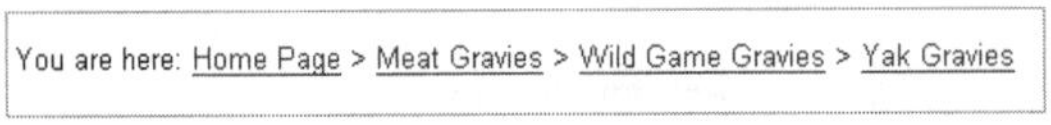

FIGURE 14.18
Breadcrumb
navigation

You are here: Home Page > Meat Gravies > Wild Game Gravies > Yak Gravies

Breadcrumb navigation shows where you are and how you got there. In the case of Figure 14.15, it's clear to most web users that they're on a page devoted to Yak Gravies, and that they got there from the home page through three intermediate pages. Breadcrumbs don't give you a sense of how to move forward; you can't tell from this portion of the interface what your choices are for continuing with your drilldown. But they do provide you with an easy way to move back as many levels as you want. If the user realizes that Yak Gravies are not what they want, they can back up directly to the Meat Gravies page and start over.

Breadcrumbs are lightweight, unobtrusive, and don't take up much space. If your site includes a hierarchical navigation system with more than two levels, it's worth including breadcrumb navigation as well.

What's New Pages

Most of the navigation tools I've discussed thus far are aimed at both new visitors to your site and repeat customers. What's New pages are different; they're almost entirely for people who have been to your website before. A well-designed What's New page will answer the question "What's changed since the last time that I was here?" Figure 14.19 shows a typical What's New page, this one from the U.S. Environmental Protection Agency's website.

FIGURE 14.19
What's New page

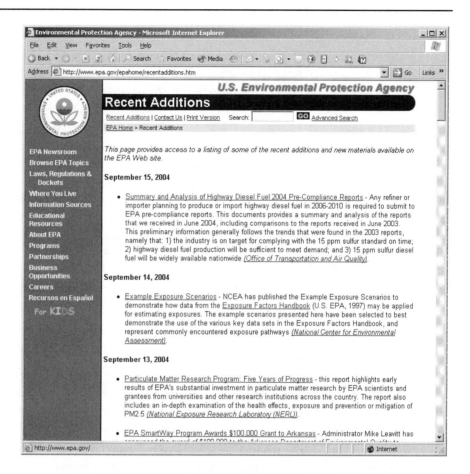

What's New pages are generally arranged with the newest items at the top. That way, users can read in a natural order until they get to things they recognize, rather than scrolling to the end of the page and reading up. Most What's New pages are simply links, possibly with short explanatory text.

Not every site needs such a page. On a news site, where there is new content on a fixed schedule that's always in the same place, such a page would be superfluous. Sites that are unchanging obviously don't need such a page either, although this is rare on the Internet.

NOTE   Many weblogs are nothing but a single page with a What's New arrangement: short items in reverse chronological order.

Adaptive Websites

Developers sometimes realize that a website does not have to be the same for every visitor. There are two ways to personalize a website for each visitor. The first is to depend on information that the visitor enters himself. For example, a news site could provide a registration form that collects information including which categories of news the visitor is interested in. When that person visits the home page of the website, it would display news only from the selected categories.

A more sophisticated approach is to depend on what the user does, rather than what he says, in customizing the website. This leads to an *adaptive website*, which learns from the user's actions. For example, Amazon.com keeps track of each user's purchases. When you visit the Amazon site and sign in, you'll be greeted with customized sales and suggestions based on what you've purchased in the past as well as what Amazon's computers have deduced about your tastes.

WARNING   Be careful about making personalization too aggressive. If you let people turn off the display of some content or turn it off automatically, make sure that there's a way to turn it back on. Otherwise, you'll be locking users out of some part of your website that they might later change their mind and want to see.

Creating Web Applications

It's relatively easy to offer advice for traditional websites. They've been around long enough to build up a body of knowledge and convention. Web applications are a different matter. The migration of desktop applications to the browser has really gotten underway only in the last several years, and developers are still struggling with how best to make the transition.

Web applications can replace almost any activity that the user might perform on their desktop computer: putting together an HTML page, balancing a checkbook, registering for classes, or cataloging books, for example. Web applications are often more complex than websites, and they usually involve interacting with a database on the server side of the connection. Though websites require upfront planning (how else, for example, would you get a consistent navigation structure?), web applications typically require even more design. It's not unusual for a web application to go through the same formal design process as a desktop application.

The actual mechanics of creating a web application depend heavily on which tools you use: ASP.NET, Java, or other alternatives. But some general guidelines can help get you thinking in the right direction:

- Don't try to mimic the design of a complex desktop application exactly in a web application. Multiple open windows might work well in a desktop application, but are normally just confusing in a web application. Complex custom controls often do not translate well to the Web, either.

- Keep the individual pages of the web application as simple and lightweight as possible. Remember that users might have limited bandwidth or browser limitations that prevent complex pages from working properly.

- Code defensively in the database layer because you don't get any explicit notification if the user abandons the application in midstream. Always allow for and clean up any lingering stale connections.

- Make sure that any requirements, such as accepting cookies or using a browser that can handle CSS, are made clear to users before they get deeply into the application.

- Keep the web application flow simple, with as few branches as possible (ideally none).

- Keep track of the application's state in a persistent location such as a cookie so that it does not become confused if the user clicks the Back button to revisit a page.

Although these guidelines make sense for most Web applications, you need to use your judgment when applying them. If you're in a position to control the user's browser (as you may be for intranet applications), and the application requires a complex user interface, by all means create one. For example, Figure 14.20 shows the user interface of Microsoft Outlook Web Access, a Web application that can retrieve e-mail from Exchange Server and perform other tasks similar to those built into regular Outlook.

FIGURE 14.20
Outlook Web Access

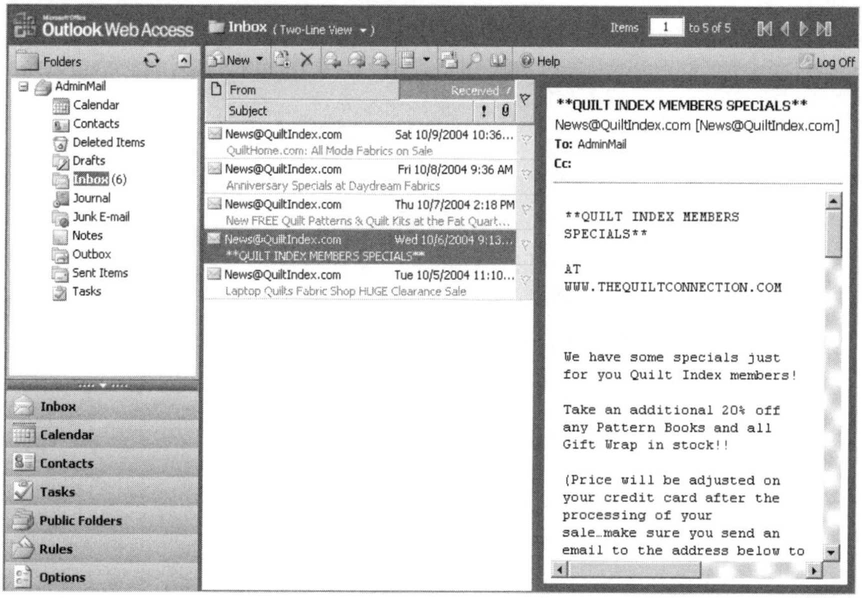

Microsoft went to a lot of trouble to make Outlook Web Access look and feel like the desktop version of Outlook. But there are several tradeoffs to this approach. First, the application only runs well in a current version of Internet Explorer. Second, it requires considerable bandwidth compared to simple pages. Finally, it's nearly as complex as the desktop version, requiring training for new users. But as a way to get your e-mail remotely when you're already committed to Microsoft technologies, it works well.

Summary

Although the Web is a blank canvas, and HTML is reasonably flexible, you can't do whatever you want and still have a successful user interface. By sticking to web conventions as far as possible, you can ensure that users have a productive and enjoyable experience with your website or web application. Using standard pages and navigational techniques help make the user feel at home and get them over the confusion (and sometimes fear) of using an unfamiliar application.

Most of the pages that I've discussed so far have been static, concerned with presenting information but not collecting it. In the next chapter I'll focus a bit more on interaction patterns between users and dynamic web pages.

CHAPTER 15

Common Web Interaction Patterns

- Thinking More About Search

- Handling Electronic Commerce

- Form Annoyances and Fixes

When you move beyond static web pages, you need to spend time thinking about how users will interact with the pages. Although the Web is more flexible than Windows, there are still general principles that you can learn to guide you to more effective pages. In this chapter, I'll discuss some of the alternatives that you can use when setting up search on a website, consider the design of effective e-commerce sites, and then dive into some of the pitfalls and techniques for setting up usable web forms.

Thinking More About Searching

In Chapter 14, "Common Web Design Patterns," I talked about the importance of having a search feature on your website. Now I'll take a closer look at the actual design of search. There are three basic ways that you can implement searching for a website:

- Simple search
- Advanced search
- Outsourced search

Let's look at each of these in turn.

Simple Search

Most users don't want to be bothered with options when they're searching (or else they're not prepared to deal with search options). For these users, a simple search interface is best. In fact, a standard interface has evolved for this purpose, as shown in Figure 15.1.

Because this interface is so standard, you should resist the temptation to dress it up or alter it. Don't use any term other than "Search" to label it; even though "Find" is a reasonable synonym and might fit in with your own design ideas, it's not what people will be looking for.

A simple search box is often part of the persistent navigation for a site. As such, you should keep it near the top of the page, and in the same relative position on every page. Many sites seem to use the right edge of the persistent navigation controls for this purpose, so if you do the same, your search interface will be even easier for people to find.

One thing you do need to consider is just how much of your site the simple search box will actually search. What most users are most likely expecting is full-word search with stemming (matching other forms of the search term). That is, entering "pose" should match "poser" and "posing," but not "adipose." Depending on your tools, you might find this difficult to set up, in which case I'd suggest a simple search that matches the term—no matter where it's found in a word. If the user enters multiple terms in a simple search box, treat them as being separated by OR. If they enter multiple terms surrounded by quotation marks, treat them as a phrase search.

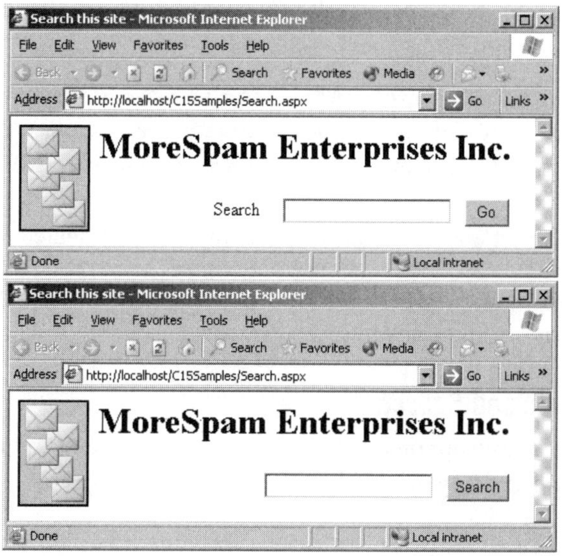

FIGURE 15.1
Standard forms for
simple search

Simple search should generally search the entire site. But there are exceptions to this rule. For example, on a shopping site you should probably just search product pages, not things such as shipping instructions or terms and conditions.

Advanced Search

In some cases, simple search won't do the job. This generally happens when the number of results returned by the simple search is overwhelming. In such cases, you need to offer the user tools for finding what they want within the simple search results. The normal way to offer such tools is through an advanced search page. Here are some of the options you can offer on an advanced search page:

Search in results   Perform another simple search, but this time only search the pages returned by the first search instead of the entire website.

Limit results by date   This is usually implemented by allowing users to specify that a page must have been added or changed in the last n days.

Limit results by category   This provides the user with subsets of the website to search. For example, Amazon lets you decide to search only books, only software, and so on. A university site might allow searching by department.

Easy Boolean search   You can implement the basics of Boolean search by providing four data entry boxes, as shown in Figure 15.2. Users don't need to know that these generate search expressions "behind the scenes."

Full Boolean search   Allow users to enter complex search expressions such as (`lion or tiger`) `and not grass`. This allows the user to construct very powerful searches, but might be difficult for many visitors to grasp and use effectively.

TIP   You might want to include a link to the advanced search page from your persistent navigation area, but there's an even better place to put such a link: on the search results page. After all, when does a user know better that they need to limit their search than right after a simple search has returned too many results?

Outsourced Search

A third search option is to let someone else do it. For example, Google offers its SiteSearch service, which lets you add HTML to your own pages to display a Google search box, as shown in Figure 15.3.

Details on Google's free search services are available at `www.google.com/searchcode.html`. In addition to the site search, you can also set up a plain Google web search from your page, either with or without their "SafeSearch" filter (which removes adult-oriented content from the results).

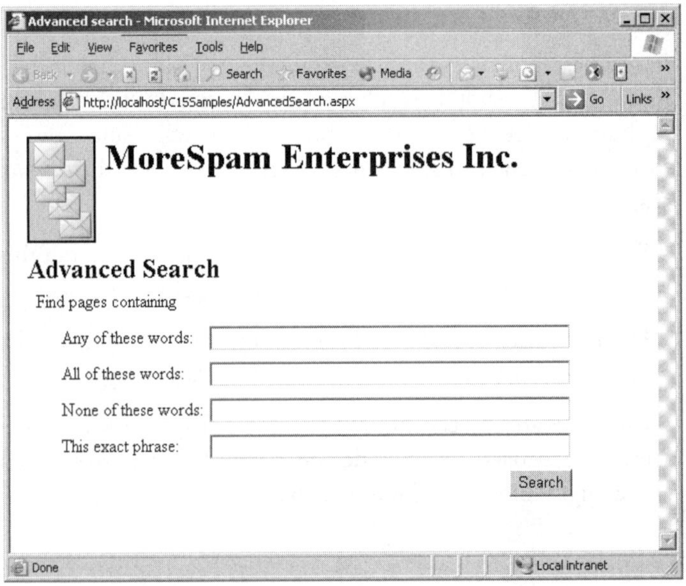

FIGURE 15.2
Easy Boolean search

Using a major search engine to search your site has pros and cons. On the plus side, users are likely to recognize the search box more quickly if it's associated with the logo of a major search engine, and might have more faith in the results. On the minus side, you have no control over the format of the results, or even which of your site's pages will be indexed. On the whole, I suggest avoiding the outsourced search alternatives unless you have no means to program a customized search.

If you are planning to program a custom search, you can still consider an outsourced solution by using a programmatic interface to one of the major search engines. Google, for example, offers the Google Web API (www.google.com/apis/) in beta as I write this. If you can make a web services call from your software, you can use this API for free to perform up to 1,000 searches per day.

NOTE   For more details on using Google programmatically, see *Mining Google Web Services: Building Applications with the Google API* by John Mueller (Sybex, 2004).

Handling Electronic Commerce

Some of the largest and most successful websites, such as Amazon, are built on the notion of electronic commerce, or *e-commerce*: buying and selling things over the Internet. No matter what product you're interested in, chances are that you can order it online these days. But that doesn't mean that there's no more room for new e-commerce sites. As time goes on, more and more existing businesses are opening storefronts on the Internet, so the need to design new e-commerce sites is likely to remain with us for some time.

Good design for a web storefront can mean the difference between happy customers who come back for repeat visits and dissatisfied customers who go elsewhere. In the real world, it can be inconvenient or impossible to drive to a competitor's place of business when you're an upset customer; the nearest competitor might be 50 or 500 miles away. But on the web, the competition is a single search and a mouse click away. That makes the creation of effective e-commerce sites an important skill for the web designer. Here are some factors to take into account when building such a site:

- Keep easy navigation in mind. At any time, the user should be able to figure out how to get more details on a product, to back up to a more general category, or to get help. The use of breadcrumb navigation (discussed in Chapter 14) is ideal for any e-commerce site with a complex hierarchy of products.

- Make it easy to find products. This means not just including top-down navigation, but including an effective search mechanism. Ideally, you should include a search box on every page of the site, so there's never a need to back up and start over if the user decides that they want a different product.

- Keep pages small and quick to load. Though this is important for any site, it's especially important if you want people to stick around and spend money. If you're using product images, include a low-resolution image on the main product page and let users click on it if they want to see a more detailed image.

- You can also keep pages small by presenting a variable level of detail. Start by showing just a product's name, image, price, and a brief description. Then include a prominent link that the user can click to get more detailed information.

- If you carry alternative products (for example, more than one type of left-handed monkey wrench) make it easy for the user to compare the alternatives. One way to do this is by allowing the user to pick a selection of products from a search page, and using that selection to build a comparison page on the fly.

- Don't force the user through the checkout process. At any point they should be able to inspect the contents of their shopping cart, and even begin the checkout process, without being locked out of the rest of the site. Even if they've done everything except click the Save Order button, you want it to be easy for them to go back and add more items to their order.

- Do save unfinished shopping carts. People may navigate away from your site for a variety of reasons. Perhaps they want to check on deals elsewhere, or perhaps their boss just walked into the office. Either way, when they come back to your site, you have a better chance of making a sale if you didn't throw away the results of their previous visit. One way to do this is by saving a unique shopping cart ID in a cookie (but remember to mention this in your site's privacy policy).

- Give users reasons to come back to your site. The more time they spend there, the more likely they are to buy something. Two tools that you can use for this are a newsletter to announce new products and a page of unannounced special pricing.

As an e-commerce site grows in complexity, there are many other features that you can add. For example, personalization is an increasingly important force in e-commerce. When you revisit a site that you've previously purchased from, you may be offered special prices or featured items that are intended to appeal to you, based on your past purchases. When you're ready to add this level of sophistication, you should consider buying an off-the-shelf solution such as Microsoft Commerce Server (www.microsoft.com/commerceserver/) rather than building everything from scratch yourself.

Form Annoyances and Fixes

Web forms are relatively simple things. As you've seen in earlier chapters, you only have a limited number of components to work with when defining a web form. Despite this simplicity, web forms can be very challenging from a design standpoint. Several factors combine to make it hard to come up with really usable web forms:

- Users typically approach web forms and web applications with little or no training and few expectations.

- Users must figure out what the web form does and how they're supposed to fill it out without any prior knowledge.

- Users typically fill out a web form once and then move on, so there's no opportunity to benefit from experience.

But there's one more factor that contributes heavily to the difficulties that users have with web forms: Many web forms are designed exceedingly poorly. This factor, fortunately, is under your control. In this section, I'll offer some notes on what you should do—and avoid—when building forms for the Web.

Handling Required Fields

Most web forms have at least one required field. Leave that field blank, and at best you'll get a polite reminder on the page to fill it in; at worst you'll get an ugly error message. Why, then, do some web forms not notify the user in advance which fields they must fill in? There's really no excuse for this.

There are two standard ways to mark the required fields on a form. The first is to add some sort of text message, as shown in Figure 15.4. The other is to use a marker (typically an asterisk or bullet) next to the required fields, as shown in Figure 15.5.

TIP   If you use markers to indicate required fields, be sure to include an explanation of the marker somewhere on the form. Don't assume that people will deduce the meaning of the marker symbol on their own.

Handling Formatted Data

You'll often want to collect data in a particular format—for example, Social Security numbers or credit card numbers. In these cases, it's important to make data entry as easy as possible. You can do two things to help the user: Be explicit about what you'll accept and be forgiving about the way it's entered.

FIGURE 15.6
A poor phone number
entry control

Enter phone number:

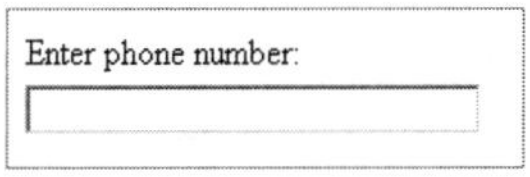

Consider phone numbers, for example. Figure 15.6 shows a first attempt at collecting phone numbers.

Without any guidance, a user might choose to enter their phone number in any of these formats, among others:

- 555-1212
- 206-555-1212
- 206.555.1212
- (206) 555-1212
- (206)-555-1212
- 1-206-555-1212
- +1 206 555-1212

If your backend application is expecting only one of these formats, and the user chooses another format, unpleasantness will result. The first step of dealing with this issue is to tell the user what you're expecting, as shown in Figure 15.7.

FIGURE 15.7
Improved phone
number entry control

Enter phone number:

Example: 206-555-1212

But you can do better than this. As long as the user enters both the area code and phone number, a little programming on the server can convert any of these formats to the one that you want to store. So why make the user do extra work? Figure 15.8 shows a user interface design for a more forgiving phone number entry control.

The same technique can be applied to other data with variable formatting. For example, you should allow users to enter credit card numbers with any combination of spaces and dashes, and just strip out the extraneous information when you store the data that was entered.

FIGURE 15.8
Even more improved
phone number entry
control

Enter phone number with area code:

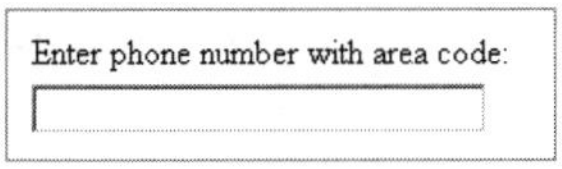

Limiting Data Entry

A lot of the data that gets input through forms ends up in databases, which means that it's subject to various limits: limits on length or on acceptable values are the most common. You need to take these limits into account when designing your forms, preferably in a way that makes them clear to users.

The easiest fields to handle are those that accept only one of a fixed range of values. For these fields, you should use a choice control such as radio buttons (for a small number of possible answers) or drop-down lists, as shown in Figure 15.9. Either of these alternatives prevents the user from entering an unacceptable value.

FIGURE 15.9
Limiting data entry
with choice controls

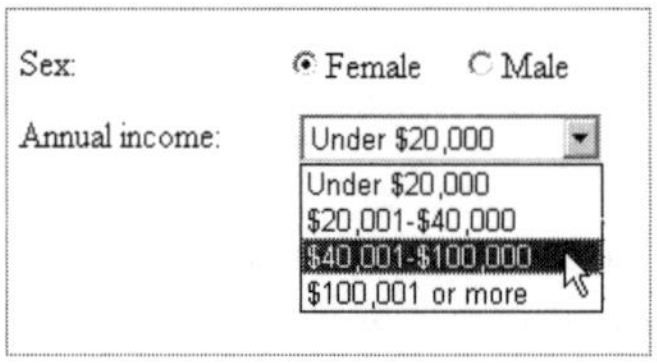

In some cases, you might choose to populate drop-down lists dynamically from a database. This is a good technique to prevent having to change pages frequently. But if you do so, you need to make sure that the dynamic content still matches up with the static content. Figure 15.10 shows an example of what *not* to do.

FIGURE 15.10
Mismatch between
dynamic and static
content

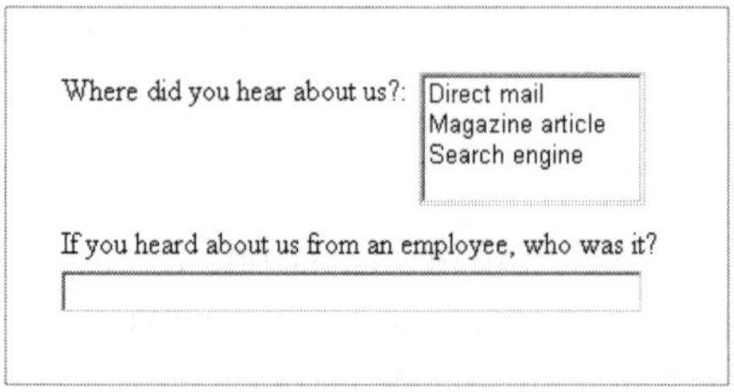

Apparently the list box included the choice "Employee referral" at some point, and the text box beneath it made sense at that time. Now it doesn't. The best solution to this problem is not to combine dynamic form content with static content; either generate everything from the database, or make everything static and modify it by hand as needed.

When data is free-form, limiting the data entry is a bit trickier. Often the only limitation is on the length of the data that you can store in the database. That's fine; no one expects to be able to enter a whole novel when asked for the name. But as with other limits on web forms, you should make this limit clear to the user right on the form.

Suppose that you're prompting for the user's name for your records, and your database accepts 30 characters in this field. If you just drop a text box on the form and let it go at that, all will be well until some user enters 31 characters. At that point, you'll be stuck trapping an error message again.

One thing you can do is notify the user after they post the form, as shown in Figure 15.11.

FIGURE 15.11
Violation of length
limits

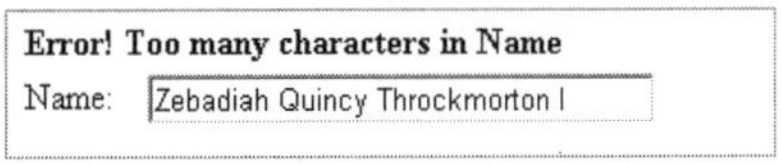

> Error! Too many characters in Name
>
> Name: Zebadiah Quincy Throckmorton I

But there's no need to make the user wait for a round-trip to the server in this simple case. HTML text boxes support a maxlength attribute that dictates the number of characters that they will accept. If your database takes only 30 characters from a particular text box, set the maxlength for that text box to **30**.

But that's still not quite enough for a good user interface. If the user is typing quickly, they might not notice that their entry in a text box is truncated. Or, worse, they might notice and spend a while banging on the keyboard trying to figure out why they can't enter what they want to. The solution is to make the limit explicit, as shown in Figure 15.12.

FIGURE 15.12
A well-designed limited
text box

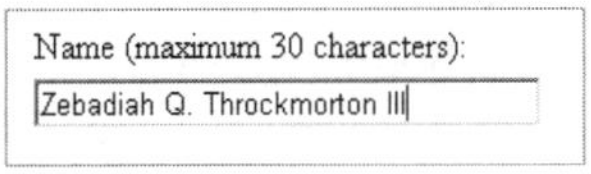

> Name (maximum 30 characters):
> Zebadiah Q. Throckmorton III

NOTE   As a general rule, you should validate as much data as you can before a form is posted back to the server. Even if you can't validate with attributes, you can use client-side scripting for validation, which lets validation occur practically immediately as the user is typing, rather than making them wait for the server to process the request and send back the response.

Handling International Input

Limiting the width of fields (in your database or on your web pages) can get you into hot water in other ways as well. Suppose that you put in a five-digit Zip code field. The first time you get a potential Canadian customer, you have a mess because they use six-character postal codes in Canada.

The Web being what it is, just about any page will eventually be used by people from countries other than your own. You can approach this issue in three basic ways:

- Just flat-out refuse to deal with it, perhaps with a note at the top of the form saying "U.S. Residents Only."
- Attempt to determine the user's location and present appropriate data-entry controls.
- Develop a "one-size-fits-all" form.

Unless you're absolutely sure that you don't have, never will have, and never will want any international customers, the first of these alternatives is pretty unappealing. The second is feasible, although it's nearly impossible to determine automatically where a particular user is browsing from. Still, you can prompt them to select their country from a list and jump to an appropriate customized form when they do.

However, developing one form per country will increase your costs substantially over developing a single standardized form. Most organizations will find the third option here the most palatable. To properly handle international input, no matter where the user is located, requires you to consider several different factors:

- Addresses are a huge source of confusion. In addition to the different sizes of postal codes, there are differing standards for how many lines an address should take up, which state abbreviations are appropriate, and the use of punctuation, among other things. Generally, you'll need to provide people a way to enter two address lines, plus a city, state or province, postal code, and country. You might find Frank's Compulsive Guide to Postal Addresses (www.columbia.edu/kermit/postal.html) useful in showing you how postal addresses are treated worldwide. Some fields that you think of as required probably aren't. Not every country uses postal codes or Zip codes, for example.
- Telephone numbers, too, vary in both their formatting and the number of digits. As I discussed previously, you can deal with some of this on the server. The best bet might be to have one box for the country code and another for the phone number, where people can use whichever format they prefer.
- People's names can also be a source of confusion. If you're a developer in the United States you're used to thinking of people as having first, middle, and last names—but this is not a universal convention. There are areas where middle names are uncommon. There are areas where a patronymic is inserted between the first and last names. Unless you really need to sort and search by the various parts of the name, you should provide just a single text box when you need to prompt for someone's name.

Handling Large Forms and Slow Users

Although keeping forms short and simple is a worthwhile goal, it's not always a practical one. A shopping site, for example, needs to confirm quantities and products, allow the user to choose a shipping method, collect a shipping address and a billing address, and prompt for payment information as part of the checkout process. Putting this all into a single huge form makes the process daunting for many users.

Instead, you should break large forms up into several smaller forms, with each form displaying the next when the user clicks the Submit button. Try to choose logical subsets of information for each form in the series.

There's another problem lurking here, though. When you break a single form into multiple forms, you need to track the user's state between forms. Otherwise, you can't (for example) match up the shipping and billing information. The usual solution for this is to use a temporary cookie on the user's computer. If you do this, be sure to not set the timeout of the cookie too low. For example, if your cookie times out in 30 minutes, and the user takes a lunch break in the process of filling out the series of forms, they'll have to start all over.

In many cases, you'll want to save some of the user's information permanently for future entry. If you can stash a customer number in a permanent cookie, for example, you can automatically fill in the last known shipping and billing addresses the next time that the customer visits your site. In the user interface, this is generally implemented with a check box, as shown in Figure 15.13.

FIGURE 15.13
Asking permission to
set a cookie

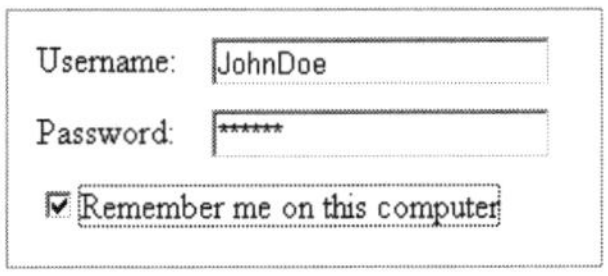

Handling Movement Issues

You might think that moving around a web page would be so simple as to be foolproof, but that's not the case. There are several things to keep in mind when designing web pages for navigation:

- HTML controls that can receive the focus have a TabIndex property. You need to make sure that this is set for every control and that the numbers go in a sensible order. If you neglect to do this, users can't navigate with the Tab key.

- Sometimes sites use client-side scripting to automatically advance the cursor when a field is completely filled-in. I'm not a fan of this technique, for the same reason that I don't like it in Windows applications: Users find it disconcerting to have the focus move around when they didn't explicitly tell it to do so.

- Any user who can manage to load a web page is comfortable with the Next and Back buttons on the browser, so there's no need to provide your own implementation of these tools. On multipage applications, however, you might still want to provide a way for users to tell where they are in the process, and to jump forward and backward. For example, Amtrak's ordering process, shown in Figure 15.14, shows clearly where you are at any given time, and offers an easy way to go back and review previous steps by clicking the step number.

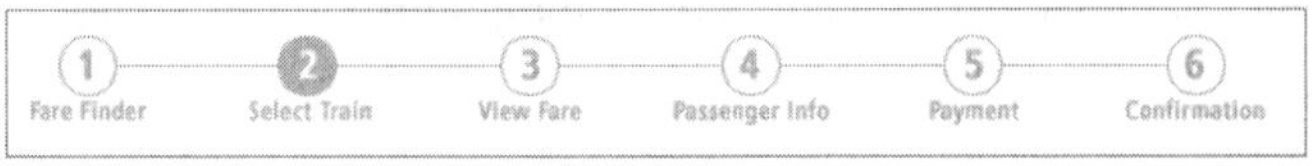

FIGURE 15.14
Navigation for a
multistep process

Avoid the Reset Button

The HTML specification provides two standard buttons for forms, Submit and Reset (although they might have different captions, of course). The Submit button is the one that sends your data to the web server, where it can be processed. The Reset button clears the contents of every control on the form, placing the form back in its initial configuration.

I'm sure that the Reset button seemed like a good idea at the time, but it's not the sort of idea that I want to present to most users. The problem is that the Reset button is potentially devastating and irreversible. When you've just spent 20 minutes filling out a complex web form, the last thing you want to do is click in the wrong place and have all of your precious data erased.

You can mitigate the danger of the Reset button somewhat with a few extra steps:

- Locate the Reset button after the Submit button in the tab order.
- Locate the Reset button physically far away from the Submit button, so it's harder to click by accident.
- Use client-side scripting to confirm Reset button clicks before processing them.

But why bother? Users these days know that they can clear a web form by closing and reloading it, or they can simply type over the data that they want to replace. The Reset button has very little function and a big downside, so it's best to just dispense with it entirely.

Summary

In this chapter, you learned about good HTML form design. The Web presents challenges (and solutions) that differ from those of Windows applications. But keeping the user in mind and making the best use that you can of the available tools will result in usable Web applications.

For the final chapter of the book, I'll look at a new user interface paradigm that combines some of the features of the Web and Windows: the user interface that's coming with Windows "Longhorn" and other Windows versions over the next several years.

Looking Forward to the Next Generation: Designing User Interfaces for Avalon

Things never stand still in the world of computer programming. Although it's been tweaked and adjusted since then, Microsoft most recently did a complete overhaul of the Windows user interface with the release of Windows 95 a decade ago. But that will change in the next year or two, when Windows "Longhorn" is scheduled to ship. In this survey, I'll discuss what we know (or think we know) about user interface design for the next generation of Microsoft Windows.

"Longhorn," "Avalon," and "Aero"

Microsoft has been working on the replacement for Windows XP for a long while now. In fact, some parts of the project appear to have been underway for at least a decade, although publicly released details are sketchy. The first public demonstrations of the new operating system, code-named "Longhorn," were made at the Microsoft Professional Developers Conference in the fall of 2003.

Since then, Microsoft has opened the floodgates for information, and there is quite a large section of the Microsoft Developers Network website devoted to Longhorn. This makes it possible to discuss the new operating system with some hope of getting the broad picture correct, although inevitably details will change between the time that I write this in late 2004 and the time that Longhorn ships (estimated to be some time in 2006).

For developers, Longhorn offers quite a few advances over the current generation of Windows operating systems. Although many of these improvements have no direct impact on user interface design, it's worth having some idea what's coming, so I'll briefly review them. Then I'll discuss the parts of Longhorn that most directly affect user interface design, code-named "Avalon" and "Aero."

WARNING   Screenshots and most of the information on Longhorn in this appendix are based on build 4074, which was released as a preview in mid-2004. This release, sometimes called M7.2, is pre-alpha and not feature complete. I can't emphasize strongly enough that details will change before the product actually ships.

"Longhorn"

Microsoft Windows "Longhorn" (Microsoft typically uses code names for its products until their release is imminent) is the successor to Windows XP as a client operating system. Key features for developers in this next-generation version of Windows include:

- A new programming model known as WinFX. WinFX, a superset of the .NET Framework, is built entirely of managed code. In Longhorn, WinFX replaces Win32 as the fundamental interface for programming the operating system.

- A new presentation subsystem, code-named "Avalon."

- A new user experience paradigm code-named "Aero." Aero, which is built using the Avalon APIs, determines the look-and-feel of the operating system.

- A new communications subsystem code-named "Indigo." Indigo will bring together Web Services, Microsoft Message Queuing (MSMQ), and COM+ into a unified way to expose functionality remotely. Indigo is the successor to the Web service and remoting communication APIs introduced with Microsoft .NET.

- A new command shell code-named "Monad." Monad offers an object-oriented way to add functionality to the command line.

- A new way to create user interfaces, by writing declarative code in an extensible markup language (XML) dialect known as extensible application markup language (XAML).

WARNING If you hunt around the Web, you'll also see references to an object-oriented file system named WinFS being part of Longhorn. Although WinFS was in the first Longhorn betas, Microsoft has now announced that it will not ship as part of Longhorn; it will be a separate add-on to be delivered later.

NOTE There will also be a server version of the Longhorn operating system, but Microsoft has released very few details and no code for that version. In this chapter, I'll be dealing strictly with the Longhorn client alpha code.

All in all, Longhorn is shaping up to be an extremely significant operating system release for Microsoft. For developers, Longhorn represents both an opportunity and a threat. The new application programming interfaces (APIs) and interfaces offer the opportunity of building cutting-edge applications with features that are simply impossible under the current versions of Windows. But the sweeping changes in the programming model mean that developers need to invest considerable time in learning before they can be productive writing code for Longhorn.

NOTE Microsoft revealed in mid-2004 that Avalon, Indigo, and WinFX would all be available for Windows XP and Windows 2003. We don't yet know the timing of these releases or whether they will differ in details from the versions that ship with Longhorn.

TIP Microsoft Developer Network members have access to preliminary Longhorn builds and documentation today. If you're at all interested in the next decade of Windows development, it's worth being signed up. Details are at http://msdn.microsoft.com.

"Avalon"

Avalon blurs the boundaries between desktop programming and web programming by using a markup language (XAML) for defining user interfaces. XAML offers new ways to perform old tasks, as well as new capabilities. In this section, I'll show you some of the basics of XAML, so you can get a flavor of what writing user interfaces may be like under Longhorn.

> **NOTE**   Although XAML is raw XML, you shouldn't assume that you'll need to write XML files by hand to create applications that use Avalon. Expect to see development tools such as Visual Studio automate XML creation, hiding the complexity of the XAML behind friendly visual designers.

Avalon Overview

Avalon applications typically combine two pieces: a declarative user interface piece written with XAML, and a procedural code piece written with a .NET language such as C# or Visual Basic.

> **NOTE**   Declarative languages specify what you want to create, rather than how it should be created. Hypertext markup language (HTML), for example, is a declarative language; you write tags to define what should be displayed, but it's up to the web browser to decide how best to display the results.

When you compile an Avalon application, the XAML and procedural pieces are compiled together. The XAML parser creates a partial class from the markup, with each tag mapping to a class, and each attribute mapping to a property. This partial class is combined with the partial class defined by the procedural code to create the complete application.

If your application is pure XAML (markup only, with no procedural code or events), it can be displayed in the web browser on Longhorn. If there is any code, the application needs to be compiled, after which you can run it from Windows Explorer. But any compiled Avalon application can be hosted in the browser by setting a single attribute. Switching back and forth is trivial.

In addition to the new model for creating applications, Avalon brings in new capabilities. For example, 3D graphics and multimedia interfaces are native parts of Avalon.

> **TIP**   If you want to experiment with XAML today, you don't have to install the Longhorn alpha code. Because Microsoft has released a fairly complete XAML specification, others can try to beat them to market. You can choose from an open-source implementation named MyXaml (www.myxaml.com/) or a commercial implementation named Xamlon (www.xamlon.com/) to build and deploy XAML interfaces today. There's no guarantee that either will precisely match the final Microsoft release, but they should be close enough for most purposes.

Hello XAML

The source code for the simplest Avalon application looks like this:

```
<DockPanel xmlns="http://schemas.microsoft.com/2003/xaml">
    <Text>Hello XAML</Text>
</DockPanel>
```

Not much to it, is there? But `DockPanel` and `Text` are special tags that have significance to the XAML parser in Avalon. Save this file with an .XAML extension and double-click it. You see the display shown in Figure A.1.

FIGURE A.1
Simple XAML file displayed by Longhorn

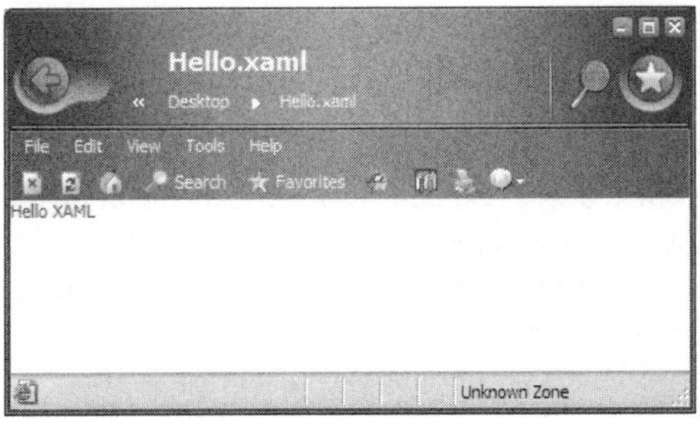

Using XAML Panels

The basic device for layout in XAML is the *panel*. A panel is a container that can hold controls. There are five built-in panel classes in Avalon:

- `Canvas`
- `DockPanel`
- `FlowPanel`
- `GridPanel`
- `TextPanel`

The `Canvas` allows you to position elements absolutely. A `Canvas` element can be positioned with x and y coordinates relative to its parent, so if you nest other elements within the `Canvas`, you can control their location as well. If you overlap elements, the z-order is controlled by the order the elements specified, with the last element being drawn on top of all the others. For example, this XAML file positions some text and two filled squares:

```
<Canvas ID="root"
    xmlns="http://schemas.microsoft.com/2003/xaml"
    Height="300"
    Width="400">
```

```
    <Canvas Height="100" Width="100"  Top="0" Left="0">
      <Text>This is some text</Text>
    </Canvas>
    <Canvas Height="100" Width="100" Top="100" Left="100">
      <Rectangle Width="100" Height="100" Fill="black"/>
    </Canvas>
    <Canvas Height="100" Width="100" Top="50" Left="50">
      <Rectangle Width="100" Height="100" Fill="gray"/>
    </Canvas>
  </Canvas>
```

Figure A.2 shows this file open in the Longhorn browser.

Note that the Canvas elements themselves are invisible, but that their attributes control the placement of their child controls.

The DockPanel allows you to dock child controls to its edges. When you place a control within a DockPanel, you can set its DockPanel.Dock attribute, as shown here:

```
<DockPanel ID="root"
      xmlns="http://schemas.microsoft.com/2003/xaml"
      Height="100%"
      Width="100%">
    <Text DockPanel.Dock="Top" FontSize="24">Top</Text>
    <Text DockPanel.Dock="Bottom" FontSize="24">Bottom</Text>
    <Text DockPanel.Dock="Left" FontSize="24">Left</Text>
    <Text DockPanel.Dock="Right" FontSize="24">Right</Text>
</DockPanel>
```

Figure A.3 shows the result.

FIGURE A.2
Using a Canvas element for positioning

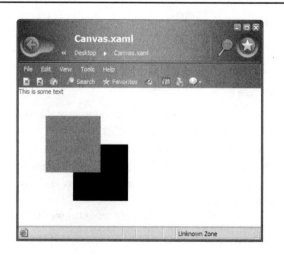

FIGURE A.3
Using the DockPanel

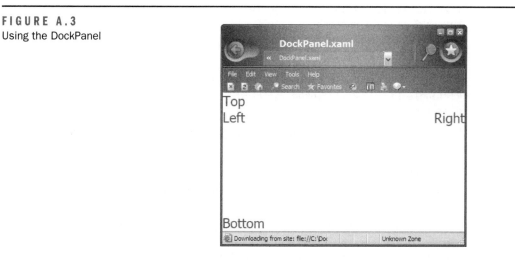

Use the FlowPanel when you want child elements to "flow," rearranging themselves to fit the available space (similar to the way that controls are laid out in a web browser). Here's an example of the FlowPanel in use:

```
<Canvas ID="root"
    xmlns="http://schemas.microsoft.com/2003/xaml"
    Width="200"
    Height="300">
    <FlowPanel Width="200" Height="300">
        <Rectangle Fill="gray" Width="75" Height="75" />
        <Rectangle Fill="black" Width="75" Height="75" />
        <Rectangle Fill="white" Width="75" Height="75" />
        <Rectangle Fill="gray" Width="75" Height="75" />
    </FlowPanel>
</Canvas>
```

In this example, the FlowPanel is defined to be 200 pixels wide. Longhorn starts laying out the child elements left-to-right, but it runs out of room after two of the rectangles have been created, so it wraps the other two rectangles to another row as shown in Figure A.4.

The GridPanel, as you can guess from its name, is used to arrange controls on a grid. When you create a GridPanel, you specify how many columns it should have; the child controls are arranged in that many columns within the grid:

```
<GridPanel ID="root"
    xmlns="http://schemas.microsoft.com/2003/xaml"
    Columns="3">
    <Text FontWeight="Bold">Column 1</Text>
    <Text FontWeight="Bold">Column 2</Text>
```

```
    <Text FontWeight="Bold">Column 3</Text>
    <Button>Button 1</Button>
    <Button>Button 2</Button>
    <Button>Button 3</Button>
    <Rectangle Fill="gray" Width="75" Height="75" />
    <Rectangle Fill="black" Width="75" Height="75" />
    <Rectangle Fill="gray" Width="75" Height="75" />
  </GridPanel>
```

Note that you can put any control you like in the grid. Figure A.5 shows this example open in the browser.

Finally, the TextPanel exists to hold text. However, unlike the simple Text element that you've already seen, the TextPanel supports a variety of sophisticated layout properties that let you control such things as the number of columns, the direction of flow, the minimum number of lines of a paragraph, and so on. Here's a small sample using the TextPanel:

```
<TextPanel ID="root"
    xmlns="http://schemas.microsoft.com/2003/xaml"
    Width="400" ColumnCount="2" ColumnGap="5">
This is some lengthy text to be displayed within a TextPanel
in two columns. The TextPanel takes care of all the layout
chores. You can use the attributes of the TextPanel element
to achieve a variety of complex text layouts.
</TextPanel>
```

Figure A.6 shows how this sample is rendered.

FIGURE A.4
Layout using the
FlowPanel

FIGURE A.5
Controls in a GridPanel

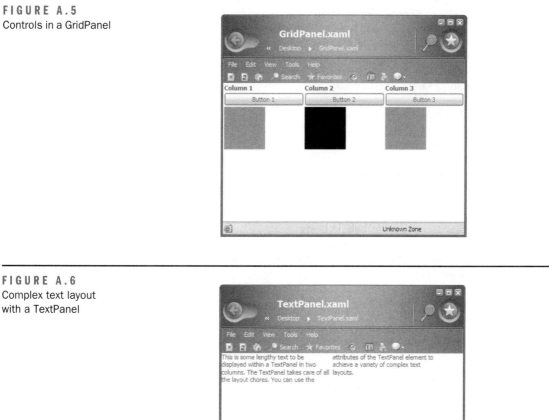

FIGURE A.6
Complex text layout
with a TextPanel

Complex Layout in XAML

Just like HTML, you can use XAML to create almost arbitrarily complex layouts. By employing a variety of tags and nesting them, you can cause Longhorn to display areas, text, controls, and so on. For just a small taste, consider this example file:

```
<DockPanel xmlns="http://schemas.microsoft.com/2003/xaml"
  xmlns:def="Definition" >
    <DockPanel.Resources>
```

```
<Style>
  <Text Foreground="Black"/>
</Style>
<Style def:Name="WhiteText">
  <Text Foreground="White"/>
</Style>
</DockPanel.Resources>

<Border DockPanel.Dock="Top">
    <Text>Some Text across the top of the window</Text>
</Border>

<Border DockPanel.Dock="Bottom">
    <Text>Some text across the bottom of the window</Text>
</Border>

<Border DockPanel.Dock="Left"
        Background="Black">
    <Text Style="{WhiteText}">Text in the left column in white</Text>
</Border>

<Border DockPanel.Dock="Fill">
    <DockPanel>
        <Button DockPanel.Dock="Top"
                Height="30px"
                Width="100px"
                Margin="10,10,10,10">Button1</Button>
        <Button DockPanel.Dock="Top"
                Height="30px"
                Width="100px"
                Margin="10,10,10,10">Button2</Button>
        <Border DockPanel.Dock="Fill">
            <Text >Some Text Below the Buttons</Text>
        </Border>
    </DockPanel>
</Border>
</DockPanel>
```

This code produces the user interface shown in Figure A.7.

Linking UI to Code

Although development is beyond the scope of this book, it's worth looking at a single sample of hooking XAML up to procedural code. The Longhorn SDK includes a sample called Word-game that presents a simple version of the classic Hangman game. Figure A.8 shows this game in action.

FIGURE A.7
More-complex
XAML layout

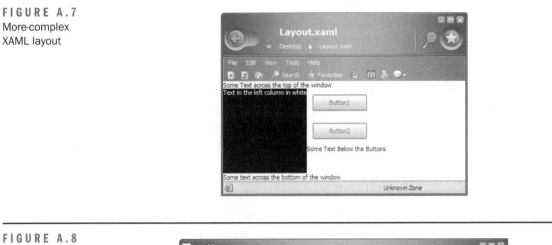

FIGURE A.8
Playing Wordgame

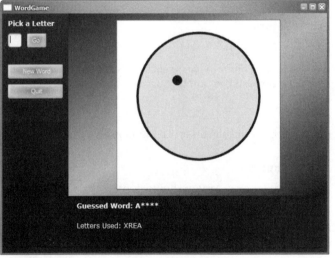

Here's a small portion of the XAML that defines the Wordgame user interface:

```
<Window xmlns="http://schemas.microsoft.com/2003/xaml"
     xmlns:def="Definition"
     def:Class="WordGame1_vb.Pane1"
     def:CodeBehind="Pane1.xaml.vb"
     Text="WordGame"
     UIReady="UI_Ready">
 …
     <Button DockPanel.Dock="Left"
          Margin="10,0,10,0"
```

```
                    Click="btnGo"
                    ID="goButton"
                    Height="25"
                    Width="35">Go</Button>
   ...
   </Window>
```

The Window element for the user interface (UI) defines a class and a code-behind file for the UI. This element is what tells Avalon that there is code associated with this user interface. Any individual element, such as the Button element shown here, can use its attributes to specify particular events to hook up. If you look in the corresponding Visual Basic source file, you'll find the code that this button calls:

```
Sub btnGo(ByVal Sender As Object, ByVal e As ClickEventArgs)
   Dim selectedLetter As Char
   Dim goodGuess As Boolean
   Dim i As Integer

   If guessedChar.Text = "" Then 'Check for empty text box
      Return
   End If

   selectedLetter = guessedChar.Text(0)
   _lettersUsed = _lettersUsed & selectedLetter
...
End Sub
```

The appropriate parsers and compilers take care of hooking everything up behind the scenes.

Avalon Controls

By the time it ships, Avalon should contain versions of all the familiar controls (such as the buttons and text boxes you saw in Figure A.8). In Build 4074, Avalon includes implementations of these controls:

Button	RadioButton
CheckBox	RadioButtonList
ComboBox	RepeatButton
ContextMenu	ScrollViewer
HorizontalScrollBar	TextBox
HorizontalSlider	Thumb
HyperLink	ToolTip
ListBox	VerticalScrollbar
Menu	

Most of these controls are familiar from previous versions of Windows. RadioButtonList offers a way to create an entire series of radio buttons as a single control. RepeatButton is a button that autorepeats, firing its associated event multiple times if the user holds down the button. ScrollViewer is a horizontal scroll bar coupled with a vertical scroll bar, providing a container for other controls that can be scrolled in two dimensions. Thumb is a small draggable control that's used to build up other controls such as scroll bars.

Avalon also includes several panel types other than the DockPanel that you saw previously. For example, Figure A.9 shows a simple use of the GridPanel control, which allows laying out of two-dimensional grids. You can expect to see it show up in many database-backed applications.

Properly speaking GridPanel isn't a control; it is a container for controls.

Layout with GridPanel

"Aero"

If you think of Avalon as providing the basic ingredients for cooking dinner, Aero is a specific style of cooking that Microsoft is defining as the native look and feel for Longhorn. You could build many other user interfaces from the Avalon components (just as you can cook a French meal or a German meal from the same basic foodstuffs), but following the Aero guidelines will make your Longhorn applications behave in ways that are consistent with the things that Microsoft plans to ship in the box.

Visual Changes

For starters, Aero includes the new styling for controls, borders, and so on. Your applications will get this "for free" when they're run on Longhorn, just as they look different depending on whether they're run on Windows XP or Windows 2000. Figure A.10 shows a representative Longhorn application: Windows Explorer.

You can see quite a few of the Aero enhancements in this figure:

- More-rounded and softer edges to various screen elements
- Crisper anti-aliased fonts
- Increased use of soft colors and gradients
- Larger and more-detailed icons

- Web-style navigation, with forward and back buttons on the upper left

- A "glassy" semi-transparent look

What you can't see in Figure A.10 is that many of these screen elements are animated, changing their appearance as you move the cursor over them. Aero will make good use of next-generation video cards (and you'll probably want to disable some of these features when working with older systems).

Longhorn also introduces the Sidebar to Windows. Figure A.11 shows the Sidebar, which is a permanent area to the right side of the screen.

The Sidebar is home to *tiles*, each of which is a small package of functionality. In Figure A.11, the tiles include a slide show of images, a feed of news headlines, search, system messages, and an analog clock. You can use the Longhorn programming tools to create more tiles as well. The Sidebar provides you with a place to host applications that's intermediate—between a full Windows application and a notification area icon. Tiles can contain controls, and the user can interact with those controls, just as in any other application.

Because tiles are limited in size, they're best suited for applications that don't require many controls, and that provide functionality the user is likely to need frequently regardless of what else they might be doing.

FIGURE A.10
Windows Explorer

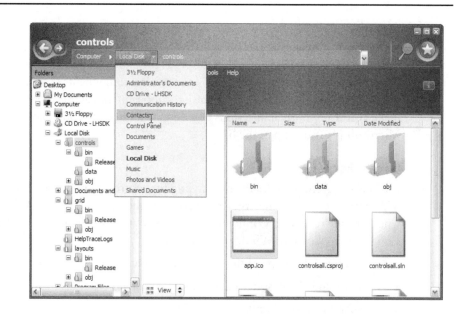

FIGURE A.11
The Sidebar

New Help System

There's more to Aero than just new visual styles. One of the other important pieces is a new help system designed to make it easier for users to find high-quality assistance when they run into a problem, or when they just want to know more about your application. Figure A.12 shows a sample of Longhorn help in action.

You create help for Longhorn using Microsoft Assistance Markup Language (MAML), which is yet another XML dialect. At runtime, Longhorn uses CSS stylesheets and other transformations to display MAML in a user-friendly form. One advantage of an XML authoring format is that Longhorn can change help delivery by changing style sheets—for example, any native Longhorn help file can be transformed to DHTML for browser-based delivery.

TIP   As with XAML, you shouldn't plan on writing MAML by hand. Help-authoring vendors will undoubtedly produce tools that put a friendlier face on the MAML authoring process.

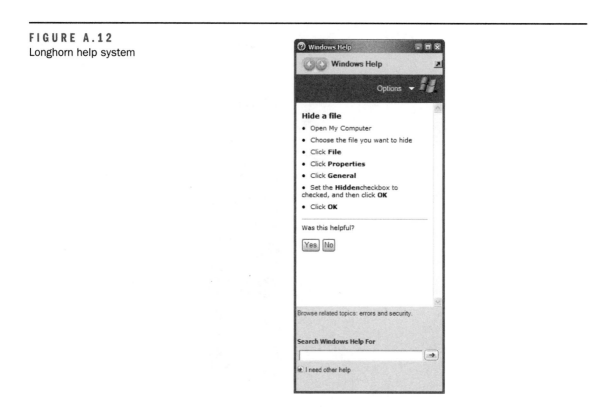

In Longhorn, all help is displayed by a single Help Pane application, rather than each application having its own separate help window. As the user navigates between applications, the Help Pane keeps in sync, showing the help for the current application. The Help Pane can float free or it can be docked to the side of the screen. When it's docked, the Help Pane reduces the working area for applications, so the user can automatically see both the application that they are working with and the help at the same time.

TIP   Of course, you can ship old help files with Longhorn applications. But if you do, you won't get the benefits of the new help system. Considering the importance of help in making applications usable, it's likely to be worth the effort to use the new technologies in this case.

Longhorn help also emphasizes several other cutting-edge features:

Task-based help   The user works from a list of potential tasks rather than the traditional index and table of contents.

Active help content   Allows help authors to script help behaviors so that the help context changes based on the user or current state of the machine.

Online updates   Continuously download new or improved content when the user is connected to the Internet.

Privacy and Security

Given the state of the computer industry, it's no surprise that Microsoft is also emphasizing user privacy and security for Longhorn and applications that are designed for it. If your application collects any user data, Microsoft recommends explicit attention to privacy and security. In particular, your application should follow these rules:

- Include an explicit privacy policy written in clear, non-technical language.

- Keep the user's data private by default. For example, if your application has the ability to log the user's actions, don't turn this feature on unless the user explicitly requests you to do so.

- Keep the application secure by default. Any settings that might compromise the security of the user's data should be kept locked down unless the user requests otherwise.

- Provide a way for the user to contact your organization for more information on privacy and security policies.

Application Archetypes

Longhorn introduces the concept of application archetypes. You can think of an *application archetype* as a pattern for an application's user experience. Each archetype identifies a class of applications and specifies guidelines for those applications:

- Document editor applications
- Database applications
- Production/development environment applications
- E-commerce applications
- Information/reference applications
- Entertainment applications
- Utility applications

Bear in mind that this list might change before Longhorn ships, and even some of the suggestions for working with Longhorn might change. But because many applications fit into these categories, it's worth looking at them in a bit more detail.

Document Editor Applications

Many applications exist to edit particular documents. For example, Microsoft Word and Excel fall into the category of document editor applications. For these applications, Longhorn suggests the following:

- Supplying thumbnail images for documents that Explorer can display
- Supporting live collaboration over the network
- Using the Longhorn versions of the File Open and File Save dialog boxes
- Using a task pane for user assistance

Database Applications

Database applications are rife in business today. With so much data stored in databases, it's natural that there are many applications to work with the data. Such applications often need to display a range of records, and then allow the user to edit, delete, and add single records.

Longhorn recommendations for this archetype include the following:

- Including ways to filter and sort records
- Using web-style navigation for browsing
- Using task-based data entry for inexperienced users
- Storing and transmitting information securely
- Linking any people stored in the database to Windows contacts
- Offering a built-in search tool
- Linking the database to Longhorn's own search
- Enabling offline use

Production/Development Environment Applications

Production/development environment applications handle the most demanding tasks that users perform. Examples of such applications include video manipulation applications and integrated development environments such as Visual Studio. For these applications, the Longhorn guidelines include the following:

- Use tabbed child windows instead of old-style MDI windows
- Build up projects from multiple documents rather than storing disparate data in a single document

- Enable collaborative editing
- Provide tools on dockable palettes

E-Commerce Applications

We've all used e-commerce applications by now. Microsoft is encouraging vendors to integrate e-commerce tightly with Longhorn. For example, in addition to a traditional website for e-commerce, a vendor could supply a rich client application that runs on Longhorn and that uses the Internet to communicate with the vendor's website.

Guidelines for such e-commerce applications include the following:

- Allow users to sort and filter lists of products
- Create shopping carts with standard functionality
- Ensure that user data remains private and secure
- Add user ratings to products
- Provide a way for users to get immediate online assistance

Information/Reference Applications

Information and reference applications include encyclopedias, magazine archives, reference databases, and so on. These applications allow the user to navigate through large amounts of information, typically in a browser-like application. For this archetype, Microsoft recommends the following:

- Use a navigation bar to provide the user information about where they are in the hierarchy
- Integrate web-hosted and local content
- Include search tools
- Include multimedia content in the data
- Use group discussion tools to enhance the information

Entertainment Applications

Entertainment applications such as games and interactive books are unique in Windows in that they usually take over the entire computer. When playing a modern computer game, users are not usually multitasking. Indeed, the standard Windows interface (such as the Taskbar and Sidebar) is usually not even visible while the game is running.

In the Longhorn timeframe, Microsoft recommends these features for entertainment applications:

- Allow users to find other users online
- Include text, audio, or video chat features
- Allow upgrades from a demo version to a full version
- Provide the ability to manage multiple saved games

Utility Applications

Utility applications perform one focused task. For example, Windows itself includes the Character Map tool and the Disk Defragmenter. Such applications are typically very simple, and the guidelines are simple as well:

- Don't require any installation beyond copying files to the hard drive
- Provide user assistance that helps the user remember how to perform infrequent tasks

Inductive User Interfaces

Microsoft is also promoting a user interface model that it calls the inductive user interface for Longhorn applications. *Inductive user interfaces (IUIs)* are designed to make it easier for users to understand and navigate through functionality in large applications. The name is chosen to contrast with the common style of presenting a user with a single application full of controls, and requiring the user to *deduce* the use of the different controls. In an IUI, the user is presented with only a few controls at a time, with the application's functionality broken up into screens and explicit navigation between screens.

Inductive User Interfaces are very similar to wizards (recall the discussion of wizards in Chapter 8, "Common Windows User Interface Elements"). The main difference is that wizards generally assume a linear set of steps that should be followed from start to finish, whereas an inductive user interface might include the ability to perform a task multiple times or to navigate in both directions among multiple tasks.

The key task of an inductive user interface is to answer two questions at all times:

- What am I supposed to do now?
- What can I do next?

To answer the first question, an inductive user interface generally includes a carefully chosen title for each page and some short explanatory text. To answer the second question, the interface provides navigation hyperlinks and web-style forward and back buttons instead of (or possibly in addition to) menu-based navigation.

For example, Figure A.13 shows ExpenseIt, one of the sample applications from the Longhorn software development kit. Note that the screen is uncluttered, that it's focused on a single task, and that there are hyperlinks to proceed to another task. A new user faced with this interface can probably figure out what to do, even without any assistance.

TIP   Inductive user interfaces represent a tradeoff. Although an application with such an interface might be easier for novices to use, it can be annoyingly tedious for more experienced users. If you create an application with such an interface, consider including an expert mode with a more traditional user interface. As an alternative, limit the inductive user interface to portions of the application that are less frequently used.

FIGURE A.13
Inductive user
interface

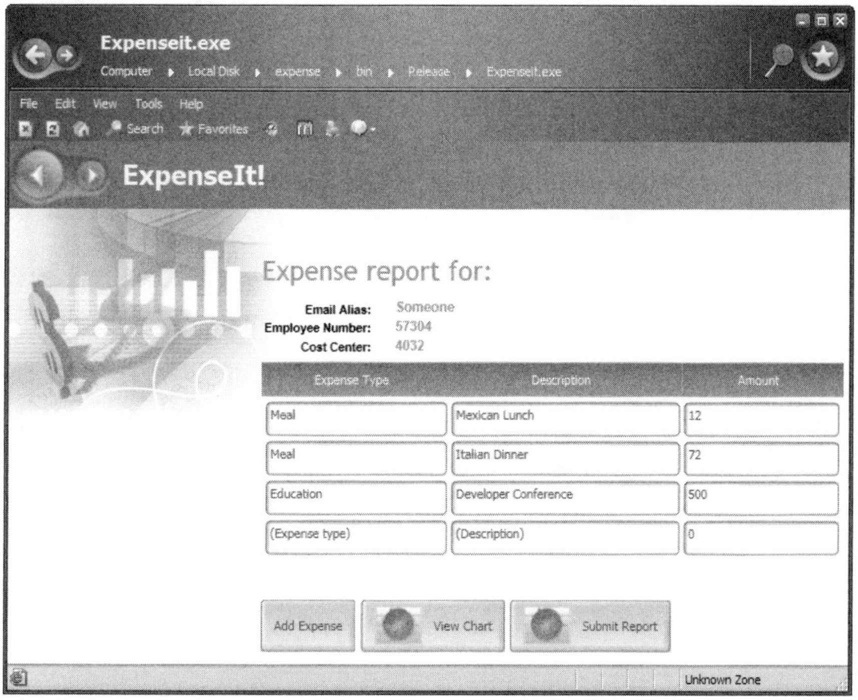

Summary

In this survey, I introduced you to some of the user interface changes that we can expect to see with the release of Windows Longhorn in the 2006 timeframe. Although many of these changes will have a significant impact on application design, one fact remains constant: Building an application that conforms to the design guidelines will result in more satisfied users than going off in your own idiosyncratic direction. For Longhorn, this means paying attention to the Aero guidelines, using application archetypes to help guide feature sets, and considering an inductive user interface where it's appropriate.

Index

Note to the reader: Throughout this index **boldfaced** page numbers indicate primary discussions of a topic. *Italicized* page numbers indicate illustrations.

SYMBOLS

A

E

S

U

X

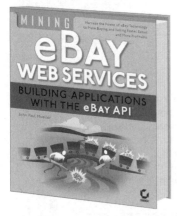